The New Local Government Series
No. 5

THE *REFORMED*
LOCAL GOVERNMENT SYSTEM

The New Local Government Series

Series Editor: Professor Peter G. Richards

THE *REFORMED* LOCAL GOVERNMENT SYSTEM

BY

PETER G. RICHARDS

Professor of British Government
University of Southampton

Revised Third Edition

London
GEORGE ALLEN & UNWIN
Boston   Sydney

First published in 1973
Third edition 1978

© George Allen & Unwin (Publishers) Ltd 1973, 1975, 1978

ISBN 0 04 352 068 5 paperback

Printed in Great Britain by
Biddles Ltd, Guildford, Surrey

PREFACE

The Local Government Act, 1972, takes effect on 1 April 1974. It provides for the most radical change in our local government system since 1888. In particular, the basic distinction then created between counties and county boroughs has disappeared. The new divide is between metropolitan and non-metropolitan areas. In these circumstances a fresh introductory volume was needed for George Allen & Unwin's series of books on local government, replacing my volume *The New Local Government System*. More than that, the series required a new title, for the old name *The Town and County Hall* Series reflected the importance of the county/county borough division that has gone. So this volume introduces a fresh series title, *The New Local Government Series*.

The purpose of this book is to provide students and all those interested in public affairs with an explanation of why fundamental change was needed, together with a description of the new institutions and of the political, social, economic and administrative framework in which they operate. Over the years the study of local government has developed a much broader content. The original introductory volume to this series, *The English Local Government System* by the late J. H. Warren was first published in 1946 and was concerned almost wholly with law and administration. Now many other aspects of the subject must be included. Party politics has a much greater effect on local government than in the immediate post-war period, partly because of political activity at local elections and partly because of the close relationship between central and local government. There is a stronger sociological element in the study of local government as we have become more conscious of the effect of behaviour patterns on the working of formal institutions. There is also growing concern with management. The study of management techniques is basically an examination of administrative method, but the tendency to think in terms of 'management' rather than 'administration' is more than a change of fashion in the use of words, because management does imply a continuous quest for efficiency. So this book, granted the limitations imposed by its length, attempts to bring together political, sociological and managerial approaches to local government.

It will be clear to all readers that this work looks to the future.

PREFACE

What is described here is not local government as it exists on the day of publication but as it will be under the new Act.

I am grateful, indeed continuously grateful, to Mrs Dunn and Mrs Powell, who do my typing with great care, and to Miss Diana Marshallsay, B.A., Dip.Lib., who gave advice and assistance with the index. My wife carried out her customary task of putting a final polish on the material before it went to the printer.

PETER G. RICHARDS

University of Southampton

PREFACE TO THE SECOND EDITION

The favourable reception given to this book has now created the need for a new edition. Substantial changes have been made. These reflect events over the past two years and, in particular, some problems of bringing the reformed system of local government into operation on 1 April 1974.

PETER G. RICHARDS

University of Southampton
November 1974

PREFACE TO THE THIRD EDITION

The need for a further edition provides an opportunity to keep a book fully up to date. Perhaps the major event in local government in the last two years has been the Layfield Report. Accordingly Chapters V and VIII have been substantially revised to take account of the Layfield recommendations.

University of Southampton   PETER G. RICHARDS
July 1977

CONTENTS

CONTENTS

Chapter I

INTRODUCTION THROUGH HISTORY

The present system of local government in England and Wales cannot be fully appreciated without reference to the past. Yet the history of local government is a vast subject on its own—witness the magnificent works of Sidney and Beatrice Webb. In an introductory book the historical element must be a mere sketch. This chapter is a sketch of the development of local government, but one that concentrates on the interrelationship of local administrative areas, local services and local resources. It also tries to link the growth of local services with the dominant trends in political thought at least since 1834. How people react to social problems depends on what they feel to be morally right: the moral drive behind much of local government is one aspect too often overlooked.

TRADITIONAL UNITS AND THEIR DECLINE

The three traditional units of local government in England and Wales have been the county, the parish and the borough. Each has had its own functions which were exercised with a large degree of independence, although the county justices had supervisory powers over parish officers. However, the sense of separateness was so strong that the idea of a *local government system* with major and minor local authorities with interlocking responsibilities did not emerge clearly until the latter part of the nineteenth century. By modern standards, the local units of government also suffered little central control. Central interference varied with the political situation of the time—the later Stuart Kings, in particular, tried to ensure that local positions of influence were held by their supporters—but local institutions were left to deal with local problems in the way they thought best. Since national grants were unknown until the eighteen-forties, the scale of county, parish and borough activity was minimal. Indeed, much effort was expended in the eighteenth century on the promotion of new local bodies to carry out tasks which the traditional authorities were unable or unwilling to undertake.

The county has its origins in feudal times when it was the territory granted by the King to an earl in return for acceptance of feudal obligations. After the feudal period justices of the peace chosen through the King's representative, the Lord Lieutenant, became responsible for county government. Initially the justices were essentially concerned with the maintenance of law and order. Thus their functions were primarily judicial. However, they had some administrative responsibilities, mainly for prisons and bridges, and they had to settle disputes arising out of the actions of parish officers. Visiting justices made irregular visits to parishes to inspect their poor law accounts.

Boroughs were based on charters granted at different times by the monarchy. These charters were valuable because they gave a small town the right to have its own justices and, therefore, to have its own court: this saved much difficulty and expense since disputes could be settled locally and without the need for a possibly unpleasant journey to the quarter sessions. Charters also gave the right to hold markets and so assisted trade and prosperity. They also provided for separate parliamentary representation, but this was commonly regarded as a mixed blessing because of the cost and danger of travel to Westminster. Often borough charters were granted by the King in the expectation of being able to control the nominations to the House of Commons made by the borough. The borough corporations themselves were usually renewed through a process of self-co-option.

The parish was originally the smallest unit of church organisation. It gradually acquired non-ecclesiastical functions, starting with highways in the sixteenth century and the care of the poor in 1601. Frequently the word 'vestry' was used instead of parish because meetings to discuss parish business were held in the church vestry. The names 'open vestry' and 'closed vestry' described how far parish business was open to all parishioners; in a closed vestry decisions would be taken by the local elite—the people who were the largest ratepayers in the parish. Whether any particular vestry was open or closed generally depended on local convention rather than law.

For the common people the parish became the most important local unit of government as it had the greatest effect on their lives. The ancient liability that highways should be repaired 'by the inhabitants at large' was enforced through the parish. By the Statute of Highways, 1555, each parish had to appoint two surveyors responsible for the repair of roads in the parish, and the inhabitants were required to devote four days labour to this work of maintenance. The more wealthy members of the community chose to pay a highway rate instead of doing the work themselves and the money collected was used to pay the poor for working on the roads. The administrative duties of the parish became truly burdensome after 1601 when it was made responsible for the relief of the poor. The

Elizabethan poor law required each parish to appoint an overseer who would impose a rate on the local inhabitants to raise money for the purchase of materials on which the poor could be put to work. The theory was that the goods made would be sold and the revenue could then be distributed to relieve poverty. Thus the poor would be helped, but they would also have to work to help themselves. The theory was commendable, but in practice, the idea could not work. The administration required was too complex for an unpaid parish officer to carry out: even where working materials were provided, paupers were often so old, ill or unskilled, or living in such bad conditions that useful work could not be done. The scheme collapsed and was replaced by the gratuitous distribution of relief financed by a parish rate. Especially in times of bad trade the cost of the poor law was heavy and often caused dispute within a parish.

Each parish carried out its duties through four types of unpaid officer—the overseer of the poor, the surveyor, the constable and the churchwarden. The duties of the first two have already been described. The constable was responsible for keeping the peace and took offenders before the magistrates. The churchwarden was responsible for the maintenance of the fabric of the parish church and, if necessary, collected a rate from the parish to pay for this to be done. Often the necessary funds were subscribed by the wealthy and church rates were rarely required. Necessarily they provoked opposition and indignation from nonconformists who did not attend the parish church. In 1837 the Braintree vestry refused to agree to a church rate and when the churchwarden tried to collect the money without authority his action was successfully challenged in the courts. In 1868 the Gladstone Liberal government abolished church rates and cut another link between ecclesiastical and civil administration.

The parish officers were appointed at the vestry meeting. Since the work was substantial in amount and sometimes unpleasant, it was not always easy to find persons willing to serve. However, the system worked because of a general feeling that good citizens should accept a share of social responsibility. Often the jobs were passed round at the end of a year's duty. Some parishes had an understanding that a parish officer could nominate his successor. The overseer had the heaviest task and in some places a payment was made to him for his trouble; this might be done quite unofficially by means of private donations from the well-to-do inhabitants. Yet the whole system depended on part-time service and goodwill. It was quite unable to accept any wider responsibilities, so when demands came forward for extra and improved local administration the parish was by-passed. More efficient and more complex social provision required better qualified, paid and full-time staff which, in turn, required a larger unit of organisation than the parish. Equally, the county and the borough were ill-placed to obtain extra duties, especially those involving the expenditure of public money. They were not representative bodies and not responsible to the public. So there were obvious grounds for refusing them any further taxing powers. In addition, some borough corporations and, indeed, some magistrates in urban areas were widely accused of corruption—of using official positions to secure personal gain. In the pre-railway age the larger counties were also regarded as too large a unit to be convenient for local administration.

Since the parish, the county and the borough were unsuitable to deal with the social problems arising from the growth of trade, the industrial revolution and the growth of population, new local government institutions were created. The three most important were the turnpike trusts, the Improvement Commissioners and the poor law unions.

The turnpikes were urgently needed to improve the state of the roads. In the eighteenth century there was a dramatic increase in the amount of road transport largely because of more trade but also because people started to travel more for pleasure or for health reasons. To place responsibility for maintaining roads on the parish was both inefficient and unfair. The largest parishes in terms of area were normally those in sparsely populated countryside, while the smaller parishes were in the more thickly populated districts. There was no correlation between the resources of a parish in terms of money or labour and the extent of its highway responsibilities: a parish with a tiny population could have a long stretch of a road running through it which linked major towns. Turnpike trusts were established by Acts of Parliament to charge tolls on travellers for using a road and the proceeds of the tolls could meet the cost of repairing the roads. Today many old toll houses can still be seen situated by the side of main roads.

The growth of towns aggravated many problems of urban living. As in the countryside there was a greater need to maintain roads, but there was also a need for drainage and for the effective maintenance of law and order, particularly the prevention of robbery. Many of the new industrial towns had no municipal corporation: elsewhere the corporations were in the hands of a limited clique and were not respected by the greater part of the citizens. So throughout the country bodies of Improvement Commissions were established by locally sponsored Acts of Parliament. The Commissioners were nominated in the local Act and renewed by co-option, but by the early days of the nineteenth century the principle of ratepayer election was introduced. Their powers varied and were defined in each local

Act. In towns adjacent to rivers or the sea they often provided docking facilities and were known as Harbour and Improvement Commissioners. In general, they were responsible for lighting, paving and draining streets and for providing a watch—an embryonic police force.

Undoubtedly, the most expensive and most contentious branch of local administration was poor relief. During the eighteenth century the parish was already losing control of this function. Various Acts strengthened the power of the justices to supervise the distribution of relief. In 1795 the magistrates of Speenhamland drew up a scale of payments which related the amount of relief payable to the size of a pauper's family and to the price of bread; this Speenhamland scale was widely adopted by justices and overseers. Parliament also permitted parishes to work together in dealing with the poor. An Act of 1723 allowed parishes to join together and form unions which could build workhouses where the poor could live and work. This power was not widely used but another Act of 1782 authorised parishes to join together in unions so they could appoint paid officers to carry out the distribution of relief. These poor law unions were controlled by Guardians, originally appointed by the justices, but subsequently elected by ratepayers.

Two features dominated the law of local administration—it was both local and permissive. Only some main traffic routes were cared for by turnpikes; others were covered partially or not at all. Only some parishes agreed to join poor law unions. The powers of Improvement Commissioners varied as did their relationship, if any, with the local municipal corporation. Until late in the nineteenth century nothing existed that could be described as a coherent system of local services—instead there was a chaos of institutions, areas and rates.

NINETEENTH-CENTURY REFORM

The political upheaval which produced the 1832 Reform Bill had an immediate impact on local administration. The first major change concerned the poor law. In 1832 a Poor Law Commission was appointed to report on the working of the existing arrangements and the Commission sent out investigators to examine conditions in about 300 parishes. These investigators may be considered as the forerunners of the present-day inspectorate. The Commission's Report portrayed a situation of confusion, incompetence and waste. The Poor Law Amendment Act, 1834, based on the Commission's recommendations, provided a new and uniform basis for poor relief. A central body in London, the Poor Law Commission, was to supervise the whole system—the start of central control over the detailed administration of local services. The central body united parishes into convenient areas for poor law purposes and in so doing ignored other traditional divisions. Thus many unions overlapped county boundaries. The poor law unions were also *ad hoc* bodies, i.e. they were formed to carry out a particular service. This was not a new idea in 1834 for turnpikes had then existed for many years, but the poor law unions were the first example of a pattern of *ad hoc* authorities covering the whole country; now there are many examples of this kind, water and health authorities and the area organisations of public corporations. The Poor Law Commission laid down strict rules covering the distribution of relief. The unions were to build workhouses and the distribution of relief other than to the inmates of the workhouse was banned: the regime in the workhouse was to be spartan to deter applications for admission. Local Boards of Guardians were elected by the ratepayers to run the workhouses, subject to national control.

The other major reform of the eighteen-thirties applied to the municipal corporations. Once more a Commission of enquiry was appointed and Assistant Commissioners were sent out to examine how the corporations were conducted. Again the Report was damning. Some corporations were so decayed as to be virtually non-existent; many did nothing of value for the local inhabitants; some were corrupt. The Municipal Corporations Act, 1835, gave the boroughs a new constitution and insisted on proper financial management. Borough councillors were to be elected by the ratepayers and the House of Lords required that a quarter of the council should consist of aldermen elected by the councillors. All borough revenues were to be paid into a single fund to be used for the benefit of the inhabitants. The administration of justice was divorced from the administration of services and the borough justices were separated from the borough council. But in contrast to the Poor Law Amendment Act, the amount of central control was negligible. The major task of the borough was the maintenance of law and order and the 1835 Act decreed that a quarterly report from the local Watch Committee be submitted to the Home Secretary. A borough could also make bye-laws for the good rule and government of its area which were subject to approval of the Privy Council. The Treasury was empowered to stop the sale and long leases of corporation-owned land. Yet the total effect of these controls was small. The 1835 Act did nothing to change the area of boroughs. It was applied to 178 towns. Other places which claimed borough status were ignored and the corporations deprived of recognition faded away. The City of London also managed to avoid coming under these provisions:

many attempts in the following fifty years to reform London government were frustrated by the powerful financial interests of the City.

These two Acts demonstrate a remarkable difference of approach.
The poor law reform was based on central control, uniformity,
rationalisation of areas and the *ad hoc* principle. The Municipal
Corporations Act emphasised the authority of local representatives
subject to a minimum of central direction, maintained existing areas
and created an organisation capable of dealing with a wide range of
services. All these contrasts recur in the subsequent history of local
government. Indeed, they form the basis of much of the recent
discussion about the shape of future local government reform.

In the eighteen-forties public attention was concentrated on the
question of health. This concern was largely stimulated by Edwin
Chadwick, Secretary of the Poor Law Commissioners, who was
convinced that disease was the main cause of poverty, and that the
best way to help the poor was to remove the causes of sickness.
Reports of official enquiries, heavily influenced by Chadwick, slowly
created public willingness for government action. The two major
reports on the Sanitary Condition of the Labouring Population
(1842) and the State of Large Towns (1845) revealed almost unbeliev-
able conditions of filth, squalor and a lack of drainage and pure
water supplies. The Public Health Act, 1848, authorised the establishment of local Boards of Health to provide water supply and drainage,
either where the inhabitants requested it or where the death rate
exceeded 23 per 1,000. Municipal Corporations became the Boards
of Health for their own areas. The work of the local Boards was to
be supervised by a Central Board of Health. Earlier, in 1846, the
Poor Law Guardians had been given limited powers to deal with
insanitary nuisances in rural areas.

The public health legislation to a large extent followed the model
of the poor law reform. However, there were differences, which
grew larger as time passed. The element of central control was present
and more *ad hoc* bodies were created. However, more scope was
allowed for local initiative and the Central Board of Health never
achieved the dominance of the Poor Law Commission. The Central
Board was reorganised in 1854 and dissolved in 1858, its functions
being divided between the Privy Council and the Home Office. (The
original Poor Law Commission had been displaced in 1847 by a
Minister, the President of the Poor Law Board, who was directly
answerable to Parliament: but the central direction of poor relief
remained firm.) The opposition to central direction on health questions was due to the disappearance of epidemics and the dislike of
spending large sums of money that had to be raised by local taxation.
Yet even when the *laissez-faire* reaction swept away the Central

Board of Health in 1858 there remained 670 local Boards of Health which continued to promote more civilised conditions in urban areas.

After a decade of inaction at national level, the Royal Sanitary Commission was appointed in 1868. Its Report in 1871 set out the requirements 'of what is necessary for a civilised social life' which included a pure water supply, sewage, burial arrangements and the inspection of food. A new government department, the Local Government Board, was created in 1871 to deal with these matters. In 1872 the whole country was divided up into urban and rural sanitary districts, the urban authorities being given wider powers. The urban authorities were boroughs, Improvement Commissioners and local Boards of Health: Poor Law Guardians became sanitary authorities for the parts of their union not included in the above. Thus while the Guardians combined both town and country for poor law purposes, they dealt with public health matters solely in the countryside. This separation of urban and rural areas was a reversal of one of the principles of the 1834 poor law reform and created the basis of the later distinction between urban and rural districts.

At this period the question of highway maintenance became acute as the turnpike trust system was breaking down. The new steam railways provided an alternative means of transport and adversely affected the revenues of the turnpikes, so reducing their ability to keep roads in good repair. There was also increased public opposition to the payment of tolls. In South Wales rioters destroyed turnpike gates. Consequently Parliament refused to renew the powers of the turnpike trusts when they lapsed and the disturnpiked roads reverted to the care of the parish. Even in the eighteenth century it had been widely accepted that the parish was not competent to maintain the roads and the obvious need was for the creation of a highway authority based on a larger unit than the parish. The county was unacceptable since the county justices were not elected. The alternative was to form unions of parishes on the model of the poor law. In 1862 the county justices were given powers to create such unions, but often these were based on the areas of the justices' petty sessional districts, not on the areas of the poor law unions. This added substantially to the confusion of local administration in rural areas. Highway districts were highly unpopular. They imposed a financial obligation upon the parish rate which had no connection with the extent of the traditional liability of the parish to maintain its own roads. Parishes suffered if small in area with substantial population; parishes gained if large in area with a small population. In some cases the gains and losses were heavy. Many large villages managed to opt out of a highway district by adopting the Public

Health Act, 1848, and forming their own local Board of Health which entitled them to separate highway powers. In 1863 this trick was stopped by an Act which stipulated that only parishes with a population of at least 3,000 could adopt the Public Health Act. Meanwhile some very small pre-1974 urban districts owed their existence to the scramble to avoid inclusion in a highway union. The resistance to highway unions was so acute that in some areas they were never formed. In other places they were allowed to decay and responsibility for the roads again fell back on the parish. Elsewhere the areas were rationalised and made to conform with the poor law unions, yet this was often difficult because the poor law unions frequently overlapped county boundaries.

Today many local authority areas are anomalous: in the nineteenth century they were fantastic. Over a thousand parishes included one or more parcels of land completely detached from the main body of the parish; in the west of England the separated parts were occasionally situated in a different county. This jigsaw necessarily complicated local administration. The parish of Threapwood in the Wrexham poor law union was partly in Cheshire and partly in Denbighshire and so was part in England and part in Wales. A woman in the village, a pauper, went mad and had to be sent to an asylum. In England the charge for maintaining a pauper lunatic was 14s a week, in Wales it was only 8s a week. The question arose whether the woman was domiciled in the English or the Welsh sector of the village. The Clerk of the Wrexham Union discovered that the house where the woman was born was astride the county boundary. However, he was able to establish that the woman was born in the Welsh piece of the house and so saved his authority 6s a week. This cameo is drawn from evidence presented to the Select Committee on Parish, Union and County Boundaries which reported in 1873. Gradually parish boundaries were rationalised, but the process was slow.

Parish boundaries achieved greater importance because of both roads and education. In 1870 Gladstone's first Liberal Government imposed on the parish the responsibility of providing a school if an adequate one had not been provided by voluntary agencies—i.e. the churches. School attendance became compulsory in 1876 and free in 1891. The eccentric boundaries had effects which appeared inequitable. The main part of a parish could have a satisfactory church school but no provision for children in a detached piece some distance off; the whole parish was required to contribute to the provision of a school for the detached part. Even in 1870 the parish was obviously too small a unit to be a satisfactory education authority. However, since many parishes already had schools it was impossible to create school unions in which the cost could be pooled: such an arrangement would have aroused even more antagonism than the highway unions.

Over the years various pressures developed which made a democratic reform of county government long overdue. Agricultural labourers gained the parliamentary franchise through the third Reform Bill, 1884. The anomaly that boroughs, but not counties, enjoyed representative government had existed for half a century. The administrative duties of the county justice had grown steadily and so had the size of the county rate demand. In particular, the village constable was replaced by the county police force in 1856. It became clear that further services, notably highways, ought to be made a county responsibility in order to achieve better and more uniform standards of repair and to spread the cost over a wider area. Finally, administration in the London area was seriously in need of reform. London had grown far beyond the area of the City, which had successfully avoided all attempts to modernise its constitution. Many important services were provided by the Metropolitan Board of Works established in 1855 which was based on a system of indirect election through a pattern of district boards. The Metropolitan Board had been responsible for substantial redevelopment in the West End but had become corrupt. Beyond question, London needed unified and democratic local government. These pressures, combined with the influence of Joseph Chamberlain and the Liberal Unionists within Lord Salisbury's Conservative Government, succeeded in making a major reform. The Local Government Act, 1888, remained the foundation of our present system of local government—outside London—until the coming into force of the Local Government Act, 1972.

The 1888 Act had three major aspects. It created a new system of county councils elected on a ratepayer franchise; it defined the relationship between the county councils and the boroughs; it reorganised the financial relations between central and local government. When originally introduced the Bill had a further section covering the reform of smaller authorities within the county, but this had to be dropped for lack of parliamentary time. After a delay of six years this part of the reform was enacted in 1894.

The new county councils did not correspond entirely with the historic counties. Some were divided for administrative convenience because of the size of the county, e.g. Yorkshire, or its shape, e.g. Sussex. To a great extent these divisions often represented existing practice in that the county magistrates had met in separate centres and had levied separate rates. The bisection of Suffolk was based on acceptance of current arrangements. The problem of the metropolis was solved by carving a new county, the London County Council, out of Middlesex, Surrey and Kent, the LCC boundaries being based on those of the superseded Metropolitan Board of Works. Two years after the Act was passed the Isle of Wight was also made a separate county. Thus the trisection of Yorkshire and Lincolnshire, the division of Cambridgeshire, Northamptonshire, Hampshire, Suffolk and Sussex, together with the new county of London created a total of 62 county councils out of the 52 geographical counties.

Initially the powers given to the counties were limited. Their major task was to care for those roads designated as county roads. A joint committee was formed with the county justices to supervise the county police force. They also inherited from the county justices an assortment of administrative duties, many relating to the issue of licences for various purposes. In subsequent years the counties acquired a wide range of functions. Indeed, the history of local government in the twentieth century can be largely summarised by listing the extensions to county responsibilities.

Much parliamentary time was consumed by the representatives of boroughs fighting for their independence from the new county councils. As originally drafted the Bill excluded only the very largest towns with a population of 150,000 from the aegis of the counties. This implied that all other boroughs would be subordinate to the county councils and would have to pay the county rate. Previously boroughs with their own quarter sessions had been exempt from the county rate because the administrative duties of the county justices had been carried out by their own borough bench. Under pressure from borough MPs the size of boroughs with county powers—i.e. county boroughs—was reduced to 50,000 population, and four smaller boroughs, Burton-on-Trent, Canterbury, Chester and Worcester, were also admitted to the select band.

The financial sections of the 1888 Act were an attempt to secure some order and principle for methods of giving monetary aid to local authorities. At various dates since the Chadwick era Exchequer grants had been given in respect of education, police, highways, criminal prosecutions and some aspects of the poor law. The grants were designed to encourage better standards of provision in these fields and had grown steadily in amount. To place a limit on the cost of these grants to the national taxpayer, it was agreed that most of the specific grants mentioned above be replaced by a single combined grant, to be paid from a separate Local Taxation Account. This Account was to be supplied with 40 per cent of the product of certain national taxes—the so-called assigned revenues. The system did not endure because the proceeds of the assigned revenues did not rise as fast as the expenditure of local authorities and because successive

Governments were unwilling to increase the range or percentage of the revenues paid to the Local Taxation Account. Although a failure, the assigned revenue idea is of much significance. It was an attempt to isolate central aid to local government from other types of national expenditure and thereby to reduce central supervision of local administration. It was also the start of a continuing argument about the relative desirability of general grants to local authorities as opposed to grants for specified purposes—a controversy examined more fully in Chapter V.

As noted above, the reform of the small units of government in county areas was delayed until 1894. The urban and rural sanitary districts became urban and rural district councils of the pre-1974 model. In urban areas the change was little more than one of name. In rural areas the effect was more complex because the Local Government Act, 1894, provided that a rural district area should not overlap a county boundary. Since the rural sanitary areas were based on the poor law unions which ignored county divisions, some reshaping of authorities was required. Rural districts acquired the duties of the rural sanitary districts, the highway responsibilities of the parish or those of the highway districts where such existed. The relationship with the Poor Law Guardians was reversed. Previously the powers of the rural sanitary district were exercised by those Guardians representing rural parishes: after 1894 the rural district councillors also served as members of the Board of Guardians. The parishes were also overhauled and given, like the districts, a ratepayer franchise. However, the powers of the parish had largely been transferred to larger authorities. Some parishes were too small to justify the creation of a council: the Act decreed that parishes with 300 inhabitants must have a council, those with less than 100 could not, and those between 100 and 300 could choose. In the absence of a parish council, parish business has to be transacted at a parish meeting. London was left untouched in 1894. This final remnant of eighteenth-century chaos was removed by the London Government Act, 1899, which replaced a miscellany of district boards and parish authorities in the LCC area by 28 Metropolitan Borough Councils, which were thought of as a counter-weight to the LCC which the Conservative Government feared might become too powerful—a suspicion aggravated by what appeared to be its permanent Radical majority. Although the Metropolitan Boroughs were given responsibility for public health, housing, rating, libraries and recreational services, they never achieved parity of importance with the LCC. Due to the centralising tendency of modern times, as new duties were bestowed on local authorities they tended to go to the top tier, the LCC.

The passage of the London Government Act, 1899, completed a

new pattern of multi-purpose authorities elected on a ratepayer franchise. The complete system can be illustrated by a simple diagram.

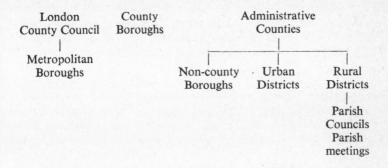

This structure remained until a fresh reform of London government took place in 1963.

Looking back over the nineteenth century it can be seen that it witnessed a constitutional revolution in local government. The Public Bill steadily replaced the Private Bill as the main instrument of change. A reconstructed system of elected, multi-purpose authorities emerged; the *ad hoc* principle went out of fashion. Separate organisations each devoted to a particular function have advantages. They can have areas most suitable for their particular purpose; they can generate specialised enthusiasm; they are not distracted by other tasks. However, the drawbacks of *ad hoc* bodies are substantial. They create a complex jumble of administrative units that is highly confusing for the public; if they are representative, the result must be a multiplicity of elections; the necessary co-ordination between them is difficult or impossible to arrange; either they cover a wide area and become remote or they are too small to use skilled manpower economically. Since the later Victorians were keener than we are now to uphold the representative principle, the move towards multi-purpose local authorities was wholly logical.

The intellectual forces advocating reform were powerful but not homogeneous. Sometimes they came in conflict with each other: this is one reason why the pace of change varied. The interaction of these ideas provides some explanation for the pattern of events and requires some attention.

The eighteen-thirties and forties were dominated by utilitarianism, the creed spread by Jeremy Bentham and his disciple James Mill. They argued that human affairs should be so organised as to secure the greatest happiness of the greatest number, that institutions should be judged by their utility, i.e. by the extent to which they contributed to the sum of happiness. This is not the place to examine the philosophical and moral limitations of the utilitarian view: a study of local government must be concerned with its consequences. It was essentially a radical doctrine. It implied that existing arrangements and institutions should not be accepted unless they satisfied the test of utility. The chaos of local administration was so complete that patently it failed the test. But utilitarianism did not require a wide extension of the functions of the state. On the contrary Bentham tended to accept the principle of *laissez-faire*—that the government should leave things alone. State action was required only where it was necessary to increase the total of human happiness—if it produced more pleasure than pain. Today utilitarianism is out of fashion, partly because it is unsatisfactory in terms of ethics and partly because the measurement of pleasure and pain presents obvious difficulties. Nevertheless Bentham probably has a greater effect on contemporary thought and action than is commonly admitted. Of course, the concepts have evolved. Utility has been replaced by efficiency. Instead of a calculus of pleasure and pain, the modern calculus is of cost and benefit which can be measured, or estimated, at least in monetary terms.

Another influential concept was representative government. This idea has a long history. It had a great impact at the time of the English Civil War. In the eighteenth century the American colonists revolted over the principle 'no taxation without representation'. Any claim for representation raises immediate practical questions—who should be represented and how should their representation be organised? Throughout the nineteenth century an increasing number of public bodies were elected and the franchise was extended; in the early years voting was restricted to some ratepayers and the number of votes each enjoyed might vary from one to six depending on the rateable value of their property, but by the end of the period each ratepayer had one vote. So there was progress towards a ratepayer democracy. But those who urged the need for representative government were not necessarily favourable to democracy. It was widely accepted that those who contributed to the local rate should control the spending of the money raised. John Stuart Mill, the son of James Mill, argued convincingly that participation in the process of government was a valuable education in public affairs which helped to produce a sense of responsibility in the community and stimulated the creation of local leadership. Yet to give the vote to all implied that policy might be controlled by the wishes of uneducated people—and of people who contributed little or nothing to the rates but derive benefit therefrom. However, the franchise for both parliamentary and local elections was steadily widened, partly because any limit appeared arbitrary and was awkward to defend politically, partly through the rise in educational standards and partly because limitation of the franchise caused administrative difficulties.

Utilitarian philosophy and demands for representative government reinforced each other in national politics. At local level they tended to come into conflict, at least before 1861. Chadwick regarded local self-government as potentially a vehicle for corruption. Utilitarianism demanded some element of central supervision of local administration to ensure that it was adequate and competent. The claim that the ratepayers, or their elected representatives, should decide how much to spend and how to spend it could easily clash with attempts to impose national standards. Controversy of this nature was widespread in connection with the development of drainage and other environmental health services. And the wider the representation, the greater the proportion of the populace to have the vote, the more likely were such clashes to arise: the poorer classes were more willing to take their chance of cholera and other diseases if this meant paying less in local rates. Opposition to central control led to the break up of the Central Board of Health in 1858. However, John Stuart Mill's *Representative Government* published in 1861 modified utilitarian doctrine in that it accepted the need to work with and through educated local opinion.

The third powerful force in local government was a feeling of humanity. This is an ageless sentiment; throughout time there has been some compassion for the poor, the ailing and the disabled. In a period when the Christian religion achieved great strength, one would expect humanity to influence public policy. However, it easily comes into conflict with other principles and baser motives. The administration of the poor law provides a clear example. Utilitarianism required a rigid, controlled and harsh regime to reduce cost, to stimulate self-help, in order to produce the greatest happiness for the greatest number. A humanitarian approach needed more flexibility, more charity and more expenditure. The reform of the poor law in 1834 was a triumph for utilitarian principles but slowly these were softened by slightly more generous administration.

Humanitarian thought stressed the dignity of the individual. It believed, to use a Victorian phrase, that people should be encouraged to better themselves. The argument can be presented with varying emphasis and degrees of sophistication. It is better for the country as a whole if everyone works hard to improve their position. God has given to each individual certain potentialities—it is therefore appropriate that these potentialities be used to the full. The same view can also be put without reference to God. Thus a climate of opinion was created favourable to state assistance to education, an attitude powerfully supported by the obvious need for a more highly skilled work force in an economy based on industrial processes of growing complexity.

Agreement that the state should take steps to promote human welfare necessarily required an erosion of support for *laissez-faire*. This doctrine, widely accepted in the early years of the century, argued that material prosperity was obtainable most speedily by fostering the spirit of free competition and leaving every man to work for his own interests. The role of the state, on this view, was minimal, limited to the preservation of internal order and security from external attack, and perhaps to provide bare essentials of life for those manifestly too weak to enter into the mêlée to acquire higher standards of comfort. But *laissez-faire* had no convincing solution to the problem of poverty caused through unemployment, to problems of public health or illiteracy. Even on questions of economic organisation it could not apply to the provision of services which required a heavy initial capital outlay and much interference with public and private rights. Free competition between railway companies, tramways, water and gas companies was obviously wasteful and undesirable. If price competition forced down standards of maintenance of equipment, the result was public danger. So the Victorians came to accept that there were natural monopolies that had to be controlled by the state, or provided by public authorities, to prevent exploitation of the consumer. Thus many towns provided their own water and gas supplies and later in the century electricity and tramways were added to the list of municipal trading services.

Support for representative institutions and humanitarian and utilitarian principles provided the driving force for change. But powerful pressures also worked against reform and hindered progress. Essentially these were the spirit of conservatism and the inevitable unpopularity of raising more money through taxation. These generalisations apply both to the nineteenth century and to our own time. It is easy to argue that things should be left as they are; that proposed changes are fraught with hidden difficulties; that the benefit of reform is exaggerated in relation to its cost. These attitudes will be promoted by wealthy persons and those in positions of authority who feel themselves threatened by change. Sometimes these established interests—Bentham called them sinister interests—have been so powerful as to be able to frustrate demands for reform: the history of the City of London in the nineteenth century is a paramount example of this situation.

TWENTIETH-CENTURY DEVELOPMENT OF SERVICES

The present century has seen a vast growth in the scale of services provided by local authorities. This has been accompanied by an increase in financial aid from the national Exchequer and an increase in supervision by central departments over local administration. The structural changes have been less impressive, and have failed to keep pace with the development of functions.

It is possible to summarise the structural alterations fairly briefly. The two major *ad hoc* authorities, the School Boards and the Boards of Guardians, came to an end in 1902 and 1930 respectively, the greater part of their duties being transferred to county boroughs and county councils. A number of towns achieved county borough status before 1926, when the population qualification was raised to 75,000 and the obstacle to this promotion was made more difficult by changing it from Provisional Order procedure to a Private Bill: between 1926 and 1964 only one new county borough was created. As the larger towns expanded, their suburbs overspilled their boundaries; by agreement between the councils concerned there were a large number of adjustments to county borough boundaries which substantially increased their population, acreage and rateable value. A number of urban districts obtained borough charters and thus achieved added civic dignity, if only very few extra powers. The areas of urban and rural districts (but not the non-county boroughs) were also rationalised in the nineteen-thirties by the reviews carried out by county councils under the provisions of the Local Government Act, 1929. As a result of these county reviews the total of urban districts was reduced from 786 to 573 and that of rural districts from 650 to 477. The policy of the counties varied. Rutland and Radnor, the two smallest counties, were excused by the Minister of Health from making any review at all. Other small counties undertook reviews but left the number of district authorities unchanged—e.g. Huntingdonshire and Flintshire. In some large counties, like Devon and Somerset, the review was also notably ineffective. Elsewhere, as in Cumberland and Northumberland, the county pruned out the tiny urban authorities but left the rural councils virtually untouched. Other counties followed the reverse policy, Northamptonshire and Shropshire amalgamated rural districts and left the urban councils alone. Finally, some counties, e.g. East Sussex and Hampshire, took strong action in both urban and rural districts. The greatest concentration of small districts was in Wales. Essentially this is because the Welsh counties enforced a minimum amount of change, but in areas of sparse population it can be argued that lower population figures for rural districts are essential otherwise their areas will become inconveniently large.

While the total amount of change has not been inconsiderable, the constitutional framework established in 1888 and 1894 remained basically the same until 1972. London is the exception. The London Government Act, 1963, pushed the metropolitan boundary out to embrace most of its suburbia and redefined the distribution of responsibilities between the upper and lower-tier authorities. There has been almost continuous discussion since the last war of the need to redesign the local government system: the various schemes of reform are examined in the following sections of this chapter.

To revert to the growth of services—the first big move forward in this century came in the field of education. In 1900 the school leaving age was raised from 12 to 14. This created an immediate difficulty. The School Boards had been given powers solely to provide elementary education: if 'elementary' was defined as being limited to the basic skills of reading, writing and arithmetic, then children of ability aged 12 and 13 would simply waste their time at the Board schools. Many of these schools started to provide more advanced instruction. In 1901 the Cockerton judgement held that the London School Board had no legal right to give advanced courses and provoked a crisis that demanded immediate action. The Education Act, 1902, abolished the 2,500 School Boards and transferred their responsibilities to the multi-purpose authorities. County councils and county boroughs were empowered to provide elementary and secondary education, but non-county boroughs with 10,000 population and urban districts with 20,000 population were made responsible for elementary education. Here is a principle that has not been widely used in local government—that the powers of an authority depend not only upon its status but also on its population. Since there was no arrangement for towns which subsequently achieved these population limits to acquire powers over elementary education, the result became anomalous: by the nineteen-thirties many boroughs and urban districts had grown rapidly and had no education powers although they were significantly larger than many authorities with these powers. The Education Act, 1944, concentrated education in the hands of counties and county boroughs, with the stipulation that limited powers should be delegated by county councils, especially to towns with a population above 60,000. Since 1944 the school leaving age has been raised to 16 and there has been a truly enormous expansion of further and technical education. There has to be increasing co-operation between local education authorities over the organisation of advanced courses in order to prevent wasteful duplication.

The abolition of the Poor Law Guardians was recommended in the 1909 Report of the Royal Commission on the Poor Law. The Report revealed wide disparities in poor law administration. Many of the Boards gave out-door relief with varying generosity and provided medical services for those who could not fairly be described as paupers. This policy was defensible on both humanitarian and economic grounds: if the working population had medical attention and kept healthy, they were less likely to become a burden on the poor rate. The Royal Commission's Report was not unanimous because a Minority Report urged more drastic remedial action to remove the stigma of poverty and to break up poor law administration by dividing education and health aspects from the relief of poverty. The Liberal Government introduced old age pensions and compulsory health insurance and so eased the Guardians' task. Yet no action was taken to transfer the Guardians' duties to the major local authorities, perhaps because the Cabinet was immersed in many other violent controversies, perhaps because of reluctance to entrust the poor to county councils largely dominated by Tory landowners. It is also true, as was stressed by the Minority Report, that many Guardians had carried out their unpopular task with humanity and imagination. So the Guardians survived for twenty years more. In the nineteen-twenties more Unions were controlled by Labour majorities; these were accused by their opponents of extravagant expenditure. The Poplar Guardians led by George Lansbury at one stage refused to pay their share of the expenditure of the London County Council owing to the high cost of poor relief in Poplar. Allegations of corruption by the Guardians were widespread. An Act passed in 1926 gave the Minister of Health power to take over the duties of the Guardians if he found their administration to be defective: this was done in three places, Bedwellty, Chester-le-Street and West Ham. Ultimately the Guardians disappeared in 1930 under the terms of the Local Government Act passed the previous year. Their duties were taken over by the county councils and county boroughs and divided up between committees dealing with health, education and public assistance. The latter function was transferred to central government agencies in two stages with the establishment of the Unemployment Assistance Board in 1934 and the National Assistance Board in 1948. Also in 1948 came the final break up of the poor law when the Children Act and the National Assistance Act redefined the powers of counties and county boroughs to care for children, the aged and the infirm.

Personal health services remained in an administrative tangle until 1964. Hospitals had three origins—voluntary organisations, the Boards of Guardians and public health authorities. The Guardians were concerned with medical services for the poor while the health authorities were required to isolate persons suffering from infectious disease. After 1930 the medical wards of workhouses were taken over by the health committees of the counties and county boroughs and turned into general purpose hospitals. County boroughs, counties, and some other boroughs and urban districts were made responsible for maternity and child welfare from 1907 onwards and had opened clinics for this purpose. The National Health Service Act, 1946, transferred all hospitals to the new Regional Hospital Boards, but an expanded range of medical duties, including the aftercare of hospital patients, the provision of health visitors and home helps was allocated to counties and county boroughs.

The construction of council houses and flats was started before the end of the nineteenth century. It was then thought of as an aspect of public health because the slums were breeding-places for disease and their progressive replacement was a medical requirement. After the First World War the public provision of housing was accepted as a social need, and various Acts were passed which gave national financial assistance towards council building. Housing powers went to the boroughs, urban and rural district councils. This is the one modern service not allocated to county councils. Indeed, without the housing function it is difficult to see how many district councils could now justify their existence.

In the nineteen-twenties there was a great rise in the popularity of motoring. The increase in traffic created demands for higher stand- ards of road maintenance. It will be remembered that highways were then the responsibility of the boroughs and districts, save that the counties maintained the more important 'county' roads. The Local Government Act, 1929, sought to improve the state of the roads in the countryside by transferring the powers of rural districts to the county councils. Towns with a population above 20,000 were allowed to 'claim' highway powers over county roads within their boundar- ies and all urban authorities remained responsible for minor roads. Rural districts and towns below 20,000 could also be given delegated powers over county roads, but this sort of delegation was never very important or satisfactory and has been steadily reduced. Care of roads demands highly skilled supervision and equipment which becomes more complex and expensive: here the case for centralisation of responsibility is strong on economic and technical grounds.

Town and country planning is a further example of the transfer of functions to the higher tier of local authorities. All the earliest planning legislation from 1909 to 1932 had given boroughs and districts the opportunity to introduce local planning schemes. But this multiplicity of planning authorities proved a serious hindrance to the effective control of development—there were, for example, 133 planning authorities in the area served by London Transport. In fact, only a small part of the country had been covered by operative planning schemes prepared by borough and district councils, partly because of the intricate procedure and also due to fear of liability to pay compensation. The Town and Country Planning Act, 1947, centralised responsibility in the hands of counties and county boroughs and introduced a comprehensive system for the control of development. Again, there were also limited powers for counties to delegate decisions to non-county boroughs and district councils.

The police and the fire brigade provide further examples of the transfer of functions to fewer and larger units of operation. After the Police Act, 1946, the remaining non-county borough forces were absorbed into the county police; in the nineteen-sixties the centralisation process continued with the amalgamation of county and county borough forces. Counties became the fire authority under the Fire Brigades Act, 1947. Other powers have been taken away from local authorities altogether. This started with the creation of Regional Traffic Commissioners in 1930 and the loss to them of the power to license road passenger services. Relief of the unemployed went to the Unemployment Assistance Board in 1934. In the post-war period gas and electricity undertakings were nationalised and hospitals were taken over by regional boards. The loss of powers continued with the transfer to *ad hoc* authorities in 1974 of personal health services, water supply and sewerage.

For a century after the reform of the poor law in 1834 local authorities enjoyed a steady growth of their responsibilities. In the post-war period while some further powers have been obtained, others have been taken away. Increasingly, the losses outweigh the gains. Local government is in competition with other types of public body. It faces the challenge of rival institutions.

How can this change of fortune be explained? There were two main reasons for the burgeoning of local government after 1834. The agreement that public provision of services should be allowed to develop was a hesitant agreement, for this period was the heyday of individualistic doctrines. The sentiment that government of any kind is but a necessary evil leads also to the supposition that local government is a lesser evil than national government because it is more susceptible to public control. The great indignation aroused by the attempts of national government to influence local affairs in the Chadwick period is eloquent proof of the force of this attitude. The second reason can be stated quite simply—local government had no competitors. The highly competent Civil Service of today evolved very slowly in the latter part of the nineteenth century. Even in the early years of this century the organisational resources of government departments were rudimentary except for tax collection. Public corporations did not appear until the nineteen-twenties. Thus the administrative capacity of local authorities, however deficient it may have been by modern standards, held a dominating position.

All this has now changed. Collectivism is in fashion rather than individualism: technical requirements demand large-scale production to achieve economies of scale: the need for efficiency and uniformity is held to require fewer and bigger units of organisation. Take the particular example of the health service. There was an undeniable case for bringing together under one management the three original sections of the National Health Service—the personal health services provided by local authorities, the hospitals and the various individual practitioners. Why could they not be unified within the context of a democratically controlled local government system? The traditional objection, that local authority areas are unsuitable, might have been met if the needs of the health service had been taken into account when local government areas were reshaped in 1972. However, there were three other powerful factors working against the claims of local government. The professional interests involved, particularly the doctors, feared the loss of freedom if they were subject to the direction of local councillors. Local authorities have inadequate financial resources to provide all health services; they would require either new powers to tax or massive additional grants from the central government. And if national government money is being spent, then Ministers like to be able to control how it is done. There is no doubt that the reluctance of many local authorities to provide family planning facilities has aroused irritation in Whitehall.

Thus local government is on the defensive. In any discussion about how a new service should be provided, or how some existing service could be reformed, the case for local government no longer dominates; on the contrary, it is increasingly difficult to sustain. Besides the challenge from government departments, public corporations and *ad hoc* boards, a new competitor to local authorities is threatening to emerge in the form of regionalism. What form this threat may take depends on the future pattern of regional institutions, a question that is discussed further in the final section of this book.

THE NEED FOR REFORM

The pre-1974 structure of local government was fashioned at the end of the nineteenth century by three Acts of Parliament which constituted a noble embodiment of the reforming democratic spirit of late-Victorian England. In geographical terms they commonly utilised boundaries which already existed, including county boundaries which can be traced back to feudal times. The structure as it stood in 1972 had been created in a different age for the needs of a different age, when the duties of local authorities were far more limited and before the internal combustion engine had revolutionised means of transport. Prior to 1972 little had been done to modernise the Victorian legacy. True there had been some changes. Between 1888 and 1929 just over 20 new county boroughs were created; in the nineteen-thirties the number of county districts was substantially reduced; boundaries of boroughs were widened to embrace advancing suburbia; some urban districts achieved the dignity of borough status and so became able to parade a mayor and aldermen on ceremonial occasions. But the pace of change has been slowed down by the clash of local interests, particularly between counties and boroughs. The counties managed to prevent the establishment of any new county boroughs between 1929 and 1964, motivated by the fear that new county boroughs would mean loss of some rateable value by the counties.

Thus the local government map failed to adjust to movements and growth of population. Anomalies inherited from the Victorians became more glaring while others emerged. In 1972 the largest administrative county, Lancashire, had a population over one hundred times greater than that of the smallest county, Radnor, and over eighty times greater than that of Rutland, the smallest English county. In the county borough class, Birmingham was thirty times the size of Canterbury. There were also second-tier authorities with a population three times that of Canterbury. Over 30 county districts, most of them in Wales, had less than 2,000 inhabitants. It was even possible to find third-tier authorities, suburbanised parishes in rural districts, with a population not far short of that of Radnor.

The existence of many small county districts had a profound effect on the allocation of local government duties. Legislation has assumed, with minor exceptions, e.g. libraries, that all local authorities of any one type must be given equal statutory rights in respect of any function. It was also held that functions cannot be subdivided, so that if a county must be given a particular part of a function, like education, it must have the whole of it. Yet highways were a notable exception to this rule. But the total effect was to drain functions away from the second-tier authorities and to change the pattern of local administration not by a comprehensive scheme of reform but by *ad hoc* measures relating to individual functions. Thus the second-tier authorities lost powers over elementary education, planning, fire service, personal health services and rural roads to the county councils. This aggravated tensions between counties and the larger county districts and led to demands for the delegation of county responsibilities to the larger districts—a clumsy compromise that often worked badly.

Another outdated concept that stayed until the 1972 Act was the differentiation between urban and rural districts. Nineteenth-century legislation was based on the belief that the countryside needed fewer services than the towns, notably in relation to sewerage. This view is no longer acceptable. Subsequently the difference in powers between urban and rural districts was often reduced, but twin organisations with virtually identical tasks were often located in the same small town where an urban district or borough served an inner area and was divided by an antique boundary from the rural district serving the hinterland. At the top-tier level the same duplication arose between county council and county borough with more serious results. An extreme case was at York where different sectors of the boundary of the independent county borough adjoined the separate Ridings, each with its own county council. Ultimately at national level the urban rural differentiation produced the conflict between the County Councils Association and the Association of Municipal Corporations that did much to inhibit basic structural reform.

The main failing of the pre-1972 system, however, was that many of the top-tier units were too small. Specialised services which demand the use of highly qualified staff, purpose-built accommodation and expensive equipment can only be provided economically for a substantial population. Planning also cannot be carried out effectively except over wide areas. The minimum size for top-tier units has been a matter of constant argument, but estimates continually increased. In 1888 the minimum population for county borough status was 50,000 and four exceptions below that figure were permitted. In 1926 the minimum was raised to 75,000; in 1958 to 100,000. Evidence given by government departments to the Redcliffe-Maud Commission was thinking in terms of 200–300,000 while the County Councils Association envisaged half a million. Government departments are attracted by the idea of fewer and larger local authorities as being easier to supervise in the interests of uniformity. Local authorities slowly accepted the need for bigger units out of fear that they would lose functions to other sectors of public administration.

If the case for change was so strong—one may well ask why so much time elapsed before any effective reforms were achieved? What were the obstacles? Reformers commonly fail to appreciate the extent and value of local patriotism. Councillors who had given much devoted service to a local authority could not be expected to welcome its demise and tended to resent any implication that their council had not been efficient. Local government officers, especially chief officers, feared the effect of change on their personal status. Ratepayers often feared, without firm evidence, that proposed alterations would adversely affect the local rates Behind these forces of local opinion stood the national pressure groups, the associations of local authorities, always ready to try to safeguard the interests of their members. Inevitably the different types of authority, notably counties and county boroughs, had opposing ideas as to the optimum pattern for local government. Successive Governments have been weak in being unwilling to enforce basic alterations in the absence of a general consensus among the interested parties. Politically reform of local government was an awkward topic. Many councillors are leading local personalities well able to make their views known to a local MP, and faced with sufficiently strong and influential local pressure a Government backbench MP might even find it expedient to ignore the party whip in the House of Commons on this issue. And there is a great difference between accepting the need for reform in principle and accepting a particular scheme which would drastically upset the established arrangements for representation and administration in your own area.

VARIED PROPOSALS 1945–70

During the last war, considerable interest developed in the need for local government reform. In part, this was an aspect of the nationwide discussion on post-war reconstruction; in part it was stimulated because the existing structure of authorities was seen to be ill-adapted to meet the emergencies of war. Various plans were put forward, e.g. by the Labour Party, the Association of Municipal Corporations and NALGO, each of which recognised the need for larger areas of administration for some purposes. These reports now belong to the history of local government but they helped to create a climate of opinion which caused the Government to take action.

Almost the last measure of the war-time coalition Cabinet was to promote the Local Government (Boundary Commission) Act, 1945, which established a Boundary Commission authorised to propose limited changes outside London. The limitations were all important, for the Commission was given no power over functions, so it could not introduce any new *type* of authority. Any prospect of regional government was eliminated from the start. (Local authorities were very hostile to the regional concept because of their dealings with the war-time Regional Commissioners.) Also excluded was any new arrangement to deal with the special problems of conurbations. The Commission had to work within the traditional model of local government: it could divide and amalgamate counties, demote county boroughs, create new ones, or amalgamate and divide them, and change the geographical arrangement of second-tier authorities. The Commission studied their problem for over two years, then reported that their powers were insufficient to initiate the changes needed and set out the details of a wholly new structure. One-tier local government was to be kept in only 17 of the largest cities with a minimum population of 200,000, to be known as one-tier counties. The remainder of the country, including the Lancashire-Cheshire conurbations, was to have a two-tier system. The major authorities would be reshaped counties, again with a minimum population of 200,000, so that the smaller counties would be amalgamated and in a few cases the largest counties would be subdivided. Within these counties would be boroughs and urban and rural districts, together with a new type of authority confusingly termed 'county boroughs' which would exercise all powers except for planning, police, fire service and main roads. The new county boroughs would be Liverpool, Manchester and other towns in the population bracket 60,000–200,000. Thus there were to be three categories of town, one-tier counties, county boroughs and other boroughs: this plan had the advantage of easing the sharp contrast in status between the wholly independent county boroughs and other urban authorities. The changes proposed were far too sweeping to be easily acceptable and in 1949 the Boundary Commission was dissolved and its ideas were consigned unloved to civil service archives.

The issue then remained dormant until 1953 when the Conservative Government asked the associations of local authorities to re-examine the problem. It seemed that the Government hoped that the associations might arrive at an agreed set of principles that could provide the basis for reform. The hope was delusory. The associations produced two conflicting schemes for reform and it was clear that there could be no agreement on principles for fundamental change. The only way in which the Government could gain broad consent from the associations was to propose a scheme which would lead to relatively minor adjustments in the existing structure. There was also a general acceptance of the need to examine whether further powers could be delegated by counties to districts with a population over 60,000, a quite remarkable contrast to the style of discussions which took place ten years later.

The Local Government Act, 1958, thereupon established two fresh Boundary Commissions, one for England and one for Wales. The Commissions were instructed to carry out their tasks within the present framework of county and county borough organisation. Thus they could propose the creation or amalgamation or demotion of county boroughs; they could suggest boundary adjustments between top-tier authorities. The English Commission had wider powers in the conurbations (described in the 1958 Act as the special review areas of Tyneside, West Yorkshire, South-East Lancashire, Merseyside and the West Midlands) where it could propose the establishment of a 'continuous county' in which the distribution of functions between the county and the second-tier authorities might depart from the normal pattern. The English Commission divided the country into areas and studied them piecemeal. As a start, the Commission held preliminary consultations with local authorities and then issued draft proposals. Before changes could take place, there was a long road to travel. The procedure designed for consultations, enquiries and appeals was so complex that some five years elapsed between the start of local discussions and the operative date for any actual changes. Plenty of opportunity was given for public opinion to make itself felt; the force of opinion might cause a Commission to change its mind or lead the Minister to reject the final plans of a Commission. There was a marked tendency for each stage of decision-making to reduce the amount of change.

A number of factors led to the decline of the English Commission. Wales is considered separately below. The morass of procedure for dealing with objectors strangled any impetus in its work. Some of its schemes seemed to be designed to arouse a maximum of ill-feeling while achieving a minimum of benefit. Does it really matter whether Lyme Regis is in Dorset or Devon? The Commission would have proceeded more speedily and probably with more influence had it concentrated always on major issues. But on major issues the Commission got little support from the Government. The reprieve of Rutland was the most glaring example. With only 25,000 people Rutland was forced to rely heavily on its neighbours to assist in the provision of services. After Rutland the Commission lost credibility and its status was further damaged when the Government refused its request to expand the Manchester and Merseyside Special Review areas and so close the gap between them.

The final death blow to the Commission, and perhaps it was a happy release, came from the appointment of a Minister of Housing and Local Government, Mr Richard Crossman, who was determined to accomplish radical reforms. A few sentences of his address to the 1965 Conference of the Association of Municipal Corporations at Torquay are worth quoting. He argued that '. . . the whole structure of local government is out of date, that our county borough and county councils as at present organised are archaic institutions whose size and structure make them increasingly ill-adapted to fulfilling the immensely important functions with which they are charged. The greatest obstacle, in fact, which prevents efficient councils from retaining public confidence is the obsolete constitutional framework within which they had to operate.' From a responsible Minister these were striking words. After some further delay the English Commission was wound up in 1966 and was replaced by a Royal Commission which could examine the whole subject afresh and with a clean sheet.

In contrast with their hesitant action in the provinces the Conservative Government took a much firmer line over the reform of London government. One reason was that action in London imposed virtually no strain on party loyalties. As the London County Council was commonly dominated by a Labour majority, a Conservative Cabinet had few political inhibitions about promoting change. In 1957 a Royal Commission had been established to study the special characteristics of the capital and the surrounding area which, therefore, was excluded from the operations of the English Commission established by the 1958 Act. The central difficulty in London was the absence of any local authority which embraced the whole of the built-up zone. The London County Council had inherited the 1855 boundary of the Metropolitan Board of Works which a century later had ceased to have any connection with geographical realities. London spilled over into large sections of Kent, Surrey, Hertfordshire, Essex and the whole of Middlesex. Little more than a third of the population of Greater London lived within the LCC area, and the LCC population of 3,200,000 was still declining slowly. There were also three county boroughs in Greater London—Croydon, East Ham and West Ham—so nine top-tier authorities in the London area were each responsible for broad issues of planning policy. No single local authority could have a synoptic view of the issues connected with the redevelopment and zoning of Greater London, the movement of population and the construction of main traffic arteries.

In brief outline this was the situation facing the Royal Commission on London Government. Its Report, Cmnd 1164 of 1960, unanimously urged drastic changes. The Commission was of opinion that a Council for Greater London should be established to be responsible for overall planning, main roads, fire and ambulance services. It would also share responsibility for education, housing, planning applications and certain other services with a new type of second-tier authority—Greater London Boroughs. These Greater London Boroughs would have the status and constitution of municipal boroughs except that the City of London would be permitted to retain its ancient institutions. The Commission's scheme envisaged 52 of these Boroughs with populations between 100,000 and 250,000 —except, again, for the City of London: they would be responsible for health and welfare services, child care, local roads and libraries, in addition to the duties shared with the Council for Greater London. Reorganisation on this scale involved the disappearance of the LCC, Middlesex and three county boroughs, substantial loss of territory and rateable value by four county councils, and extensive amalgamations of county districts and Metropolitan Boroughs. These proposals aroused considerable opposition in the Labour Party and also in some suburban fringe areas which heartily disliked the prospect of integration with the metropolis.

In this instance, however, the Government were not deflected by local hostility. They accepted the broad lines of the Royal Commission's Report and the London Government Act, 1963, now provides an opportunity for the co-ordinated planning of the whole metropolitan area. There were some modifications to the Commission's proposals. The number of London Boroughs was reduced from 52 to 32. There were two reasons for this change: first, some fringe areas were excluded from the London area altogether and remain in Surrey and Essex; and second, and far more important, the minimum population of London Boroughs was doubled. This rise to 200,000 was due partly to the further decision that London Boroughs shall have full powers over education—save in the former LCC territory where a committee of the GLC, the Inner London Education Authority, representing the area concerned, has this responsibility.

To return to the problems of provincial England, the Royal Commission was appointed in February, 1966, under the Chairmanship of Lord Redcliffe-Maud with these terms of reference:

'To consider the structure of local government in England, outside Greater London, in relation to its existing functions; and to make recommendations for authorities and boundaries, and for functions and their division, having regard to the size and the character of areas in which these can be most effectively exercised and the need to sustain a viable system of democracy.'

It will be noted that this phraseology contains a hint of the perennial conflict between efficiency and democracy. The choice of chairman was also significant: one expected Lord Redcliffe-Maud to produce a structure in harmony with the ideas of the earlier Maud Committee on the internal management of local authorities which showed a heavy emphasis on efficiency.

The views of government departments presented to the Commission showed quite remarkable similarity. All favoured larger units of local government in the interests of efficiency and uniformity. No doubt they felt that fewer local authorities would be easier to supervise. The Ministry of Transport wished for 30–40 major transport authorities to replace the then 823 highway authorities and 1,190 parking authorities. Indeed, all departments favoured 30–40 major authorities. How did these magic figures occur separately to so many minds? Within the overall figure of 30–40 authorities there was some variation of approach. Education sought a population of 500,000 with a minimum of 300,000, but Health was prepared to go down to 200,000. There was also difference about the need for second-tier authorities: Housing and Local Government accepted the need for a second-tier, the Treasury assumed all-purpose authorities while Transport was unsure—'there is no advantage in creating lower-tier authorities in areas which could be adequately governed at first-tier level'.

Evidence from the associations of local authorities was less uniform but more forward looking than on previous occasions: delegation of county functions to second-tier authorities attracted little interest. The County Councils Association naturally proposed a two-tier system in which the top-tier authorities should have a minimum of half a million population with second-tier authorities of 40,000 to 150,000—the lower figure being appropriate for sparsely peopled areas. Had the CCA suggested a lower figure for major authorities, they would have opened the way for an increasing number of large towns to claim independence and maintain existing county borough status. The suggested distribution of functions between upper and lower tiers was not greatly different from the present arrangements, except that no recommendation was made about the allocation of responsibility for personal health, children and welfare services. The Association of Municipal Corporations was much less specific. It urged a two-tier system of elected provincial and local authorities but did not specify population limits for each type of authority: the intention seemed to be that provinces should be smaller than the existing economic regions but larger than the top-tier bodies envisaged by government departments and the County Councils Association. The difference is explained by the fact that the AMC proposed only a limited range of functions for their provinces. It would include planning and some further education, perhaps police, fire and water supply.

The departmental view that education authorities required a population of 500,000 implied that the London Boroughs were far too small to be effective education authorities. This was curious since these authorities were created as recently as 1963, and minimum sizes of authority are generally thought of as being *higher* in densely populated areas. Further, the evidence submitted by the inspectorate in the Department of Education and Science indicated that the quality of service suffered where the population of an LEA was below 200,000: however, the inspectors judged authorities in the 200–250,000 bracket to be superior to those in the 300–400,000 bracket and equal to those in the 400–500,000 range. Thus the 500,000 standard and absolute minimum of 300,000 suggested by the Department are open to objection. Another problem concerning education is whether the education function can be split between two tiers of authorities. If an upper-tier authority is requisite for further education, must primary education also be provided by the same category of authority? The departmental view has been that education is an interrelated whole and cannot be divided. The contrary view is that there is a clear break between school education and further education, both in relation to geographical location and the type and method of education provided. The question of whether a function can be divided also arises elsewhere—can house construction usefully be separated from house maintenance, can highway construction be divorced from traffic control? But it is in education that the divisibility of the service is a most crucial issue.

The Report of the Royal Commission (Cmnd 4040) was published in July 1969. It is impossible for a brief summary to do full justice to the Report and the Memorandum of Dissent by Mr Derek Senior. The Commission found six weaknesses in the local government system each of which are discussed elsewhere in this book; the six problems were the division between town and country, the division between county boroughs and counties, division of responsibility within counties, the small size of many authorities, the relationship between local authorities and the public and between local authorities and the central government. Obviously, these items were interrelated. The distinction between town and country, county and county borough, aggravated relations between central and local government because Ministers and civil servants had to deal with separate local authority associations. The minute size of some authorities tended to raise levels of central supervision over all councils. The division of functions between different types of authority was confusing to the public. Councils were often deeply concerned by problems that were the responsibility of another authority. This analysis pointed clearly to two solutions—bigger authorities and a greatly simplified system.

The Commission (except Mr Senior) therefore proposed that the greater part of England be divided into 58 unitary authorities which would be responsible for almost all executive action in relation to local government services. Unitary areas would embrace town and countryside. The major towns which provide a focus for the commerce and cultural life of the surrounding area should also constitute the centre for local government. The administrative map would be made to coincide as far as possible with contemporary economic and social geography. Inevitably, this concept fitted some parts of the country better than others. The population of the 58 units suggested by the Commission varied from 195,000 for the Halifax area to well over a million in Sheffield and South Yorkshire. The Report accepted that there would be serious disadvantages in terms of size and remoteness if the population of an all-purpose unitary authority was much more than a million. So a quite different two-tier system was proposed for the three largest conurbations; this was similar but not identical, to the pattern that has operated in London since 1963. In these three areas, the West Midlands, Merseyside and Selnec, i.e. South-East Lancashire and North-East Cheshire, the top-tier or metropolitan authority would have been responsible for planning, transportation, water supply, sewerage, refuse disposal, police, fire and ambulance services; some tasks were to be split between upper and lower tiers, notably housing and provision of entertainment and recreation facilities; all other duties would rest with the 20 lower-tier metropolitan districts. This plan would have given the districts a very important role with responsibility for personal services including education. The whole scheme involved a direct reversal of traditional wisdom about local government: it had been assumed that single-tier authorities were suitable for compact urban areas but that more sparsely populated rural areas required a multi-tier system. The Royal Commission argued that the single-tier arrangement is appropriate for mixed urban and rural areas while the two-tier system should be reserved for the greatest urban concentrations.

It is true that the Commission also proposed the establishment of local councils within the unitary authorities and, where desired, in metropolitan areas. Initially their areas were to correspond with the displaced county and non-county boroughs, urban districts and parishes. The variations in size were extreme. These local councils would have only one duty—to express local opinion by making representations to the unitary authority: they would also have optional powers to provide local amenities and might, with the agreement of the unitary authority, assist with some of its functions.

Set above the unitary and metropolitan authorities already described, the Commission recommended the establishment of eight provincial councils covering areas coinciding with those of the economic planning regions. Provincial bodies were to be largely recruited by indirect election, i.e. elected by the unitary and metropolitan authorities, and would co-opt between 20 per cent and 25 per cent of their membership. A quotation from the Commission's Report best describes their purpose, 'The (provincial) council's chief task will be to create a broad strategic framework for the exercise of main authorities' operational responsibilities.' This section of the Report has been criticised for vagueness. However, it is clear that the provincial councils were expected to exercise supervision over planning, further education and other highly specialised fields, e.g. education for handicapped children and cultural activities. They might undertake major development projects of benefit to a number of authorities within its area. Provincial councils would keep in close touch with the regional offices of government departments. The obvious objection is that the provincial councils were not to be directly elected. This would damage their status and inhibit their activities. No doubt the Commission was conscious of the hostility to elected regional councils among both the main political parties, local authorities and government departments. If an advisory body ignores political considerations the chances that its recommendations will be accepted must be greatly diminished.

Other proposals from the Commission reflected the views of the Report of the Maud Committee on Management issued two years earlier. Aldermen should be abolished. No council should have more than 75 members. The number of committees should be small. A central committee should work out priorities. Every authority should appoint a chief executive, chosen regardless of professional background. Delegation to officers should be freely exercised. Local offices should be established where the public can seek advice.

The main issue facing the Commission was the choice between essentially one-tier and two-tier local government. Here a dispute arose between the Commission and one of their number, Mr Derek Senior. Mr Senior was a journalist specialising in local government and had committed himself, before appointment to the Commission, to the concept of 30–40 City Regions as being the optimum basis for local government reorganisation. It is arguable that anyone who is already committed to a particular solution to a problem is unsuitable to serve on a body designed to advise upon it. Not surprisingly, Mr Senior pursued his idea of a City Region and became estranged from his colleagues. There is some similarity between his City Region concept and the unitary authorities since both ensure the amalgamation of town and country. But the 35 Senior City Regions were larger: 20 of the 35 regions would have had virtually a million or more inhabitants. All members of the Commission were agreed that units of this size were too large to be all-purpose authorities and so the Senior plan proposed 148 district councils. The Senior City Regions would have been responsible for planning, transportation, water supply, sewerage, police, fire, education and 'capital investment programming': other more personal services would be left to the district authorities. Mr Senior also proposed minor local common councils and five indirectly elected provincial authorities. The differences between the Majority Report and the Senior dissent can be illustrated by a diagram.

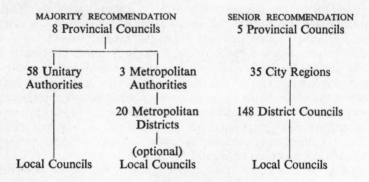

The crucial clash was over the principle of unitary authorities. Thirty-five City Regions would certainly fit in well with the evidence presented by government departments. Why then did the Commission reject this plan? Essentially because the majority of members were convinced of the value of all-purpose county borough type authorities: where responsibility for local government is undivided, then co-operation between services is much easier. Since the Senior units were too big to be all-purpose authorities, smaller units had to be found. The Report noted that the evidence of the DES inspectors did not support the Department's claim that an education authority should have a population of half a million; Lord Redcliffe-Maud and his colleagues were therefore prepared to accept unitary authorities of 250,000 people, or even less in a few cases. They also tried, in contrast to Senior, to respect existing local boundaries wherever possible. The argument against unitary authorities is that it is impossible to define areas which are suitable for the operation of all local government services. One is forced to choose either areas suitable for planning purposes which are too large and remote for personal services, or a framework suitable for personal services, that is too small for planning.

The views of the Labour Government on these problems were set out in a White Paper, *Reform of Local Government in England* (Cmnd 4276), published in February 1970. In general, the ideas of the majority of the Commission were accepted. However, two further areas were added to the two-tier metropolitan category—South Hampshire and West Yorkshire. This reduced unitary authorities from 58 to 51 and increased metropolitan areas from 3 to 5 and metropolitan districts from 20 to 28. In effect, seven unitary areas were demoted to metropolitan districts and an extra district was created for the Isle of Wight which previously would have been wholly absorbed in the Portsmouth unit. The White Paper immediately raised the criticism that boundaries designed for unitary authorities were not necessarily appropriate for second-tier districts but it did accept that there would have to be further consultations about boundaries. It also proposed two other main amendments to the Royal Commission's plan. Education in the metropolitan areas was to be an upper-tier not a lower-tier function; this would have divorced education from other social services. Secondly, the Government felt that local councils should not share the executive tasks of unitary authorities as this could cause duplication and confusion. Instead, district committees should be formed to supervise a more decentralised system of administration within the unitary authority: local councils would nominate members to these district committees. This suggestion was contrary to the Maud theory that councillors should concentrate on broad policy and remit the detailed execution of policy to officials.

Public reactions to the unitary authority idea were hostile. The Conservative Party favoured a two-tier system. So also did the County Councils Association and the Urban and Rural Districts. Rural areas feel strongly that a two-tier system reduces the danger that the interests of the countryside will be disregarded and swamped by urban centres. Almost in isolation the AMC favoured the unitary scheme. There was much sympathy among local councillors for the Senior alternative because it provided for more local councils and seemed less remote, but this ignored the fact that the Senior scheme would have produced fewer and larger education authorities and that his proposed boundaries would do more to disturb present administrative and social patterns. All the pressure was for more representation, more 'democracy' and, in general, to water down the scale of reform. The election of a Conservative Government in 1970 ensured that the concept of unitary authorities was dead.

As a postscript to the discussion of proposals for structural reform, mention must be made of the separate developments in Wales. Here the local authorities, except in South Wales, tended to be weak in terms of population and rateable values. In spite of very considerable financial aid from the national Exchequer it had been difficult to maintain a standard of service comparable with that enjoyed in other areas. The 1958 Commission for Wales intended to deal with this situation by a drastic plan of county amalgamations which would have reduced the number of Welsh counties from thirteen to seven. Anglesey alone was to remain intact. Inevitably, the plan was hotly opposed in Wales. Local patriotism was incensed by the complete disregard of existing county boundaries and some of the new counties proposed were both large and inconvenient in shape. Inevitably these proposals were rejected. Subsequently an inter-departmental working party was established to review Welsh problems. Its conclusions, published in 1967, were that Merthyr Tydfil should cease to be a county borough and that the counties be reduced from thirteen to five by a process of amalgamation of whole units. Subsequently this number was raised to six when the Government agreed that North Wales should form two counties instead of one. The four new counties suggested were:

Clwyd   —a combination of Denbighshire and Flintshire.
Dyfed   —a combination of Cardiganshire, Carmarthenshire and Pembrokeshire.
Gwynedd—a combination of Anglesey, Caernarvonshire and Merionethshire.
Powys   —a combination of Breconshire, Montgomeryshire and Radnorshire.

Glamorgan and Monmouthshire, renamed Gwent, were to remain. Thus with the three remaining county boroughs, Cardiff, Newport and Swansea, there would have been nine major local authorities in Wales. At the second-tier level the proposal was to reduce the number of councils from 164 to 36.

No action was taken on these plans in spite of the wide measure of agreement to support them. The Redcliffe-Maud Report and the Labour Government's acceptance of unitary authorities for England injected a new element into the situation. If county boroughs were to disappear in England, then the retention of three 1888-style county boroughs in Wales became anomalous. So the Secretary of State for Wales announced a new plan in 1970 to create three Maud-type unitary authorities in South Wales, one for Newport and Monmouthshire, one for Cardiff and East Glamorgan and a third for Swansea and West Glamorgan. This would have reduced the number of major authorities in Wales to seven. The application of the unitary principle to South Wales caused a storm of protest, not least because it involved the dropping of district councils within the unitary areas. A fresh anomaly was created: in England, two-tier local government was to be restricted to the main centres of population, but in Wales it was to apply to the less populous areas, Clwyd, Dyfed, Gwynedd and Powys. This dilemma was also resolved by the election of a Conservative administration wedded to the concept of two-tier local government.

Chapter II

PREPARATIONS FOR THE NEW SYSTEM

THE EMERGENCE OF THE 1972 ACT

The new Government in 1970 grasped the nettle of local government reform with commendable vigour. The Ministry of Housing and Local Government was renamed the Department of the Environment to stress the breadth of its responsibility to promote good living conditions. Early in 1969 a Commission on the Constitution had been appointed with wide terms of reference—'to consider the relations between the central government and the several countries, nations and regions of the United Kingdom'. Clearly, this broad inquiry would have provided a good excuse to postpone changes in the structure of local administration. The opportunity for delay was ignored. The new Secretary of State, Mr Peter Walker, moved ahead and quite rapidly prepared a fresh policy.

A White Paper published in February, 1971, *Local Government in England* (Cmnd 4584), argued that regional or provincial areas would be too large for the operation of local government services so that local government reorganisation could proceed independently of other changes that might be made subsequently in regional administration or representation. The White Paper itself was remarkably brief. A mere dozen pages outlined the basis of a new system of local government. The detailed geographical application of these principles was set out in a separate document, Department of the Environment Circular 8/71. The White Paper recognised the ever-competing claims of efficiency, which demanded larger units of organisation, and representative democracy which favoured smaller units. A fair compromise had to be made between them but where the arguments were evenly balanced the White Paper promised that the case for fuller representation would be decisive. So the tasks of local government were to be divided between two tiers of authorities, counties and districts. The allocation of functions was to differ between the main industrial areas with heavy concentrations of population and the remainder of England which is predominantly rural or semi-rural. Thus there are two styles of local government system, the metropolitan and the non-metropolitan.

The crucial distinction between the two lies in the distribution of responsibility for education, including libraries, and the personal social services. It was argued in the White Paper that the effective organisation of these functions required a population between 250,000 and one million, although these limits were not to be rigidly applied. The minimum figure was substantially below that advocated by the Department of Education and Science in its evidence to the Royal Commission. In the conurbations it is possible to form second-tier districts compact in size which fall within this population range. Here the districts can undertake education and the social services. Six metropolitan areas were proposed—Merseyside, Greater Manchester, West Midlands, West Yorkshire, South Yorkshire and Tyneside. These metropolitan counties were to contain 34 metropolitan districts. The Conservative list of conurbations differed from the Labour scheme issued a year before in that South Yorkshire and Tyneside were added but South Hampshire was omitted.

In more rural areas the second-tier authorities must have a population far below 250,000 if they are to be reasonably small in area with offices readily accessible for residents and councillors. Here the major functions remain largely with the county council and the distribution of powers between county and district remains very similar to the previous pattern. The White Paper proposed the establishment of 38 non-metropolitan counties and the accompanying DOE Circular outlined boundaries for the counties. Northumberland, the smallest non-metropolitan county in terms of population, barely passed the 250,000 limit. At the other extreme six non-metropolitan counties exceeded a million inhabitants. It is arguable that the three largest, Essex, Hampshire and Kent, are too big to be satisfactory representative bodies responsible for education and social services, especially as they are all areas that can anticipate substantial further growth in the immediate future. The DOE circular also suggested boundaries for metropolitan districts. Here the population range lay between 182,000 and 1,168,000 (Birmingham). It is notable that many of these districts had a population and rateable resources considerably below those of many demoted county boroughs. Clearly the status of a local authority was to depend not only on size but also on the nature of the area and its surroundings. A Boundary Commission was established to delimit areas for non-metropolitan districts and this body reported in 1972 with proposals for 278 districts with an average population around 100,000. As far as possible the new district map was formed by amalgamations of existing authorities. In the most remote rural areas district populations fall as low as 40,000. Largest districts are former county boroughs which the Commission felt unable to split, e.g. Bristol, but the fledgling county borough of Teesside was divided into three districts. Subsequent negotiations secured some changes in the boundaries originally proposed, but in general, the original suggestions were carried into effect.

The White Paper recognised the value of the third-tier authorities, the rural parishes. These were to continue, but with powers rather than duties. But what was to be done with the boroughs and urban districts due to lose their separate identities in the reshaping of second-tier authorities? Two solutions were offered. Either parish councils could be established in essentially urban areas or local communities might achieve some form of local representation through non-statutory bodies, which might be assisted by district councils financially or in other ways. Subsequently it was agreed that third-tier councils be formed in many of the former boroughs and urban districts within an upper population limit of approximately 20,000. Areas which had formed larger authorities were held not to need separate institutions as they would play a major role within the new district councils.

The practical effect of these changes was to vary greatly between different parts of England. In five shires, Cornwall, Hertfordshire, the Isle of Wight, Salop and Wiltshire, the only change was to district boundaries. Elsewhere there were adjustments to county boundaries and/or the amalgamation of former counties either in part or as a whole. Many of the new shires had to join with one or more former county boroughs, which, inevitably, resented their demotion. The shock was weaker where the county borough was already the geographical headquarters of the administrative county. Norwich and Nottingham were less disturbed than Plymouth, Portsmouth or Southampton. The complexity of reorganisation was greatest in the metropolitan areas because, apart from new boundaries, wholly new types of authority were to be created.

For Wales the proposals of the Conservative Government were in tune with their policy for England. The two-tier system was to prevail everywhere. The new pattern contained seven counties and 36 districts. Glamorgan was to be split into two and five other counties Clwyd, Dyfed, Gwent, Gwynedd and Powys were to be established broadly on the lines described above. The Local Government Act itself contained a further change: Glamorgan was divided into three sections. This further division is controversial because the new county of South Glamorgan is exceptional as it contains only two districts, one based on Cardiff and one on Barry. Cardiff dwarfs the remainder of the county. There are examples in England where a major city has a predominant position within a county but nowhere is this so overwhelming as in South Glamorgan. Whether Cardiff should have such exceptional treatment must be a matter of opinion.

The 1972 Act emerged after at least 25 years of intermittent official discussions about local government reform. Its passage to the statute book was relatively easy. The Labour Party opposed the Bill in Parliament, but the Party's position was weakened by its earlier acceptance of the unitary authority plan advocated by the majority of the Royal Commission, an idea that was widely unpopular. Nor did Labour's other main objections to the Bill arouse much enthusiasm. To urge that metropolitan counties rather than districts should be given responsibility for education was to move against the current of opinion demanding fuller representation and participation. Another important criticism was that boundaries had been drawn too tightly around the metropolitan areas with the consequence that these authorities would find it difficult or impossible to obtain the land needed for housing development in the foreseeable future—at least within their own territory. Obviously the 'fringe' areas immediately affected did not share this attitude. They wished to remain as rural or semi-rural as possible and so were well content that the Bill excluded them from the conurbations. Another political complaint raised the charge of gerrymandering: it was said that the Conservative Government had designed boundaries which would give them local political advantage. This claim could have some justification in that county boroughs, normally Labour, were merged in counties normally Conservative. However, the charge lost much of its bite because Labour had also proposed to merge counties with county boroughs, although in a rather different way. In any case the political effect of a given boundary is open to dispute. It may assist one party on one side of a line and the opposing party on the other. Or it may help different parties on different occasions.

During the second reading debate in the House of Commons on the Bill the most lively issue concerned a question of procedure rather than substance: it was whether the proposals for Wales should have been presented in a separate Bill. Naturally there was much argument over matters of detail. The standing committee met on no fewer than 51 occasions. The report stage was also lengthy; many amendments were considered: the Commons sat up all night several times. But no changes of principle were made. The Government agreed to various alterations of detail. It was defeated only once in the Commons; by a majority of four an amendment was passed to give non-metropolitan districts powers in relation to refuse disposal. Later the Government successfully introduced a further amendment in the Lords to reverse this decision. So refuse disposal went to the counties. But the House of Lords were successful in forcing some changes in local boundaries. There was a flood of Government amendments, mostly minor and technical, at the end of the legislative process in the last few days of the parliamentary session. As a result some details of importance did not get a reasonable amount of consideration. Indeed, the very last stages of the Bill were notable for confusion combined with an acceptance by all parties that the Bill must be allowed to pass.

Why was this fairly general acceptance obtained? In view of the tensions caused by earlier proposals this relative harmony demands explanation. One reason, certainly, was that a general weariness had surrounded the whole question. There was broad agreement that some change was essential; that without reform local powers would be further eroded by central departments. Then the 1972 scheme was in many ways easier to accept than earlier plans. The Royal Commission had ignored the extent to which the county was a social unit as well as an administrative entity and that as a social unit it commanded considerable loyalty. In contrast the Conservative plan respected existing boundaries to a far greater extent, especially in relation to the counties. The associations of local authorities broadly accepted the plan with the exception of the Association of Municipal Corporations. And the AMC, although dissatisfied, was helpless. Amendments proposed at the committee stage designed to allocate certain county functions to former county boroughs with a minimum population of 150,000 received scant support. Of course there were many cases in which individual MPs tried to secure changes on behalf of constituency interests. Organised protest lobbies at Westminster sometimes showed a public relations flair: Herefordshire produced a Hereford bull and Plymouth paraded Drake's drum. However, with a few exceptions, these campaigns were ineffectual. They were never co-ordinated and were sometimes conflicting. Undoubtedly another factor which eased the path of the Bill was that both the Opposition and the Government backbenchers were far more concerned about other social and economic issues. In 1972 local government was far from being top of the political agenda.

So the Bill became an Act. The following chapters will outline the more important of its provisions.

THE BIRTH OF THE NEW COUNCILS

Four requirements must be met before a new public body can establish itself on an effective working basis. It must have the essential legal powers, finance, staff and accommodation. The 1972 Act provided the legal and financial basis for future operations: the assembly of resources, in terms of staff and accommodation, was a matter for local action. But this represents the bare bones of the skeleton. For any organisation to work well, good internal relations are of great importance. For a democratic organisation to give satisfactory service there must be a wide measure of public support and understanding. So the new councils were faced with the twin tasks of creating a fresh administrative system and also of promoting a fuller understanding of their future activities.

The Local Government Act became fully effective on 1 April 1974. The delay was necessary in order to complete arrangements for the changeover from the old authorities to the new. There were two phases to the preparations. First, joint committees were formed composed of elected representatives from the authorities to be joined together. Second, elections for the new councils were held between March and June 1973, so these bodies had between nine and twelve months to set up shop and make themselves ready to accept executive responsibilities from 1 April 1974.

Some of the joint committees started work on a voluntary basis as early as the autumn of 1971; once the Bill became law they were placed on a statutory basis. Their task was two-fold. The committees had to organise the elections to choose their successors and make the basic decisions about time and place of the initial meetings of the new councils. Far more important was the work done in framing a mass of advice for the new regime. Detailed suggestions were made in relation to management and committee structures and over the organisation of particular services. Naturally, the extent of this guidance varied. Many joint committees drew up exhaustive blueprints. Elsewhere, particularly where there was doubt about the future political complexion of the councils, the preparations were less extensive. Of course, the detailed work was not done by the members of the joint committees themselves. Working parties were formed, composed of senior officials of authorities due to be merged together. Thus specialised professional attention was given to the problems of uniting each major group of local authority departments. In the shire counties these discussions often centred on how far services should be decentralised to area offices, possibly through agency agreements with district councils. The working parties also reviewed the availability of accommodation and the difficulties that would arise from the harmonisation of policies and administrative practices. It is important to stress the influence of these working parties: where they reached agreement their reports were normally accepted by the parent joint committee and then passed on to the new authority which, in turn, generally accepted the proposals. The new councils, of course, were advised by their chief officers who generally had been members of the local working parties. There were occasions where joint committees failed to agree due to a clash of political policy or of local interests; such disputes could be settled only by the newly-elected councillors. Sometimes, as in South Yorkshire, the location of the headquarters of the new authority produced a major conflict.

Many joint committees devoted much attention to framing models of committee and management structures. This activity was greatly stimulated by the publication of the Bains Report in September 1972. A full analysis of the Report is given in Chapter VII. It is mentioned here in order to emphasise the great impact it made on the ideas of the joint committees and subsequently on the decisions of the new councils.

The newly elected councillors arrived in the spring of 1973. They started off in the morning twilight with none of the detailed problems which arise from the normal administration of services. Instead their work had an abstract, almost academic, quality as approval had to be given to models, plans and schedules which determined how their organisation should work. Until these fundamental issues were resolved, little progress could be made on building an organisation. The first step was to appoint a Chief Executive and at least some chief officers. This was an essential prelude to forming the pattern of committees and local authority departments. Until chief officers had been chosen, departmental establishments could not be fixed. The councils which proceeded most rapidly with the selection of top officials had the widest range of choice. So everything encouraged speed. Matters which, in normal circumstances, would have caused months of discussion were settled in weeks. The point must be stressed because in this initial formative period decisions were made which, for good or ill, will influence local administration for years to come. The need for haste was the more unfortunate because often the new councillors were unknown to each other. Naturally the extent of previous acquaintance varied. It depended on how far the previous councillors and aldermen had been re-elected and on how far the authorities in the locality had been amalgamated. Experienced councillors found themselves among strangers; inexperienced councillors found themselves among strangers in a strange situation. The most common link was loyalty to a political group, so political parties tended to provide the main element of social cement in the new authorities.

In this situation the recommendations passed down from the dying authorities through the joint committees carried great weight. The first business of the new authorities was to consider these recommendations. At this stage a paradox emerges. To follow the advice of your predecessors is normally to follow the ways of your predecessors. So reliance on the wisdom of the joint committees could easily have led to minimum change in the methods of conducting business. However, this did not occur because the legacy of advice was geared to the quite radical innovations suggested in the Bains Report. Of course, some of the new authorities moved away from the blueprints prepared for them. Indeed some joint committees made far more detailed proposals than did others. Nevertheless, the chain of influence from the Bains Report through the joint committees to the committee and management structures of the new councils was very strong.

THE ASSOCIATIONS OF LOCAL AUTHORITIES

It is convenient to notice here the associations of local authorities, particularly as they were reorganised in 1974 to fit the new situation created by reorganisation. Each type of local authority has its own national association which provides its members with a collective voice. These bodies have a variety of functions. They provide advice for individual local authorities. They give an opportunity to exchange opinions and experience about current problems. They provide representation on the wide range of public bodies and advisory committees that are in some way connected with local government. They co-operate with each other and so provide a united policy for some aspects of local administration. The associations nominate representatives on the myriad of National Joint Councils which negotiate salaries, wages and conditions of employment for all those on the payroll of local authorities. Joint bodies have been established each with a specialised purpose and known by a code name devised from initial letters in the formal title of the organisation. A glossary may be useful:

JACLAP: Joint Advisory Committee for Local Authorities Purchasing.
LACSAB: Local Authorities Conditions of Service Advisory Board.
LAMIT: Local Authorities Mutual Investment Trust.
LAMSAC: Local Authorities Management Services Advisory Committee.
LGTB: Local Government Training Board.

The main task of the associations is to negotiate with each other and with government departments about proposals to change the law or any administrative practices concerning local government. In particular they engage in detailed negotiations with civil servants over the amount of financial assistance local government is to receive from the Exchequer through the rate support grant. Each association is in touch with one or more MPs who may be asked, on appropriate occasions, to put forward in the House of Commons the point of view of a particular category of local authority. It is easy to overlook these activities and to underrate their significance, because much of the work is done in private and does not receive great publicity. In fact, central departments do not generally introduce a change in policy—unless it be a major political decision—without some prior and semi-confidential discussions with the associations. Should the latter be firmly united in opposition to government proposals, then Ministers often make adjustments so that their policy becomes more acceptable. While the associations are often in conflict with government departments every effort is made to keep relationships as harmonious as possible. They try to evade issues which are not strictly local government matters and they also avoid becoming entangled in a dispute between any one local authority and a Ministry unless there are general principles involved of general concern.

The reorganisation of local government following the 1972 Act provided a unique opportunity to reorganise the associations as well. One possibility was that they might join into a single body, perhaps with a federal constitution. The advantages of such a move were apparent. There would be a great simplification in the structure of the joint organisations which the associations have formed or on which they are represented. The development of further nationally-based services to local councils would be facilitated. There would be administrative economies. Above all, local government would be able to speak to central government and the general public with a single and far more powerful voice. Discussions were held between the associations to see if a basis of unity could be found. However, no agreement was reached largely for political reasons. All the metropolitan counties and most of the metropolitan districts returned Labour majorities at the 1973 elections. So the leaders of these councils came to favour a separate national organisation for metropolitan areas in the knowledge that such a body would normally be dominated by the Labour Party. The Greater London Council, which previously had stood apart from the associations, agreed to join. So also did the London boroughs. Thus the Association of Metropolitan Authorities was born. When it became clear that unity among all types of authorities was impossible, the shire counties formed the Association of County Councils and likewise the districts formed the Association of District Councils. The third-tier authorities are now represented through the National Association of Local Councils which serves parish councils, town councils and community councils in Wales. Education authorities have had a separate national organisation since 1902, the Association of Education Committees. The value of this separate body became a matter of controversy after the 1972 reorganisation as not all education authorities supported it. In 1977 the AEC decided to wind up its affairs.

Chapter III

THE BASIS OF THE SYSTEM

TYPES OF LOCAL AUTHORITY

The reformed local government system in England and Wales is based on four sub-systems which can be illustrated conveniently by diagram. The structure for the main urban centres of population is shown on the left of the page and that for the remainder of the country on the right.

Conurbations	*Mixed Urban and Rural Areas*

English Provinces

6 Metropolitan Counties	39 Counties
|	|
36 Metropolitan Districts or Boroughs	296 Districts or Boroughs
|	|
Parishes or Towns (*in some places*)	Parishes or Towns (*except in larger urban areas*)

London	**Wales**
Greater London Council	8 Counties
|	|
32 London Boroughs	37 Districts or Boroughs
	|
	Communities or Towns (*except in larger urban areas*)

In addition to these multi-purpose authorities there exists a wide variety of special purpose bodies and joint committees formed by or in association with the major local authorities. Perhaps the most important institution of this kind is the Inner London Education Authority (ILEA) which is responsible for education in all the inner London Boroughs, i.e. those which were within the area of the former London County Council.

Changes in the structure of local government have been evolutionary rather than revolutionary. The traditional units of local administration remain—the county, the borough, the district and the parish. A map showing the top-tier boundaries of today is recognisable as a development from a map of the traditional shires. Of course there are changes. The major centres of population have produced the new metropolitan counties and in rural areas the amalgamation of counties has produced Cumbria, the new enlarged county of Cambridge and the combination Hereford and Worcester. The face of Wales, in contrast, has been changed considerably with the large-scale amalgamation of counties and the trisection of Glamorgan. The greater part of England and Wales still has a three-tier structure. This apparently cumbrous arrangement provides for a fuller range of representation of local interests and opinion than would be possible with a simpler form of organisation. It also permits functions to be distributed between the types of local authority according to the requirements of a particular service: the allocation of functions is discussed in the following section of this chapter. Areas which have but two layers of local government are those in which an urban community itself forms a second-tier authority or which has such a strong position within a second-tier authority that it is not felt to need further, separate representation. The very smallest parishes, or in Wales the smallest communities, with a population below 300 do not have a council unless a parish meeting resolves to have one. Where the population is below 200 the consent of the district council is also required. Districts exercise some general supervision over their parishes, e.g. in relation to boundary changes, elections and the compulsory acquisition of land. Where there is no parish council, the powers of the parish rest with an annual meeting which may appoint a committee to carry out any of its business.

Some districts enjoy the dignity of being boroughs. The chairmen and vice-chairmen of these councils are entitled to the status of Mayor and Deputy Mayor. To become a borough a district council must submit a petition to the Privy Council and the decision to do so must be supported by not less than two-thirds of the members voting thereon at a special meeting of the council convened for this particular purpose. If the view of the Privy Council is favourable, the district then receives a charter which may contain local provisions which appeared in earlier charters belonging to former boroughs now included within the district. In fact, every application received for borough status in 1973 and 1974 was accepted. And every metropolitan district except Sefton chose to be a borough. However, the practical effect on the powers of a district arising from borough status is negligible.

Great ingenuity has been devoted to the retention of the privileges of ancient boroughs. The 1972 Act provided three means to this end. Any parish or community council, that does not represent a grouping of parishes or communities, can resolve to choose the status of a town. This is a general right and is not restricted to former boroughs. When this course is adopted, the local council becomes a town council and the chairman of the council is entitled to be known as the town mayor. Thus former boroughs that still have their own institutions at third-tier level can retain something of their old status. It follows that an area can have two mayors, i.e. wherever a parish which opts to be a town is included in a district which has applied to become a borough. But not all former borough and urban districts were permitted to have a separate third-tier council. The Government ruled that such an authority should not have more than 20,000 population or alternatively not more than one-fifth of the population of the parent district council. These guidelines were applied with some flexibility: even so, at least 100 places were refused the right to have a parish or town council. Where a former borough is not allowed to retain a third-tier council, the method of preserving its dignities depends on whether the second-tier district authority becomes a borough. If it does, the charter rights and privileges transfer automatically to the new and larger borough. Where the district is not a borough, the district councillors elected to represent the former borough become charter trustees who are a corporate body, entitled to hold land and who can appoint one of their own number to be the town mayor.

One object which was prominent in the discussion which preceded the 1972 reform was the need to end the divorce between urban and rural areas. It was argued that a town which is a natural commercial, social and cultural centre for the surrounding hinterland should also be its administrative centre. At county level this aim has been achieved. At district level some authorities are wholly urban, some are essentially rural and some are mixed. The boundaries of many former county boroughs, now reduced to districts, were left unchanged in 1974. Extension of these towns to embrace adjacent rural areas would have created an obvious danger that the interests of rural communities would have been swamped by a dominant urban majority. So in some cases the distinction between town and country has remained at the second-tier level. Bath is a separate authority, an island wholly within another district: the same is true of Cambridge. Among third-tier authorities, the difference in status between town and parish tends to emphasise the urban/rural divide even more clearly than before the 1972 Act.

There are considerable variations in size within each category of local authority although these are far less bizarre than before the 1972 Act came into effect. Size can be measured in terms of acreage and population. Financial capacity is measured in terms of rateable

value. Appendix A gives basic statistical information about the size
of county and district authorities. Each metropolitan county exceeds
one million population; the typical metropolitan district is nearer
250,000. Non-metropolitan counties average more than half a
million people; a non-metropolitan district commonly has around
100,000 inhabitants. These figures give a general picture but there
are extreme cases which depart a long way from the norms. The
original intention was that the smallest non-metropolitan county
should be Northumberland with a population of a quarter of a
million. At a late stage in the passage of the Bill, the Government
accepted that the Isle of Wight should be treated as a special case
owing to its physical separation from the mainland. So the island is
now the smallest county with a population a little above 100,000.
Bristol is a quite different type of unusual case. It is the largest non-
metropolitan district with a population of 425,000—more than twice
that of many metropolitan districts which have much wider powers.
In terms of acreage the largest authority is North Yorkshire. In
England the average number of districts per non-metropolitan
county is a little over seven. Essex, Kent and Lancashire each have
fourteen districts, but Bedfordshire and Cleveland have four and the
Isle of Wight only two. New Town areas are all within a single
district with the one exception of the Central Lancashire new town
based on Preston, Leyland and Chorley which is split between these
districts.

The structure in Wales is similar to that in the non-metropolitan
parts of England save that the minor local authorities are termed
communities rather than parishes. Since the Anglican Church in
Wales was disestablished in 1919, it is not fitting that a name associated with church organisation should be linked to a secular unit of
local administration. The main difference is that Welsh authorities
tend to be smaller in population. Powys scarcely exceeds 100,000
inhabitants and one of the districts within Powys, the former county
of Radnorshire, serves only 18,000 people. The county of South
Glamorgan is also unusual in that it has but two districts.

Local councillors are elected for a four-year term of office subject
to transitional arrangements for the period after the initial elections.
However, London still retains the older three-year arrangement.
The pattern of elections is not uniform. County authorities are
elected as a whole in each fourth year after 1973 on the basis of
single-member constituencies. In the districts the position is more
complex. The rule in metropolitan districts is that a third of the
councillors are elected in each year when there is not a county council
election. Non-metropolitan districts are allowed a double choice.
They can opt either for whole council elections, as the counties have,

or they can have elections by thirds as in the metropolitan districts. Again, they can opt for single-member wards or multi-member wards or some combination of the two systems. The original arrangements were made after consultations with local opinion, i.e. with representatives of the former local authorities. So in these areas there may be an election each year or every other year. Under the former plan the election in three years out of four would be for district councillors; under the latter plan the timetable will run—county election, blank year, district election, blank year, county election and so on. After 1974 any resolution by a non-metropolitan district to change the existing arrangements needs a two-thirds majority to succeed. Parish and community councils, like the counties, are elected as a whole for a four-year term. They may be divided into wards; this is unusual in rural areas but normal in small towns.

The choices facing the non-metropolitan districts are worthy of further discussion. The borough tradition of the three-member wards and annual elections is favoured by political party organisations as giving local enthusiasts a regular focus for political activity which is felt to be helpful in maintaining interest. Accordingly this arrangement had been adopted in areas where party intervention in local elections is strong. However the system has major disadvantages. It necessitates larger electoral divisions and makes it more difficult for councillors and election candidates to become known to local residents. It increases the difficulties facing a non-party candidate attempting to organise his campaign. An annual election is more costly and causes more disturbance to the regular flow of council business. And where a council is run on strict party lines, if one party has a substantial majority it may be impossible to displace it at a single election, however badly it is beaten at the polls. An election at which the government is immune, even in the short term, is not an attractive concept. It must reduce public interest in the right to vote, as also does the greater frequency of elections. The one advantage that can be claimed for electing one-third of a council at a time is that it does provide some guarantee of continuity of membership and safeguards against the return of a very inexperienced assembly of councillors. No advantages can be claimed for the London borough system of whole council elections based on three-member wards: this could only have merit if some form of proportional representation or single alternative vote were to be introduced.

The representative responsibility of a county councillor may be more individual than that of a district councillor elected as one of three ward representatives for an urban area. The county councillor has to travel to the county capital to fulfil his duties and becomes something of an envoy to a higher authority: to a lesser extent the same is true of a parish representative on the district council. All this should mean that county elections are more keenly fought than other elections because the winners have functions which are more vital and important than those who serve on other types of local authority. In the past, county council elections have been more often unopposed than borough and urban district elections. The explanation is probably twofold: there is less party political activity in rural areas and because the county authority seems remote and distant there is less appreciation of the wide range of its activities. It still, however, remains true that the consultation of local opinion by county councillors can be a more complex activity than similar consultation in districts. Where a council is controlled by politics a councillor must pay attention to the views of his party colleagues and support- ers. In rural areas, where politics are less pervasive, a county council- lor will feel he should keep in touch with the attitudes of his parish councils, the district council and other local associations within his constituency. There is much overlapping of membership between the layers of local government in the counties. Some county council- lors serve on district councils; many district councillors serve on parish councils.

In the historical chapter it was noted that parishes often resisted being drawn into larger authorities, partly because they resented the loss of independence but perhaps even more because it was feared that any co-operation with neighbouring parishes would prove disadvantageous financially. Today the administrative county acts as a financial pool for the county districts within its boundaries. Counties spend far more money than districts but the latter have the task of levying the local rate. The counties impose a uniform rate on the districts. In consequence the more wealthy areas of the county tend to subsidise less well-to-do places. A prosperous town will make a proportionately greater contribution to county revenue than the ratio of its population to that of the whole of the county. This situation can generate hard feelings. Every part of a county area will wish to ensure that it is enjoying its fair share of county expenditure. Equally, the claims of a county councillor to secure benefits for his area must be judged in relation to the needs of the authority as a whole. Very often the interests of the county, especially in planning matters, will diverge from more local interests. If county councillors feel a strong need to press 'constituency' questions, who is to protect the interests of the county? There are a number of possible safeguards. Where party politics are a dominant influence, the majority party, one hopes, will take a broad view. On items of expenditure the processes of financial control impose restraint.

Elsewhere it may be that chief officials exercise considerable sway over the conduct of affairs and help to stifle unreasonable local claims.

Before 1972 a major difficulty facing local government was that administrative areas remained relatively static and failed to adjust to movements of population. The suburbs of an expanding town frequently spilled over its boundaries into the surrounding rural area. While this was both inconvenient and inefficient it also failed to arouse demands for appropriate adjustments to be made. Indeed, public opinion was likely to be aroused only when proposals were made to change boundaries. To work in the town and live in the adjacent rural district had a curious status value. Further, rateable values in rural areas were often lower for historical rather than practical reasons. An allied consequence of population movements in both urban and rural areas was that, as electoral divisions tended to be static, councillors came to represent very unequal numbers of electors. Ward councillors from decaying urban centres represented fewer and fewer people while those from the new suburbs were responsible to more and more. This produced undemocratic unfairness.

To deal with such matters in the future, the 1972 Act established two permanent Boundary Commissions, one for England and one for Wales. Each Commission must make regular reviews of district and county areas within every ten to fifteen years—or otherwise as the appropriate Secretary of State may direct. Local authorities and the general public must be fully consulted during the progress of these reviews and any Orders authorising boundary changes will be submitted for parliamentary approval. Alterations in parish or community areas will be suggested by the parent district council for the approval of the Boundary Commission. Should a district fail to make proposals, then the Commissions have reserve powers to act in default. Similarly the Commissions are to review regularly the electoral areas within local authorities and must be consulted about proposals from non-metropolitan districts to alter the local method of election.

One anticipates that there will be a considerable amount of work for the Boundary Commissions. Because the 1972 reorganisation of districts was carried out at high speed, many existing boundaries, although unsatisfactory, were left unchanged both in the interests of immediate administrative simplicity but also, no doubt, in order to minimise objections to the whole scheme of reform.

FUNCTIONS AND THEIR ALLOCATION

Local authority services fall into four groups which can be termed protective, communal, personal and trading. The paragraphs below describe these functions in general terms.

The first group of services is designed to protect the individual from a variety of dangers—e.g. fire, assault, robbery and epidemics. Thus local authorities provide a fire brigade, a police force, drainage, refuse removal, food inspectors and weights and measures inspectors. These protective services constitute some of the older branches of local administration, although rural areas lacked a comprehensive fire service until 1938 as before then much reliance was put on voluntary arrangements. Protective functions are negative in character as they promote good via the suppression of evil. All are highly necessary but scarcely exciting. The licensing of theatres, cinemas and of other premises for music and dancing has dual purpose. It is a safety measure and is also used to protect public morals. A local authority can prohibit the public exhibition of a film it judges to be offensive: this creates anomalies since licensing authorities do not always take the same view about the same film.

Communal services again provide benefit for all, but in a more positive way. In earlier centuries trade and travel were assisted by parish responsibility for the roads. The towns repaired and lighted the streets. Today the geographical distribution of population and employment is guided by planning authorities, the beauty of the countryside is protected and facilities are provided to assist its enjoyment. Parks and sports grounds are also provided, particularly in urban areas.

Personal services are of direct assistance to those individuals who need them. They form the most costly sector of local government functions. Education is the most expensive item. Other personal services include welfare services for children, the aged and the disabled. The use of these is optional. A parent need not send his children to a local authority school. A frail old lady living on her own need not apply for a home help. But the percentage of people who decide not to make use of public services is declining. Some services are free; others are partially subsidised. All are financed from the local rate fund supplemented by national grants. Where a charge is made, e.g. home helps, it may be wholly or partly remitted subject to a means test. Thus the personal services have an important equalising effect on society in that they benefit the poor at the expense of the rich—or the richer; they benefit the sick and the family man at the expense of the healthy and the childless; they benefit those who use public services at the expense of those who do not although entitled to do so. Over the years the development of free services has been urged forward by left-wing opinion. There is now pressure for these benefits to be provided on a selective basis so they are paid for by people who can afford it. Local authorities are tending to operate the means test principle more fully.

Trading services have declined since the nationalisation of gas and electricity in the post-war period. In 1974 water undertakings were transferred to the new Regional Water Authorities. However, in London and the metropolitan counties local authority control over passenger transport has been strengthened in recent years. Many local councils also subsidise passenger services, but this is a social welfare provision not a trading activity!

The division of local functions into these four groups is useful for the purposes of analysis, but the allocation of a particular service between the groups can be a matter of opinion. In a sense, all of them are communal. Education is provided for individuals, but it is a matter of communal benefit to have an educated society. And whether housing is regarded as a personal service or a trading undertaking must depend on how far council tenants pay an economic, i.e. unsubsidised, rent. Clearly, the sale of council houses is a trading activity. A few years ago it was arguable that town and county planning should be termed a protective service since it concentrated on stopping bad things, e.g. ribbon development; now it promotes environmental improvement and should be classed as a positive communal service. The introduction of tolls on new bridges is something of a reversion to the turnpikes and produces the flavour of a trading service.

Communal and personal services are those which show recent growth and these sectors offer wide and challenging opportunities for local government in the future.

It must also be noted that local authorities are not merely executive agencies. They exist not only to carry out duties but also to express opinions. This representative function has two forms. Local authorities can urge other public bodies to carry out policies which will be of local advantage. A Regional Planning Council can be asked to encourage industrial development in a particular area: Regional Traffic Commissioners can be asked to stop proposed fare increases on the buses. The second aspect of this representational activity is for one local authority to ask another, usually a larger authority, to do something. Counties receive many requests from districts. The executive tasks of a parish are small, but a parish council may be very active in pressing local problems on district or county councils.

Setting aside the minor authorities, the parishes and the communities in Wales, the essence of the local government system is the division of functions between two tiers of authorities, the counties and the districts. On what basis are functions distributed? The more expensive services tend to be allocated to authorities with greater financial resources. Specialised services, required by few people or which demand the use of highly skilled staff in short supply, go to authorities with substantial population. The top tier also has responsibility for functions which are felt to demand most uniformity or perhaps greater control by central government: the police are an obvious example. The second-tier authorities are responsible for services when local knowledge and responsiveness to local needs are held to be of paramount importance. Which of these criteria apply most forcibly to any particular local function must be a matter of opinion. Spokesmen for counties and districts argued these issues at length during the protracted discussions on local government reform.

The following paragraphs explain in general terms the distribution of functions under the terms of the Local Government Act, 1972. Formal lists of functions are given in Appendix B. However two preliminary points must be made. Distribution is not uniform as between upper-tier and lower-tier authorities because of statutory differences between metropolitan and non-metropolitan areas and, to a less extent, because of variations in Wales. Nor are duties uniform as between local authorities in the same sub-group because the 1972 Act gives a general power to authorities to arrange for another local authority to carry out specified duties on an agency basis. This power of transfer is subject to exceptions—the administration of education and the social services, the right to levy a rate, to raise a loan and, curiously, functions under the Diseases of Animals Act, 1850.

Non-metropolitan counties are responsible for education, libraries and social services, but not so the metropolitan counties. The financial effect is dramatic. The former account for 85 per cent of expenditure in their areas, the latter for only 20 per cent. It follows that the second-tier in the metropolitan areas is significantly more important. London follows the metropolitan pattern save that education in the inner London area is controlled by a committee of the GLC representing the inner London boroughs. Wales follows the non-metropolitan pattern. Another distinction is that metropolitan counties are passenger transport authorities: elsewhere this function is performed, if at all, by districts. However, all counties are responsible for promoting public transport policy in conjunction with bus operators and British Rail.

All counties are police and fire brigade authorities. (In London the Metropolitan Police are the direct responsibility of the Home Secretary.) Consumer protection, including the inspection of weights and measures, food and drugs, is another general field of county activity except in London and sometimes in Wales. Minor items on the list are road safety and the provision of small holdings. Some counties have special duties in connection with National Parks.

Other functions are shared between counties and districts, notably planning and highways. Counties prepare structure plans which determine the broad strategy of development for their areas: districts prepare local plans which set out more precisely the detailed implementation of county policy. Districts also decide whether to grant development permission, except where an application is of sufficient importance to raise issues which affect county policy, in which case the matter is transmitted for decision by the county planning authority. Districts issue enforcement orders and revocations of planning permission. Both counties and districts have powers in relation to town development. Another example of shared responsibility relates to abandoned motor vehicles; districts remove them but counties destroy them. This is a particular application of the general principle that districts collect refuse but counties destroy it. Counties are the major highway authorities and are responsible for road maintenance. Districts can claim to maintain unclassified roads in urban areas, i.e. the territory of former boroughs and urban districts: this work is carried out at county expense but subject to county cost control. Counties are responsible for local traffic orders and control of parking but districts have concurrent powers, with county consent, to provide off-street car parks. Other concurrent powers relate to recreation and leisure facilities, swimming baths, open spaces and entertainments, aerodromes and action in natural emergencies.

District functions also cover environmental and public health services, including building regulations, clean air, drainage and inspection of offices, shops and factories. Housing is perhaps the most important duty. Counties, except in Wales, have reserve housing powers but these can be used only on the request of a district council. Districts collect the rate. They can operate buses where local powers existed before 1972; in addition they can subsidise services and provide travel concessions. They can provide allotments, markets and civic restaurants, and are responsible for coast protection.

Districts are licensing authorities for theatres, cinemas, night refreshment houses and many other purposes. Welsh districts have an additional significance for they constitute the areas for holding septennial referenda to determine whether alcohol should be on public sale on Sunday in licensed premises.

Individual local authorities may obtain additional powers through private Bill legislation: this procedure is described in the following chapter. Otherwise local government is bound by a firm *ultra vires* rule which forbids the spending of money other than in ways authorised by statute. Even so there is some flexibility in that a county or district can spend up to the amount realised by the rate of 2p on any purpose which is in the interests of its area. Expenditure under this heading may include contributions to charity.

Overall the 1972 Act marked a further stage in the process of making local government less local. It reduced the number of top-tier county level authorities to less than 40 per cent of the previous total. As metropolitan districts retain education and social services, the cut in the number of authorities responsible for these functions was not quite so severe. However, the statutory provisions which permitted and sometimes required delegation of county powers have also been withdrawn. Powers over traffic orders were also moved from districts to counties. In sum, the total of centralisation was considerable. Even more serious from the local government standpoint was the loss of further functions from the ambit of local government, namely personal health services, water supply and sewerage.

To be fair, the 1972 Act did provide for some decentralisation. Previously many districts had exercised some delegated powers in relation to town and country planning but the Act gave them control over planning questions that do not affect county policy. In view of the growing public interest in planning matters, this is a major advance for district councils. Some licensing duties have also been handed down from counties to districts, and, as noted above, there is the possibility of agency arrangements to carry out county duties.

To conclude with, a review of the activities of the minor local authorities, the parishes and communities. Their powers are optional and of limited importance. They include provision and maintenance of allotments, burial grounds, public clocks, footpaths, bus shelters, recreation grounds, street lighting and war memorials. In addition they have various powers in relation to charities and common or parish land. But a major part of the business of the minor authorities is to represent local opinion to other local authorities and public bodies. It follows that parish and community councils can and do discuss many items which fall outside the scope of their executive duties. In particular they can claim to be consulted on local planning applications. There is no doubt that a vigorous parish or community council can play a valuable role in protecting the rural environment and it provides an opportunity to ventilate opinion which is sadly lacking in the wards of our large boroughs.

COUNTY/DISTRICT RELATIONSHIPS

The success of the new local government structure will be greatly influenced by the quality of co-operation between county and district councils. Both represent local opinion, albeit over different areas. Both share functions, especially planning, which cannot be exercised independently of each other. They can achieve important economies if they agree to share specialised resources. Yet there are serious hindrances to co-operation, namely separate institutional loyalties, sometimes party political differences and a widespread instinct amongst the district councils to preserve and insist upon their independence.

Closer relationships between the two tiers can be assisted through a variety of methods. There is some common membership between the two types of authorities as some councillors have been elected to both district and county councils. One local authority can provide goods and services for another; this provision facilitates joint purchasing arrangements, the joint use of computers and the employment of both district and county staff upon a particular project. Section 101 of the Local Government Act 1972 allowed one local authority to act as the agent of another local authority in the provision of services: the difficulties of this arrangement are considered below. Finally, two or more local authorities can appoint a joint committee to help them to find a common approach to particular problems.

Many counties have formed such joint committees with their districts to discuss items of mutual interest. These committees may cover a whole county or be restricted to a single district. They may constitute a general forum of discussion on local government affairs or they can be restricted to a particular function. They are purely advisory and have no executive functions. It may therefore be difficult to find useful work for them to do. They can too readily be used simply to complain about what other people are doing or not doing. There are also problems of organisation. If a single committee is used to cover a whole county and the county has equal representation with each district, then the county will be heavily outnumbered. If county representation equals that of all the districts together, then the burden of attendance on county councillors will be severe. Again, if a county establishes a separate committee for each district then the cost is heavy in terms of the time of both county councillors and county officials. Necessarily this problem is aggravated in the counties with a large number of districts, e.g. Essex, Hampshire and Kent. Where the remit of a committee is very broad, there is also a problem over the continuity of membership. Where membership is static a committee may not contain local representatives whose experience and interests are most appropriate for the business of a particular meeting: if membership is fluid and can be adjusted to suit the agenda, the committee tends to lose continuity and become a series of *ad hoc* gatherings.

Some counties have decentralised the administration of a particular service, e.g. highways. Such an arrangement may be accompanied by the establishment of area committees with responsibility for supervising the local operation of the county service. Where this is done the district councils may be invited to nominate a few members of the area committees, and so are given a modest opportunity to influence county policy. The joint committees described in the previous paragraph should be carefully distinguished from the area committees. The former are purely advisory bodies; the latter are county sub-committees with some executive responsibility.

The concept of agency, whereby one authority undertakes the work of another, caused much local controversy when the new authorities were being established. In law the powers of an agent are restricted to those that the principal has agreed to confer upon him: the element of discretion enjoyed by the agent depends on the terms of the agency agreement. So the agent is potentially in a very humble position. For a local authority—usually a district—working an agency system, it was important to secure a basic agreement which would permit a fair amount of flexibility. Nevertheless the principal— usually a county—will need to retain control of total expenditure and of major priorities as well as some right to exercise scrutiny over standards of work. It is clear that agency creates a complex situation with major opportunities for tension. Agency does not fit easily into the idea of a simplified, streamlined local government system. Why was the idea introduced?

There were three main reasons. First, where a function was transferred from one type of authority to another, it might be convenient to delay the change beyond April 1974 to allow more time for preparations to be made. This factor applied in particular to refuse disposal, responsibility for which was moved from districts to counties. Secondly, the prospect of agency was seen as a means of reducing the resentment among districts at their loss of powers to the counties. Such pique was strong in the former county boroughs. However, if agency was a mild palliative, it was not allowed to undermine the principles of the 1972 reform: the districts were precluded from trying to claw back the major functions they lost because both education and the social services cannot be included in any agency agreement. The third argument in favour of agency is that it allows more flexibility and provides an extra avenue for co-operation between counties and districts. Apart from refuse disposal, agency is being used most extensively in relation to highway maintenance. By adding to the workload of many district councils, highway agency strengthens their engineering and technical services and so helps the second-tier authorities to carry out other responsibilities directly allocated to them.

Disputes over agency agreements could be remitted to the central government department responsible for the function in question. Only in relatively few cases were decisions given in favour of the district authority. No more adjudications of this kind will be made as the power of central government to determine these disputes ended on 1 April 1974. It seems probable that the extent of agency will diminish as the years pass. The arrangements made in relation to refuse disposal are due to last two or three years and are clearly transitory. Highway agency agreements are of five years duration, but they may well decline after 1979; counties may argue that their wider resources will enable them to undertake highway work more economically.

The problems caused by concurrent powers may be of longer duration. Such powers provide splendid opportunities for co-operation between counties and districts; equally they can provide a climate in which mutual inaction flourishes. The danger of inertia arises from the possibility that a council may lose enthusiasm for a service in the hope that the other tier will exert itself and carry the financial burden. The list of these concurrent functions includes museums, art galleries, the acquisition of land, clearance of derelict sites, health education, aerodromes, action in face of natural emergencies and provision for recreation. The catalogue does not include major local government services but in total it amounts to a significant opportunity to improve the quality of life. One method of avoiding friction over these shared responsibilities is for the two tiers to strike a bargain. Thus in Tyne and Wear the arrangement is that the county shall be responsible for museums and art galleries while the districts provide leisure facilities which cater for physical exertion unless a district asks the county to take over a major project which will serve needs from outside the district.

It was noted above that planning powers are shared between counties and districts: counties are responsible for the formulation of broad strategy and districts deal with the detailed application of county policy. To examine in detail the problems of a particular local service would be to go beyond the scope of this book. But it must be stressed that this partnership in planning requires full co-operation between the two tiers if it is to work well. Counties must be satisfied that individual decisions by districts do not undermine county policy. To this end the more important development applications are classed as 'county matters' and are referred to the county for decision. This opens an opportunity for dispute about the definition of county matters and whether an individual case falls within the definition. A county may be unhappy about district decisions which fall within the boundary of district discretion. The employment of separate teams of planning officials who spend much time negotiating with each other is clearly wasteful. On the other hand, the involvement of the districts in planning can be justified because it ensures that public opinion has a stronger impact on the decisions made. The benefits of this county/district partnership should outweigh the added cost, provided the planners work together and avoid professional antagonisms.

THE COMMITTEE SYSTEM

Even in the smallest local authorities—other than parishes—it is obvious that all the detailed consideration of business cannot be done at meetings of the full council. Accordingly, committees are established. The tendency is for them to grow in number and in authority. They consume a great amount of time of both elected members and officers. It is commonly said that the committee is the workshop of local government: certainly, a realistic appraisal of committee behaviour is essential to a full understanding of the practice of local administration.

In the interests of speed in decision-making, the 1972 Act increased the powers that can be given to committees and to officers. A local authority may delegate its powers to a committee, sub-committee or an officer. Further, unless the authority otherwise directs, a committee may arrange for its powers to be discharged by a sub-committee or an officer: thus the principal *delegatus non potest delegare* is avoided. However, the full council cannot remit its power to levy a rate or raise a loan. In accordance with the Maud and Bains Reports (discussed in Chapter VII) the tendency now is for simplified structures with fewer committees and sub-committees and wider delegation. It is common practice to nominate a central committee, usually entitled Policy and Resources, to deal with major issues concerning the allocation of funds and to exercise a co-ordinating role of the work of the authority as a whole. The number of committees varies from council to council. Second-tier authorities in the shires tend to have fewer as they have fewer responsibilities. It is no longer usual to appoint a separate committee for each major function or local authority department. Instead the work of an authority is divided into broad 'programme areas' and a committee is allocated to each. The question then arises—can the ambit of a committee be too broad? This issue has arisen particularly with planning and transportation which some authorities have treated as one programme area to be controlled by a single committee; other authorities have felt the scope was too great for a single body and appointed separate committees.

The frequency of committee meetings also varies. They tend to be more often in the districts than in the shire counties. But every councillor knows that the routine timetable of meetings can be supplemented by others called for a special purpose. A committee once born becomes unwilling to die. It may be justifiable to have a separate body to consider a fresh and unexplored problem but when the new category of business contracts or becomes routine, the justification disappears.

Each local authority decides on the size of its committees. The larger the body, the wider the range of opinion and experience that can be represented on it. Conversely, the larger the body the smaller must be the scope for the average member to play a significant part in its work and the greater will be the cost in terms of time demanded of the elected members. Authorities in rural areas tend to have larger committees because there is pressure for the constituent geographical parts to be represented. Where a council is run on party lines the majority group will ensure that it has a political majority on each committee. Otherwise the selection of committee members should take into account their regularity of attendance and reputation with fellow council members. The central policy committee is the key committee of a council and the most senior and able members are usually selected to serve on it.

Is it useful for local authorities to inject more outside blood into their proceedings? The law permits this to be done. A council may include on its committees, other than a finance committee, persons with full voting rights who are not members of the parent council, providing that such additional members do not form more than one-third of any committee. This practice of co-option from outside does enable local authorities to widen the range of specialised knowledge and experience available for their deliberations. Magistrates form one-third of every Police Authority but this is tantamount to the creation of a joint committee rather than co-option. Otherwise the practice is optional. It is commonly used on education committees and boards of school governors and managers. (There is a widespread misconception that co-opted members are mandatory for education committees.) But apart from education, this device is not much used. One reason is a feeling that it is undemocratic to give authority to persons who have not been popularly elected. Council members may think that they can get adequate specialised advice from their officers. They may also fear that co-opted members would outshine them in discussion and have an unduly dominant role in committee decisions. Critics have also said that the system can be abused—that where councils are run on political lines, co-option can be a method of compensation for defeated council candidates.

One local incident is worth recalling. In 1972 the co-opted members of the Exeter Education Committee voted with the minority Labour and Liberal groups to elect another co-opted member, said to be a left-winger, as chairman of the committee. The Conservative majority on the City Council, acting under the terms of the 1944 Education Act, thereupon successfully applied to the Secretary of State for permission to dissolve and reconstitute their Education Committee. This was done to avoid a situation in which the education chairman would not have been a member of the City Council and, indeed, would have been hostile to its political majority group. This was an exceptional occurrence. In general, the practice of bringing additional people into local committee work is valuable and should perhaps be used more widely.

Meetings of committees are held in an informal atmosphere. The chief officer responsible for the committee's business or a committee clerk will sit next to the chairman in a strategic position to offer *sotto voce* words of advice. If the body is small enough it will sit round a table. Smoking is permitted unless health warnings have had effect. At the first meeting in the council year the initial task is to elect a chairman. Where an authority is subject to political control the chairmen are chosen by the majority group—otherwise the choice depends on the interplay of personalities. The normal practice is to start proceedings by approving the minutes of the previous meeting. The other items on the agenda will be to consider developments in matters that have been previously before the committee, and new pieces of business. Information on these will either have been circulated beforehand in reports prepared by the officers or there will be a verbal report at the meeting. Sub-committee reports are usually introduced by the chairmen of sub-committees. The volume of papers circulated to members to prepare them for the business varies considerably; often it is very substantial. The Maud Committee on *Management of Local Government* reported in 1967 that one of the largest county boroughs sent out 700 sheets of paper a month to each member of the council and 1,000 sheets to those on the education committee. One wonders what proportion of the papers were read. Strenuous efforts have since been made to cut down the amount of detailed business submitted to committees, and to reduce the bulk of paper circulated. In the case of education, the status of the committee is protected by law: a local education authority is required by statute to refer all matters to its education committee and must consider the committee's recommendations before taking action, except in an emergency. So the content of committee work is mixed. It is desirable that they should concentrate on issues of major policy but much time can still be consumed on trivial items that become contentious, perhaps for political reasons.

Thus committees are separate but interrelated cogs in the local government machine. How can they be made to mesh smoothly together? This raises the allied problems of co-ordination and control. Such supervision is essential otherwise committees would become wholly independent entities. Control is vital to ensure that a council remains in full charge of its policies and expenditure. Co-ordination is needed to prevent waste. It need not involve saying 'No' to a committee, but is rather a matter of showing them that their proposals can be carried out more effectively or economically if they are done in a certain way. A problem facing one committee may already have been dealt with satisfactorily by another. One committee may find that a certain piece of land or property is surplus to requirements while another committee may be seeking to buy a similar property. At this level co-ordination is increasingly the task of chief officers although formal responsibility may rest with some form of central policy committee. At lower levels, e.g. the need to maintain steady work flows for office and outdoor staff, the responsibility must rest wholly on officials.

Control of committee policy raises other issues. All spending is subject to review by auditors, internal and external, who provide a rigorous check against irregularity. The formal process of policy control takes place at council meetings at which reports or minutes of committees are presented for approval. Where a committee has delegated powers it will present a report of its actions for the information of council members and not for approval. Practice varies as to how detailed these reports are. For obvious reasons in the larger authorities the scale of delegation is greater and less detail can be included in reports if they are not to be unduly lengthy. At the full council meeting should members object to the way in which delegated powers have been exercised they can do nothing where the delegation is absolute. Of course, the council can always withdraw the delegation.

On matters that are not delegated the council can reject a committee's proposals or refer them back for further consideration. This occurs infrequently. Time at council meetings is not limited in any strict or formal sense, but the patience and energy of elected members are limited. Were a large number of recommendations to be challenged, then meetings would become unduly long. Even so, there will be many occasions when the specialised enthusiasms of a committee will be overruled on matters of principle, on issues that affect the business of other committees and especially on levels of expenditure. How is this done? Wherever a council is run on party lines, policy supervision can be expected to come from the dominant political group which will settle its internal disputes, if necessary, by vote at its 'caucus' meetings. In the absence of strong party loyalties, the situation becomes more flexible. The general policy committee can normally persuade a council to prune back any proposals for expenditure it considers excessive. The ultimate check to a committee is imposed by the balance of opinion expressed in council debate. The council must always prevail in any fundamental clash with a committee because it holds the ultimate sanction of being able to replace recalcitrant committee members with others who will heed the views of the full council.

The committee system offers substantial advantages. It ensures that all business has been subjected to prior consideration before it comes to a council meeting and thus avoids hasty decisions. This process of pre-digestion should enable a council to devote its attention to matters of major importance. Council members can specialise on particular aspects of the authority's work, thus helping them to make a valuable contribution to it. The specialisation also leads to a deeper sense of involvement and commitment; it heightens the sense of responsibility for the committee's work. And by narrowing the ambit of concentration for the elected member, the committee system enhances his education in administration. The informal atmosphere softens differentials in status and partisan opinions. So officers can intervene in discussion and offer advice to an extent that would be resented and thought improper at council meetings. And where a local authority is dominated by party loyalty, in the freedom of committee the members will not always talk and act in party groupings.

Since a council cannot take all decisions one obvious alternative is to transfer much decision-making power to an individual, be he official or elected member. But the wisdom of any one man (or woman) acting alone is open to doubt, quite apart from the force of the dictum that power corrupts. The committee enables power to be shared and brings together a variety of interests and experience which, in most cases, should produce a better and more acceptable decision. Not all members will play an equal part in moulding the collective mind of the meeting: there will be always a few who give a lead, either through stronger personality or greater experience and ability. An adviser to the committee, a chief officer, may often persuade it. In these circumstances a committee decision is perhaps not a genuine collective decision, but is rather a 'front' or support for those people who dominate its deliberations. Yet a committee, unless completely inert, is a valuable check. The leading voices still have to convince. Without committees, far more decisions would be made without potential challenge.

Equally committees are open to criticism. There must be a tendency for each one to live in a world of its own, deeply conscious of its special problems but failing to see them in the context of the full responsibilities of the council. They may be swayed too easily by the advice of officials, backed by the authority of professional qualifications which can produce undue enthusiasm and ill-balanced judgement. There is always a danger that a committee may seek to build an empire and be over-concerned with matters of status. The safeguards are to establish a central policy or executive committee to oversee other committees and to have as few committees and departments as possible. Thus the Seebohm Report of 1968 recommended that all social services provided by local government be administered through a single committee: this idea became a requirement in the Local Authority Social Services Act, 1970.

It was noted above that the power to delegate decisions to the committees is widely used. But how far should committees themselves deal with the detailed application of general policy, or how far should these matters be left to officials? The extent to which officials are permitted to act will vary. In larger authorities, delegation to officials has increased both in order to save time and to prevent committees being overburdened with detail. But there is some unwillingness among elected representatives to surrender prerogatives. There is a widespread conception of local democracy, dating from the Victorian era, which insists that it is the duty of elected representatives to take all decisions; that it is undemocratic to allow officials to exercise discretion. And some councillors do not wish to surrender matters to officials because they like dealing with details and personal cases.

A substantial cost has to be paid for any insistence that elected representatives must take decisions. Committee meetings are longer; sub-committees multiply; mounds of paper are distributed to explain the detailed business to committee members; officials spend much time in preparing these papers; if they are conscientious, committee members must spend much time on studying agendas and reports; decisions are delayed until committees, and sometimes the full council, have met. All this might be tolerable were it certain that decisions would be made under optimum conditions. Unhappily this is not the case. Often elected representatives may be less qualified to take decisions than the officers who advise them. This statement has an undemocratic flavour but frequently it must be true. Normally a happy marriage between democratic principle and expertise is possible since committees accept the advice of their professional staff. A committee would not dispute the view of its surveyor that a bridge was unsafe. School governors and managers commonly think it improper to intervene on questions of curriculum. Yet this self-denying convention may break down. What is the best course of action to take in relation to a child in care? Here any committee member may feel that his opinion is as valuable as that of an official. When a committee is faced with an aesthetic issue it is a matter of opinion whether professional advice should necessarily be followed. There is great variety in the extent to which elected members concern themselves with staff appointments, including teachers: it is arguable that this is a type of responsibility that chief officials should be expected to shoulder. There is a danger that when committee members become involved in personal cases emotion may determine action, or an undesirable element of patronage or even corruption may creep into council business. Housing is an obvious example. If council tenancies are decided by officials operating a points scheme, no favouritism is likely to arise; if a housing committee or sub-committee arranges tenancies, the basis of decisions becomes a matter for speculation.

Over-devotion to detail gives elected representatives inadequate time to concentrate on major matters of policy. Committee members snowed under with papers containing information on trivial matters will have less time to read more important documents, e.g. Ministry circulars. Indeed, where circulars are not immediately relevant to committee business, members may never know of the existence of a circular or will not appreciate its contents. Likewise at meetings, if hours are consumed by the minor items on the agenda, inadequate time is left for important business. A wily official may put a difficult matter of policy at the end of an agenda in the hope that he can persuade a tired committee to follow a certain line of action. Some committees, the weak committees, may prefer to take time over fairly routine items and then get through the major business rapidly by following the advice of their staff because the major items are too complex for members to be able to debate effectively.

In theory, one can argue that committees should decide policy and leave their officials to carry out the details of administration. In practice, the distinction between policy and administration can never be clear-cut. At what stage does a decision on how to put a policy into practice become itself a policy decision? If unexpected administrative difficulties develop which involve additional expenditure, the elected representatives must be consulted. If the operation of a policy incurs unexpected difficulties with the public, the councillors will need to know.

Under the reformed local government system the local authorities are fewer in number and larger in size, so councillors must place increasing trust on the judgement of their officers. This principle is now widely admitted, even where the need for it is regretted. But not all the problems raised in this chapter can be solved by leaving matters to officials. The influence of the Bains Report on the relationships between committees and chief officers is discussed in Chapter VII.

Chapter IV

CENTRAL CONTROL OF LOCAL GOVERNMENT

To a large extent our system of local government has been a system of local *self* government. There is a strong tradition that local communities should be able to decide how to deal with their own problems. In the introductory historical chapter it was shown how the central guiding hand of Chadwick was deeply resented. Today central supervision has come to be accepted in general terms although complaints are still frequent about particular applications of it. Clearly, if the national government did not have ultimate control over local councils the latter would tend to become autonomous units. No sovereign state would tolerate such a basic challenge to its authority unless it was prepared to become a federation of largely independent communities. At the other extreme, if local government were to have no ambit of decision not dominated by national government—then it would cease to be local *government* at all and become a mere agent of national government. So central-local relations demand a balance of control and independence, a balance of partnership and separation. The examination of why these relationships have evolved towards their present pattern is left until the final chapter. The immediate purpose is to describe the network of controls that surround local authorities.

One other preliminary note is essential. The orthodox treatment of central control divided it into three sectors, control by Parliament, Government Departments and the Courts. This fits the traditional tripartite division of political institutions into the legislature, the executive and the judiciary. However, if this model induces the idea that local government has three sets of controllers—Members of Parliament, civil servants and judges—then it is misleading. Civil servants advise Ministers how to use the powers made available to them by Act of Parliament. Members of Parliament are heavily influenced by party loyalty, so that the Commons normally accept the policy proposed by Ministers of the Government. Not all legislation is initiated by Ministers and the formal process of party discipline, the use of the whips, is not applied to Bills sponsored by backbenchers or by local authorities. But no Bill in either of these categories will pass if Ministers are deeply hostile to it. Thus both parliamentary and administrative controls over local government reflect the will of Ministers. Judicial control is a separate category; yet here again if Ministers dislike a judicial interpretation of local government law they could use their parliamentary majority to amend the law.

The threefold distinction between parliamentary, administrative and judicial control is retained in the pages that follow as it facilitates description. But it must not be forgotten that while civil servants, Members of Parliament and judges are not without influence, the essence of national supervision of local government is that it is undertaken on behalf of the Ministers of Her Majesty's Government.

PARLIAMENTARY CONTROL

The legal basis of national control over local government is that local authorities have no powers other than those conferred on them by statute. All local councils must be able to produce statutory authority for everything they do. If a council exceeds its powers, albeit unwittingly, its actions may be challenged in court where the principle of *ultra vires* will be invoked, and the extra-legal actions will be declared null and void. Thus local authorities largely carry out the administration of general principles of policy decided by the national legislature. Local authorities are not themselves legislative— i.e. rule-making—bodies except in relation to local bye-laws, and even here their decisions are subject to detailed government scrutiny and approval.

Local government law is complex, partly because it is highly detailed, partly because there are many varieties in the forms of legal power. Some statutory authority is contained in the Acts which established a particular type of local council. Thus the Greater London Council and the London Boroughs received powers from the London Government Act, 1963. More generally, however, powers are obtained from general Acts relating to a specific local authority function; obvious examples are the major statutes relating to public health, education and town and country planning. Most of the duties conferred on local authorities by Parliament are mandatory, i.e. compulsory, but in a few matters of secondary importance there is a choice of whether to use or 'adopt' powers. The Small Dwellings Acquisition Act, 1899, which enabled councils to provide mortgage loans to encourage home ownership, is an example of this optional arrangement. Another more recent case is the ability of the rating authorities to decide under the terms of the Local Government Act, 1966, whether to levy rates on unoccupied properties. In 1963 Parliament gave local authorities a general optional power to spend a penny rate in any way for the benefit of its area provided that such activity was not subject to other statutory limitations: the 1972 Act increased the permitted rate to two new pence. A third type of power is that conferred by a local Act, where Parliament has accepted a request by a local authority to give it additional authority. The procedure for obtaining such special powers is complicated and expensive; generally speaking, only the larger authorities seek to promote their own private Bills. A few pioneering ventures, notably the Birmingham Municipal Bank, have been started in this way, but many of the powers obtained from private Bills are relatively minor and raise no points of principle. The intention behind Section 262 of the Local Government Act 1972 was to enforce drastic simplification in this area. The plan is for a Government Bill to confer generally on local authorities those local Act powers which are found to be of value. Meanwhile local councils are due to consider which of their remaining local powers need to be retained. The residue of unnecessary and outdated local legislation will then be repealed—in metropolitan areas by 1979 and in the shires by 1984.

Private Bill procedure, if widely used, could have greatly broadened the span of local government. Perhaps this is why Parliament has ensured that the promotion of a private Bill is a formidable obstacle race. A resolution to promote a Bill must be passed at two council meetings by a majority of the members and public notices must be issued indicating the nature of the powers a council hopes to acquire. If all these hurdles are surmounted, a private Bill goes before Parliament where, having been scrutinised by a body of Examiners to see it is in appropriate form, it then has to go through the usual routine of three readings in both Houses. Normally these readings are a formality. Discussion is usually restricted to the committee stage which is held before a small group of Members who sit in a quasijudicial capacity hearing arguments in support of the Bill and any objections to it. Pleadings for and against a Bill are undertaken by members of the 'parliamentary bar', a special kind of barrister. The need to employ these parliamentary counsel adds greatly to the cost of the proceedings, especially if a Bill arouses objections and the committee stage is protracted. It was shown above that a Bill will not succeed if it incurs ministerial hostility; however, ministerial support is not an absolute guarantee of success, especially as the Bill has to satisfy the Lords as well as the Commons. The Conservative interest in Parliament has tended to be hostile to new extensions of local authority activity, notably in relation to municipal trading.

In addition to powers obtained directly from statutes, local government receives further powers from various types of Orders made by Ministers—Provisional Orders, Orders under the Statutory Orders

(Special Procedure) Act, 1945, and normal Statutory Instruments. These are subject to varying degrees of parliamentary scrutiny. However, since they all engage the influence of Ministers, it is unusual for any parliamentary challenge to be successful. Many Orders of purely local application, e.g. compulsory purchase and clearance orders, asked for by local authorities, are approved or not approved by Ministers, and are not submitted to Parliament at all.

ADMINISTRATIVE CONTROLS

The detailed supervision of the work of local authorities is undertaken by government departments. The extent of the direction varies greatly from function to function and between different parts of the same function. Central government is deeply involved in all major issues relating to education, police and town and country planning; it pays far less attention to the provision of public libraries, municipal entertainments and recreational facilities. The Department of the Environment is concerned with the amount of local authority house-building and the standards of design and construction, but local authorities are wholly free to select tenants on whatever basis they think best. It is also greatly concerned with major road improvements (trunk roads are entirely a government responsibility) but leaves alone the maintenance of minor roads. This variation is due largely to the uneven amount of political interest attracted by local government functions and, inevitably, the more expensive services will induce greatest attention.

Most of the supervisory activity by the central government is authorised specifically by statute, but there are a few examples of Ministers being entrusted by Parliament with a broad oversight of a particular local government function. The Local Authority Social Services Act, 1970, is the most authoritarian piece of local government law to have been passed in recent years. It requires the responsible authorities to appoint a social services committee, restricts the business coming before the committee subject to the consent of the Secretary of State, empowers the Secretary of State to prescribe qualifications to be held by a director of social services and requires local authorities to act under general ministerial guidance in relation to these functions. The Education Act, 1944, is another extreme example of conferring wide power on a Minister by generalised wording. According to the Act it is the duty of the Secretary of State for Education 'to secure the effective execution by local authorities, under his control and direction, of the national policy for providing a varied and comprehensive educational service in every area'. (In view of the current controversy about comprehensive education, it must be stressed that the word 'comprehensive' in the Education Act was used in the normal sense of all-embracing, not in the recent specialised sense which implies the abolition of selection for secondary education.) The language of the Act is strong and scarcely fits the conception that local authorities should govern: rather it implies that local education authorities are mere agents to carry out a Minister's will. This impression is supported by another section of the Act which authorises the Secretary of State if satisfied that any local education authority '. . . have acted or are proposing to act unreasonably' to give directions accordingly. In fact, these draconian powers are not used. Yet they remain in the background and must overshadow any major dispute between the Department and local education authorities.

The Education Act, 1944, is vague in another important sense. It speaks of the national policy for education without defining what the policy is to be. Presumably the policy is to be decided, and redefined from time to time, by the responsible Minister. Thus the wide powers of the 1944 Act entitle the Secretary of State for Education and Science to press forward or restrain the ending of selection for secondary education depending on the viewpoint of the Government.

Many other Acts give Ministers a strong reserve power over local authorities. If a Minister is satisfied that a council has failed to perform a particular function adequately he may be empowered to issue an order to the council to instruct it to do certain things, or he may transfer powers from a district council to a county council or he may take over the powers himself. This default power was first incorporated in the Public Health Act, 1875, in respect of sewerage and water supply but was never actually used. Similar provisions are to be found *inter alia* in the Public Health Act, 1936, the Town and Country Planning Acts, 1947 and 1962, the Civil Defence Act, 1948, and the Housing Finance Act, 1972. These certainly give Ministers a big stick to brandish at recalcitrant local councils, but they are called into effect very rarely; post-war examples relate to civil defence at Coventry and St Pancras and, more recently, to housing at Clay Cross. There is no difference between the political parties in the matter of these broad statutory powers over local government: both Conservative and Labour Governments have inserted default clauses into local government legislation.

In the nineteen-forties it was the fashion for major Acts dealing with local government functions to require local authorities to prepare development plans for ministerial approval. The idea was to force councils to take a long-term look at local conditions and to get them to commit themselves in advance to a programme of improvement. The practical effect of these development schemes varied considerably. The plans for future school-building rapidly became out-of-date and were ignored. Long-term plans drawn up under the Town and Country Planning Acts, although repeatedly changed, are the basis of all town and country planning controls. More recently in 1972 the DHSS asked local authorities responsible for the provision of social services to prepare ten-year plans which would chart the course of future growth of these services; the Department also suggested standards of provision which local authorities should attempt to achieve.

One of the oldest forms of central supervision is the use of inspection, first employed by Chadwick in 1834 to review the activities of the Boards of Guardians. Four local authority services are subject to regular inspection, police, fire, education, children. There are two aspects to an inspector's duties. Primarily he has to ensure that local services are efficient and that standards are maintained: he also advises local authorities and his own Department on matters of technique and policy improvement. The term 'inspector' is also used, rather misleadingly, to describe officials who preside over local enquiries of various kinds. Their task is essentially to hear objections to proposals and report thereon to a Minister—this function will be considered below in the paragraphs on the appellate functions of Ministers.

The process of inspection is concerned not so much with council policy as with the way in which council servants perform their duties. There are other types of control over officials. In some cases regulations prescribe their qualifications and duties. Various controls over the appointment and dismissal of local government officers are outlined below in the section describing the role of officials. The most exhaustive control over personnel is to be found in the police and fire services where the Home Secretary can make regulations governing appointment, dismissal, discipline, and conditions of service. In the case of fire brigades the supervision extends to methods of training and the provision of certain items of equipment.

Various actions of local authorities require ministerial approval. Development plans provide one example; another is any proposal for the compulsory purchase of land or property. Many Acts require a Minister to adjudicate in a conflict between a local authority and an individual, but some such disputes go to a court of law. Parliament has been careful to protect private rights against unjustifiable interference by local government, but no clear line can be drawn between the sort of issue that goes to a Minister and that which goes to a court. The policy imposed by Parliament has varied. Before 1930 appeals against closing orders—that a house is unfit for human habitation—were decided by the Ministry of Health: now they go before a county court judge. It is still a matter of doubt whether a county court judge is best suited to consider the technical issues that may arise in such disputes. A better solution might be to create a special tribunal to deal with these cases.

If an authority makes a clearance order to compulsorily acquire an area of sub-standard housing and other property for the purpose of redevelopment, any appeal goes to the Department of the Environment. The Department will send an inspector to hold a local enquiry into objections and to hear any claims that certain properties in the area have been well maintained and are, therefore, eligible for additional compensation payments: the sort of evidence heard at this type of enquiry will not be dissimilar from that presented to a county court judge adjudicating on a closing order. Inspectors hold other types of local enquiry, the most common are those arising out of refusals to agree to applications to develop land by building or extracting minerals. Other examples are enquiries into objections into the compulsory purchase of land by local authorities for housing, school-building, road-widening, etc., and disputes over footpaths. Save in minor planning cases, the inspector does not himself make the decision. His task is to listen to evidence presented by both sides to a dispute, normally to visit the site in question, and make a report with a recommendation to the appropriate Minister. The Minister is responsible for the final decision and in the vast majority of cases will uphold the inspector's opinion. Since 1958 the reports of inspectors have been published, unless considerations of national security are involved, so it is possible to see if the Minister has overruled his inspector.

Ministers also adjudicate in disputes between local authorities. Here there are no public enquiries; the councils concerned submit arguments on paper and the issue is decided within the Department. If education authorities are in dispute over which of them is responsible for the education of a child, the matter is determined by the Secretary of State for Education. If a similar issue arises over a child taken into care, responsibility is allocated by the Secretary of State for the Social Services. If a county council disagrees with a county district over whether a local plan is in conformity with the strategic county plan, the issue is referred to the Secretary of State for the Environment.

The remaining types of administrative control are all related to finance. Each new category of local authority created since 1844 has had to have its accounts examined by a government appointed auditor—now known as district auditor. Boroughs outside London were the only authorities to escape: they could choose between employing professional auditors, using district audit or choosing auditors by election—the latter method was quaintly archaic and rarely used. Except for London the 1972 Act permits councils to choose between district audit and professional audit, but an appointment in the latter category must be approved by the Secretary of State. Relatively few authorities took advantage of this new freedom. Only three counties and seven metropolitan districts use professional audit and half of these retain district audit to check some of their accounts. The district auditor must be satisfied that accounts are accurate and compiled in accordance with proper accounting principles. Any criticisms are to be included in his report to the local authority and the Secretary of State. Professional auditors report similarly. The Secretary of State may instruct the district auditor to hold an extra-ordinary audit into any accounts either as a result of local complaints or comment by a professional auditor. Penal powers of district audit are now supervised by the law courts and are considered in the following section.

Since local authorities obtain much financial aid from central government it is inevitable that these grants should form another means of central control. The nature of the control depends partly on the grant system. Where a grant is made for expenditure on a specific service, the way in which that service is developed can be greatly influenced by an alteration in the amount of the grant or by a change in the rules governing the eligibility of local expenditure to earn grant. Alternatively, the yardsticks which control the scale of expenditure on construction projects may be adjusted. In 1958 the number of local government functions which had a separate grant was reduced; central financial aid to the local rate fund is now largely distributed in the form of general grants not linked to expenditure on specific services. However, the general grant can exert much influence over the policy of local councils: if the grant is unexpectedly generous, councils will spend more freely, but if it does not increase as much as they hoped then there is encouragement to cut back their estimates. A reserve power also exists, never yet used, which enables the Government to refuse payment of the general grant to a local authority if the Government is gravely dissatisfied with the way in which the authority has been carrying out its duties.

The third category of financial control arises from control of local borrowing. When a local authority proposes to purchase or construct a capital asset which will be of benefit to the ratepayers in the future, the expenditure is normally financed by borrowing so that the cost of the asset can be spread over a number of years. Thus the need to obtain loan sanction is a powerful ministerial weapon. Originally, the requirement for loan sanction was imposed so that Ministers could ensure that local schemes were both reasonable in terms of local financial resources and were also technically sound.

This provided a safeguard for smaller authorities with less well qualified staff and enabled them to benefit from the wider experience of Ministry officials. Another advantage was that the system may promote co-operation between local authorities in that approval for a scheme, e.g. for sewerage or water supply, might be withheld on the ground that the service could be more economically organised in conjunction with a neighbouring council. Since 1939, however, the major purpose of this control has changed, for it has become a vital part of the general supervision which the Government exercises over the national economy. To this end, the total of capital expenditure allowed to all public authorities is fixed each year, and local authorities receive a ration from this amount. Thus local authorities have to fit into a national economic plan, and the amount of capital resources they are permitted to consume in any period will depend upon Government policy. In 1970 a considerable simplification of procedure was introduced. Capital expenditure was divided into two groups, key sector schemes and locally determined schemes. Departmental control was fully maintained over the key sector so that local authorities had to obtain specific consent to raise capital in connection with education, housing, principal roads, police, health and social services, water supply and sewerage. For locally determined schemes which covered all other local government functions, the counties, county boroughs and London boroughs were each given a ration of loan sanction to use as they saw fit: the county ration had to be split up between the county and its district councils by local agreement.

The wide scope of administrative control requires regular communications between local authorities and central departments. Applications for individual authorities are normally dealt with through correspondence. From their side the Ministries issue a large number of publications, many duplicated rather than printed, consisting of circulars, bulletins and handbooks of various types. The Department of the Environment issues bulletins of selected appeal decisions to show planning authorities how the planning policy of the Department is developing. Many of these departmental documents relate to technical and highly specialised matters, but the circulars often deal with questions of general policy. The importance of circulars has grown so considerably that they are commonly treated as an additional technique of central control, rather than simply as a means of communication. Their contents vary. A circular may be informative, and merely state that a new regional office of the Ministry has been established. It may explain the contents of a Statutory Instrument or how a Minister proposes to use powers given to him by statute. It may offer advice and guidance, e.g. on how to deal with a particular type of planning application. The most important circulars are those which indicate major changes in Government policy. The Local Government Act, 1972, stimulated a cascade of circulars giving details of how the reorganisation should be carried through. A file of these departmental circulars is perhaps the best single guide to contemporary developments in local government. Necessarily the literary style of the circulars tends to be a reflection of their content; those which merely provide information are flat, if not diffident, but those which demand action are more powerful.

A third means of communication is through personal contact. When a council has a serious problem it may send a small deputation of councillors and officials to London to put their point of view to civil servants or perhaps even a Minister. Civil servants also visit local authorities, but such visits are most often made by officials with specialised qualifications, e.g. engineers, surveyors and planners. Senior civil servants, the members of the administrative class who have the greatest influence on Ministry decisions, more rarely travel round local authorities. This is a possible ground of criticism. It is arguable that central control would be more flexible, that central departments would have a fuller understanding of local difficulties, if there was more personal intercourse between Whitehall and the counties and districts. Yet it is not certain that local authorities would welcome more visits from civil servants. They are, quite rightly, jealous of their independence and would resent anything that seemed to be a call from a new type of general inspector.

The total of administrative controls is very great. No doubt, a case can be advanced for each item in the catalogue. The danger, of course, is that their cumulative impact can have a deadening effect on the whole of local government.

JUDICIAL CONTROL

Government departments had few personnel and resources before the second half of the nineteenth century. Administrative control of local government in the modern sense was unknown and impossible. County justices exercised somewhat erratic supervision over parish officers, but the justices themselves and the municipal corporations enjoyed a high degree of independence. The means of redress for a disgruntled citizen was to bring a legal action against a local authority. Thus judicial control formerly had an important effect on the development of local government. Today its effect is much reduced although certain legal principles inherited from the past still exert substantial influence.

A full discussion of the subject requires an extensive description of case law and the technicalities of legal procedure. This can be found in legal text-books and will not be attempted here. However, a brief analysis of their legal position is necessary for a complete understanding of the constitutional position of local authorities.

Local government law can be divided into two sections. There are branches of general law, e.g. contract and tort, where special rules apply in relation to local government. A local authority cannot be held liable on an *ultra vires* contract because it had no power to make the contract in the first place. In general, a local authority is responsible for the tortious—i.e. wrongful—acts of its servants. Since an authority has no power to commit torts one might expect, following the doctrine applied to contracts, that it could not be liable for wrongs done by its employees. Fortunately, in this instance, the courts have not been logical or consistent. However, there are exceptions to the general rule. If a local authority employee is acting under powers conferred on him personally by statute, the authority is not liable for his actions. Local authorities also have a wide range of powers that are not possessed by a private person, rights of entry into private premises for certain purposes, rights to destroy infected goods or unsound food, etc. It follows that many things done by local government officers, which would be tortious acts if undertaken by private individuals, are legitimated by statute.

The other sector of local government law relates specifically to the way in which local authorities carry out their functions. Here again a twofold distinction can be made between provisions for appeals against council decisions and wider opportunities for ensuring that local authorities both keep within their powers and carry out their duties.

Magistrates' courts deal with disputes arising out of the application of building regulations and the naming of streets. County courts hear appeals against closing orders. The High Court hears appeals against compulsory purchase orders and clearance orders. This is a selection of examples, not an exhaustive list. But it must be noted that the powers of the High Court to review compulsory purchase and similar orders are very limited: any action must be started within six weeks of the order being confirmed and the Court can consider an appeal only on grounds of *ultra vires* or if it is satisfied that the applicant has been 'substantially prejudiced' by some defect in the procedure when the order was being prepared and considered. The time limit is necessary to prevent local authorities being required to restore houses that have been knocked down or to return land to its previous owners after work has started on the erection of new buildings.

The sector of judicial control which offers the greatest constitutional interest is that relating to the extent of local authority powers and the way in which they are used. The principle of *ultra vires* has been described above. Here it may be useful to give an illustration of how closely the principle is applied. In *Attorney-General* v. *Fulham Corporation* (1921) the issue was whether Fulham Council had the power to run a municipal laundry. The Baths and Washhouses Acts, 1846–7, gave Fulham, as a public health authority, the right to provide baths and washhouses where people could wash themselves and wash clothes. The question was whether this power allowed Fulham to provide a service whereby the servants of the Council would wash clothes in return for payments to the Corporation. The Court's answer was 'no'. There have been many cases of this kind in which *ultra vires* has been used to obtain a ruling, often a restrictive ruling, on the meaning to be placed on words used in local government statutes. Judicial proceedings can also be instituted to force a local authority to carry out its statutory obligations: such a case would now be a rarity, but in previous centuries there have been important instances relating to the maintenance of highways and the provision of drainage.

Decisions by the District Auditor in relation to *ultra vires* acts are now wholly supervised by the courts. If the Auditor thinks that any item of expenditure is illegal, he may apply to the court for a declaration to that effect. Should the court agree with the Auditor, it may also impose a surcharge on any person responsible for illegal payments, except where it finds that an action was reasonable or taken in the belief that the expenditure was lawful. Where a councillor is surcharged more than £2,000 he can also be disqualified from membership of a local authority. Another possibility is that the examination of accounts may discover fraud. Here the Auditor can order the individual responsible to repay the sum involved; anyone aggrieved by such an order can appeal to the court.

Local authorities can also be required to observe certain rules of equitable behaviour known as the principles of 'natural justice'. The two most important are that no man shall be judge in his own cause and that no man shall be condemned unheard. If an elected member participates in the making of a decision of benefit to himself, then it can be declared void by a court. In 1933 a decision of the Hendon Rural District Council to permit the construction of a roadhouse was quashed because one of the councillors present was financially interested in the project. There are difficulties and limitations connected with these declarations of interest which will be discussed in Chapter VI. The other concept that no man shall be condemned unheard, has led to the establishment of a wide range of public enquiries into the actions of public authorities, especially where these are likely to interfere with private property and other rights. It also governs the way in which these enquiries are conducted. The leading case here is *Errington* v. *Ministry of Health* (1935). The facts were that the Minister of Health had ordered a public enquiry into objections against a clearance order made by a local authority. The enquiry was duly held by a Ministry inspector, but subsequently the inspector visited the site accompanied by local authority officials but without the objectors. This was held to constitute listening to evidence from one side in the absence of the other, so the High Court quashed the Minister's decision to confirm the clearance order. It will be noted that this was not an action against a local authority, but an action against the way in which a Minister had used his supervisory powers over local government.

An outstanding example of judicial control in recent years is the Tameside dispute of 1976. Tameside is a metropolitan district in Greater Manchester created by the Local Government Act, 1972. It is one of the three metropolitan districts not to contain a former county borough and so is a 'new' education authority in a real sense. The Labour majority on the council made arrangements to end selection for secondary schools in 1976 and to operate a comprehensive system. However, the Conservatives won the local election a few months before the changeover was due and they were pledged to retain some grammar schools. After some preliminary negotiations with Tameside, the Secretary of State, Mr Mulley, issued a direction that Tameside should give up the intention to continue selective entry to some secondary schools. This instruction was based on Section 68 of the Education Act, 1944, which provides that when the Secretary of State is satisfied that a local education authority is acting unreasonably a direction may be issued to that authority such as appears to the Secretary of State to be expedient. The language of the Act is so broad that one might have thought that Mr Mulley's action was fully justified, at least in law. Yet Tameside appealed to the courts. The case was fought up to the House of Lords where Mr Mulley lost.

Their Lordships held that there was no basis on which the Secretary of State was entitled to say that Tameside was acting unreasonably. They rejected the Whitehall view that plans for comprehensive education were so far advanced that it was impractical to change them and that the difficulties of arranging a selection system in the short time available were insuperable. There was, of course, a major political aspect of this conflict. A Bill then before Parliament, now the Education Act, 1976, required authorities not already operating on comprehensive principles to submit plans for ending selection. But the courts take no notice of Bills that have not reached the Statute Book.

In the past Section 68 had rarely been used to settle a major controversy; it has been used regularly in individual cases where parents have appealed to the DES against a local refusal to send a child to a particular school. So the Section had been used to uphold parental choice. Now its force is in doubt. Any dispute between a local education authority and the Secretary of State over what is reasonable may be referred to a court and there is clearly no guarantee that the ministerial direction will be supported. Thus the judgement of a Minister responsible to Parliament can be replaced by the judgement of judges responsible to no one.

If there is disagreement over the meaning of words in a statute it is proper that the matter be settled in a court of law. To this extent, judicial control over local government is unavoidable. It remains, however, an unsatisfactory process. Local authorities are responsible to the local electorate and try to serve the public interest as they think best. They are in a quite different position to the ordinary defendant in that they rarely break the law deliberately. If they do break the law, it is normally because a law is unclear or becomes unclear when lawyers start arguing about it. Another aspect of litigation is the heavy expense, so local authorities are not challenged in the courts—other than before the magistrates—unless someone is prepared to spend a substantial sum. It follows that judicial control is partial in its operation. Some parts of local government law have been heavily contested in the courts while other parts go unchallenged. The statutes that are disputed tend to be those that affect property, i.e. rating, housing, compulsory purchase and town and country planning. The Tameside case noted above is untypical in the sense that the amount of recent litigation over educational administration has been small.

The merit of being able to appeal to a Minister rather than a judge is cheapness. Yet we recoil from the idea that a Minister should be able to interpret the law for this would place still more power in ministerial hands. There may also be a feeling that, as a dominant factor in the sphere of public administration, a Minister would be biased in favour of local authorities against individuals, or would be guided by political considerations. A judge is held to be impartial and to give decisions based on recognised rules of statutory interpretation. However, since judges often find it possible to disagree, it is arguable that a judicial decision may be nothing more than the personal preference of a judge. Even so, the personal view of a judge may still be preferable to the personal view of a Minister in that a judicial decision can be overruled by subsequent parliamentary discussion and action, whereas a ministerial decision is virtually irreversible in Parliament because of party loyalty and party discipline.

Chapter V

FINANCE

THE SCALE OF OPERATIONS

Every benefit involves cost. Because local authorities organise a wide range of social provision, they consume a considerable fraction of the nation's resources of goods and manpower: in 1976 it was almost one-seventh of the gross domestic product. To put the matter in financial terms, local councils have an annual financial turnover of the order of £15,000 million. The spending and the collection of huge sums necessarily create a number of intricate problems.

A dominant feature of local finance is the meticulous care taken to control spending. Every authority prepares annually a detailed set of estimates to govern expenditure in the financial year starting on April 1st. Once approved by the council these estimates act as a check on subsequent expenditure. 'We cannot do anything about it this year because no provision has been made in the estimates' is a common explanation for failure to take action. Strict budgetary control is reinforced by auditing, by both internal and external auditors. Complicated rule systems have evolved to determine the legitimacy of expenditure. All this helps to prevent waste and corruption, although the auditing controls themselves cost a great deal of money.

In local finance a careful distinction is made between revenue expenditure and capital expenditure. Capital spending involves the purchase of an asset which will last for years to come. Thus money spent on school building or house building is of a capital nature while the money spent on an official's salary is not. The distinction is important because local authorities can borrow to defray the cost of capital items. Not all capital spending is financed by borrowing; many small items are charged against current income. Loans have to be repaid and the cost of loan repayment including interest charges is included in revenue expenditure; such costs constitute a high proportion of revenue expenditure on housing.

Above 60 per cent of current expenditure is now financed from central government grants. This overall figure conceals local variations because less prosperous areas enjoy levels of grant larger than the national average. The local rates withstand the highest proportion of expenditure in places where rateable values are high. Trading profits now make a negligible contribution to local resources. The Exchequer grants can be divided between the Rate Support Grant which, as the name implies, is a general subsidy to local government, and a number of grants in support of specific services, e.g. police and housing. The Rate Support Grant is by far the more important factor amounting to nearly 90 per cent of the total national aid. On the expenditure side, the most costly service is education which accounts for roughly half of all the outgoings. For this reason one of the most common remedies suggested to ease the burden of the rates is to transfer the cost of teachers' salaries to central government.

While the global sums involved in local finance are immense, the financial resources of individual councils vary greatly, although the largest disparities were eliminated by the 1972 reorganisation. Figures for the rateable values of major authorities will be found in the Appendix. It has been assumed in the past, rather too easily, that low rateable value damages the quality of local services. In fact, quality probably depends more on the opinions of councillors than on the details of the local financial situation. Some of the poorest authorities, judged by the standard of rateable value per head, have maintained an excellent standard; partly this has been due to the central grant system and partly to decisions by councillors to incur expenditure that would involve a high rate poundage in the belief that their electors would accept that the money spent was well spent.

Every local council has to bear full responsibility for its own expenditure—subject to assistance from the central government. However, some expenditure is 'pooled'. This applies in the case of a specialised service which would be uneconomic for each authority to organise. So the service is provided by a particular council or some other agency in return for payment by other local authorities. Such arrangements cover advanced further education, approved schools, the training of teachers and health visitors and 'no area' pupils, i.e. pupils who are not the responsibility of any particular local education authority. Various formulae determine the details of these pooling schemes. One difficulty is that the authority providing the service may have little incentive to economise since it may itself have to defray but a small part of total expenditure. The problem has now been recognised, in particular by the Department of Education and Science, and cost limits have been placed on pooled education expenditure.

In 1974 there was a major outburst of protest against rate increases as these reached levels previously unknown. Many authorities increased their rate demands by 50 per cent; a few extreme cases showed rises of nearly 100 per cent. This massive escalation of cost was caused by a unique combination of factors most of which were related to local government reorganisation and some of which were not. Inflation and high interest rates are major influences on the rising tide of local expenditure and seem likely to continue. The Water Act, 1973, which transferred water and sewerage functions to the new Regional Water Authorities, was not an integral part of local government reform but it had a serious effect on rate levels. The new water authorities obtain their revenue from a charge which is attached to the local rates and the sums required were substantially higher than the product of the water and sewerage rates formerly levied by local authorities. These new bodies faced heavy expense in setting up their organisations; they also made large provisions to establish reserve funds and protect themselves against future inflation. Reorganisation had a number of other more direct effects on expenditure. It encouraged improvements in local services. Authorities which were merged together often provided facilities of different quality, provided different levels of benefit or imposed varying scales of charges. When these came to be evened out there was a natural tendency to adopt the better standard of service or the more generous scale. Then reorganisation led to the employment of more local officials, to major improvements in salaries especially for senior officials, to substantial payments to chief officers and their deputies over the age of fifty who took the option of early retirement and also to the payment of allowances to councillors which were more extensive than those previously permitted. Finally there were the more obvious costs of reorganisation related to the acquisition of new premises and equipment.

It has now become apparent that the present basis of local taxation —the rate—is inadequate to meet the burden placed upon it. The implications of this statement are considered in the final section of this chapter.

THE RATING SYSTEM

It was noted in Chapter I that the Elizabethan Poor Law laid the foundation for the present rating system. As local services developed their cost was met by extra rates added on to the parish poor rate: thus county rates and school board rates were linked with the poor rate. Such charges were imposed on the whole country, both town and rural areas. Urban areas had further expenses, mainly connected with sanitary services under the Public Health Acts, which were financed by a separate rate collected in boroughs and urban districts. In these areas two separate rates were imposed. Many towns obtained powers to unify the collection of money, but this wasteful and stupid duplication was not finally ended until 1925. Under the 1972 reorganisation the districts and the London Boroughs levy the rate. Other authorities, the counties, the parishes and an assortment of joint boards with special powers, obtain income by precepting on the rating authorities. The level of the rate necessarily varies with local financial circumstances. Outside London it may vary within the area of a rating authority: in particular, wherever parish expenditure has to be added to the sums required to meet district and county expenses. In the non-metropolitan counties a very high proportion of rate revenue is handed on to the county councils because they are responsible for the most expensive services, notably education. The Layfield Report wanted to stop precepting so that the public became more conscious of the charges imposed by each local authority. It suggested that separate rate demands could be included in one envelope.

Liability to pay rates falls normally on the occupier of premises. Occupation is generally thought of in terms of control of the front door: a lodger does not control the front door and so is not liable. In some cases the owner of a property may be liable instead of the occupier(s). This applies to properties with a very low rateable value and to blocks of flats. Alternatively, an owner may come to an agreement with the rating authority to collect the rates from tenants along with the rents. For this trouble he receives a compounding allowance or discount from the rating authority. Until 1966, occupation was defined as beneficial occupation: no rates were payable on empty premises. However, rating authorities now have the option of imposing rates on premises unoccupied for three months, or six months in the case of new houses and flats. Many councils have decided not to exercise this power because a high proportion of the additional revenue could be consumed by the extra costs of collection. The Local Government Act, 1974, also gave power to impose a penal rating surcharge on unoccupied office property. Some property is excused from payment. Agricultural land has been exempt since 1929. Crown land is also exempt; in practice, the Treasury makes an equivalent contribution. Property used for or in connection with religious worship, public parks, sewers, lighthouses, buoys, beacons, sheds for housing invalid chairs, and the residences of ambassadors and their servants, are also exempt; and so are certain classes of machinery not deemed to be part of a building. Almshouses and other properties used for charitable purposes enjoy a 50 per cent reduction in the amount of rates payable, and rating authorities have a discretionary power to remit their rates altogether. This discretionary power to reduce or remit rates extends to other non-profit making institutions, e.g. social clubs and educational, literary and scientific bodies.

The Rating Act, 1966, was designed to ease the situation of rate-payers with low incomes. It authorised collection by instalments and provided for remission of rates for poorer persons not in receipt of national assistance. Each applicant for a rebate has to submit to a means test and the amount of relief granted depends upon a scale which is adjusted from time to time, to take account of changes in the value of money. Ninety per cent of the cost of these concessions is met by a government grant. In fact, fewer people have applied for rebates than was initially anticipated. Considerable pressure of claims arises in seaside towns where there are many elderly persons in receipt of fixed incomes often living in quite expensive properties.

How much is a ratepayer required to pay? This depends on two factors—the valuation placed on his property (the technical term is hereditament) and the poundage levied by the local rating authority. To give a simple example: if a house has a net assessment of £120 and the poundage charged is 75p, the liability for the year will be £90. It follows that the valuation of properties for rating purposes is a matter of financial concern to every ratepayer. The valuation is an attempt to define the annual value of a hereditament. While all rating valuation is based on this single principle, various means are used to arrive at the assessment in relation to different classes of property. However, shops and houses are assessed on the basis of a reasonable rent for the property; this figure is known as the Gross Annual Value. There is a standard scale of allowances to cover maintenance and insurance costs which are deducted from the Gross Value and this produces a second and lower figure, the Net Annual Value, on which rates are actually paid. Other techniques of assessment are used for factories, licensed premises and nationalised industries.

The task of valuation has been carried out by the Inland Revenue since 1948. Originally, of course, it was the duty of the overseer. Through the years various checks had to be imposed on the overseers to try to ensure that they did not undervalue property in their parish. There was substantial advantage to be gained from undervaluation in relation to charges assessed over a wider area than the parish, e.g. the district or county, because lower valuation allowed a parish to escape with paying a lower share of the total costs. The Rating and Valuation Act, 1925, abolished overseers and transferred the valuation function to county boroughs and area valuation committees which covered a group of neighbouring county districts. Finally the system was nationalised in 1948 to achieve uniformity. As a new system of government grants was introduced at this time designed to give greatest aid to authorities with the lowest rateable values per head of population, this uniformity was essential to ensure fairness in the distribution of the grant. In these circumstances the inducement to undervalue property would have been very strong. The first valuation list produced on a national basis became effective in 1956. It showed conclusively that the earlier standards of assessment must have been extremely varied. To take the extreme examples: in 1956 the rateable value of Radnor was increased by 17 per cent, but nearby in Cardigan rateable value of the county went up by 160 per cent. Cardigan had been under assessed before while Radnor valuations had been very much higher. In theory, a completely new valuation list is produced every five years, but they tend to be postponed. The 1961 revaluation was put off until 1963; the 1968 valuation was put back to 1973; the revision due in 1978 has already been postponed until 1980. However, valuation of particular properties may be altered at any time to take account of extensions or improvements: by the Local Government Act, 1974, alterations are not to be made in respect of minor structural alterations.

Any ratepayer may appeal against an assessment and argue his case before a local valuation court. A further appeal from a decision of this body can be made to the Lands Tribunal. To succeed an appeal must show that there is some injustice in the valuation. It is useless to go before the valuation court and say that you cannot afford to pay so much in rates. But if it can be shown that similar properties have a lower assessment, or that more desirable properties have the same assessment, or that the value of a property has been adversely affected by some local development, then an appeal can succeed.

In 1929 when agricultural land was derated altogether, industrial and freight-transport hereditaments were also relieved of three-quarters of their rate liability. But since the war the law on valuation for rating has been changed frequently in response to political and administrative pressures. In the 1963 valuation list the derating of industrial and freight-transport hereditaments was ended (Rating and Valuation Act, 1961). Dwelling-houses, shops and offices are now rated also on current values, so there have been drastic upward adjustments everywhere in the assessments of residential property. Of course, the rate paid by the residential occupier does not increase *pro rata* with a rise in assessments because the rise in total rateable values, including the greater amounts accruing from industrial premises, should permit broadly equivalent reductions in the level of the rate poundage. But any ratepayer will suffer if his own assessment has risen proportionately more than the average of assessments in his area. The rate burden also tends steadily to increase as local authorities are forced to pass on the rising charges for goods and services which they require.

The rating of nationalised industries presents a special problem; their physical assets are not Crown property but are assessable to rates. Three of them, the railways, the gas industry and the electricity supply industry, have fixed plant obviously not self-contained in any rating areas. Special arrangements operate under the General Rate Act, 1967, for the ascertainment of the total rateable value of such assets in the areas of the owning Boards and the apportionment of the rate liabilities in respect of them among the rating authorities.

We now turn from valuation to the calculation of the rate poundage. The local financial year starts on April 1st, so in January and February estimates are prepared of spending in the coming financial year; these will be considered by a finance or central policy committee, possibly pruned back, and presented to the council for final approval. The detailed work is carried on by the Treasurer and his staff in consultation with the other spending committees. Obviously this involves pre-planning of future activities and requires important policy decisions to be made, so the preparation of estimates can be both a complex and controversial exercise. The final total of projected expenditure is a major feature of the local budget, but there are other factors which affect the extent of the demands made on ratepayers—national grants, local revenue from rents, fees and other charges and unspent balances, if any, from the previous year. A local authority is not entitled to accumulate surpluses on revenue account, so if expenditure in any one year is less than estimated the saving should be devoted to reducing the rate levy in the following year. Of course, an adequate working balance is permitted and a margin for unexpected contingencies.

When the figures for the various parts of the budget are available, the size of the gap between expenditure and non-rate revenue becomes apparent. This is the gap that has to be filled by local taxation. If the charge on the rate fund shows a steep rise on the previous year, there may well be demands for reductions in expenditure. The rate poundage is fixed by relating the income required from the rate to the rateable value of a local authority's domain; the latter is the sum of the net rateable values of all properties in the area. Thus if a council has a rateable value of £5,000,000 and requires to raise three-quarters of this sum, the probable rate levy is 76p in the £—the extra penny being required to cover contingencies and the loss of revenue on empty property, various remissions and bad debts. This is, naturally, a greatly simplified picture of the local budgetary process; in reality, the calculations involved are highly complex. One other concept must be noticed, that of the penny rate product which is the amount produced by imposing a rate of a penny in the pound and equals one-hundredth of the local rateable value, ignoring the effect of empty property. The penny rate product is a useful way of showing the cost of any new policy. To revert to the earlier example, an authority with a rateable value of £5,000,000 has a penny rate worth £50,000, so that a £100,000 scheme that earned no revenue of its own and attracted no national grant would cost a twopenny rate.

Until 1967 all classes of ratepayers paid the same rate in the pound. There had been, as was noted above, many shifts and adjustments in the methods of assessing various types of property, but at least the rate poundage was uniform. Now valuation is tolerably uniform but rate poundage varies because the domestic ratepayer is allowed to pay at a lower figure than other categories of ratepayer. This development is discussed more fully below.

GOVERNMENT GRANTS

When the state required local government to undertake new duties it often made a grant in aid of the new service to ease the financial burden. Alternatively, grants were given to reduce the cost of an activity obviously of national as well as local benefit; a clear example is the grant made to meet the cost of criminal prosecutions in 1834. There is, of course, room for argument over which services are of national benefit. Public health is of national interest because disease can spread across local authority boundaries. An efficient police force is of national benefit whereas a local playing field is not. Through the years views have changed on the nature and extent of the public interest and the term is now given a much wider definition than in the nineteenth century. The Victorian controversy about the exact distinction between what were described as local beneficial services and national onerous services deserving national aid now seems curiously antique. However, this distinction had an important role in the evolution of the grant system. Grants were also given to ease the burdens of the poorer areas and to ensure that minimum standards were maintained over services thought to be of national importance. Financial recompense also has had to be made to local councils when the national government reduces their taxing powers, e.g. the derating of agricultural land and the partial derating of industry in 1929 and the domestic rate relief imposed by the Local Government Act, 1966.

There has been a succession of changes in government financial policy towards local authorities. Various types of grant have been used. The main distinction is between specific grants and general grants. The specific grant is given to aid a particular local service and is usually given on a percentage basis. An alternative is a unit basis—so much per house or flat. The percentage arrangement has two disadvantages. It may encourage extravagant spending, especially if the percentage grant is high: where a 50 per cent grant applies, the local authority can expect to recover half its expenditure. In consequence, central departments have to impose some check on local expenditure, probably by setting down categories of spending that will be accepted for grant purposes. This involves more central supervision of local government and an increase in administrative cost.

The general grant is a contribution to local rate funds not tied in this way. Again, it can take one of two main forms; either it can be designed specifically to help the poorest authorities or it can be given to all councils. Distribution is governed by a formula which will either try to assess the poverty of an area or will assess need by reference to the size and nature of the population. A general grant is simpler administratively. Arguably it is more conducive to local independence and freedom from central supervision. It also encourages good housekeeping by local authorities. The amount of grant is fixed before the start of a financial year so the councils know in advance their income from the Government. Any extra sums they may be tempted to spend fall squarely on the rates. Quite naturally, the general grants method has always been preferred by the Treasury. Essentially the history of the grant system over the past hundred years is one of continuous growth but also of ebb and flow between the general and specific categories. In 1888, 1929 and again in 1958 many specific grants were swept away and replaced by (more) general grants. The education grant disappeared in 1958. Critics claimed that its termination would lead to cuts in the standards of educational provision, but this did not happen because the increase in the general subvention was more than adequate to compensate for the termination of the separate education grant. The Labour Opposition was highly critical of the 1958 decision; however, when in office they did not reverse it. Indeed, speaking on the 1966 Local Government Bill in the House of Commons, Mr Crossman laid down two criteria for specific grants, that there must be a need to control the service centrally or that the expenditure involved must be distributed unevenly between authorities. The police are an example of the first and coast protection of the second.

The main specific grants now in operation are for housing, police and transport. The Local Government Act, 1974, introduced a new transport supplementary grant (TSG) the amount of which is negotiated alongside the annual discussions on the size of the general grant—now termed the Rate Support Grant. Transport grants are related to local expenditure on highways, public transport subsidies

and traffic regulation. To explain and justify their spending programmes each county council has to submit to central government a
document entitled Transport Policy and Programme (TPP) which
contains a statement of transport objectives and strategy over the
next decade or so. The TSG/TPP system is a clear example of the
strong link between specific grants and central control; in 1977 the
transport grant for South Yorkshire was cut drastically because the
Government opposed the local policy of providing large subsidies to
keep down the level of bus fares.

The Local Government Act, 1974, also provided that central
government would meet 90 per cent of the cost of awards to students
at universities and teacher training colleges or following courses of
equivalent standard. The Layfield Report was notably unenthusiastic
about specific grants. It urges that the whole costs of mandatory
student awards be met by the government and that police and transport grants be merged into the Rate Support Grant.

Housing subsidies have been a source of contention between the
Labour and Conservative parties. Thus legislation in this sphere has
been amended frequently. The Housing Rents and Subsidies Act,
1975, reaffirmed the rights of local authorities to fix council house
rents—but not so as to make a profit on their Housing Revenue
Accounts. Earlier Conservative legislation, the Housing Finance
Act, 1972, was intended to lead to the fixing of 'fair rents', not by
housing authorities but by independent rent-scrutiny committees.
The 1975 Act also provides for a complex system of subsidy based on
sums payable under previous legislation, plus 66 per cent of loan
charges on money borrowed to buy land, build houses or improve
houses, plus additional payments for high cost areas, particularly
London. However, the Government keeps a firm control over the
number of new council houses built.

General grants commenced their tortuous history with the assigned
revenues of 1888, the failure of which was noted in the introductory
chapter. During and after the First World War a variety of new
grants was made available to assist particular services. The Conservative Government, with Winston Churchill as Chancellor of the
Exchequer, decided to reorganise methods of central financial aid
and as from 1929 all specific grants were replaced with a general
grant, apart from those for education, police, housing, certain health
functions and roads in county areas.

The post-war Labour Government favoured specific grants which
were increased in range and amount. The 1929 general grant was
replaced in 1948 by the Exchequer Equalisation Grant which gave
aid solely to the poorer authorities. This system lasted for ten years
until in 1958 the Conservatives decided on another slaughter of

specific grants, this time to include education. A new general grant took their place distributed on the basis of a formula. A basic sum was paid to counties and county boroughs on the basis of actual population plus population under fifteen years of age. Additional grants were payable under seven headings; children under five, old persons over sixty-five, a high ratio of school pupils, high population density, sparse population, declining population and higher costs in the London area. The Exchequer Equalisation Grant to help poorer districts was continued in a slightly modified form and renamed the Rate Deficiency Grant. A number of factors are taken into consideration when fixing the total—the level of relevant local expenditure (this excludes expenditure on services which enjoy a specific grant), changes in local expenditure which lie beyond local control, the need to develop local services and the extent to which development can be afforded in the light of the national economic situation. Here is a clear recognition of the need to link the fortunes of local government with the general economic situation of the country.

The latest form of general grant is the Rate Support Grant initiated by the Local Government Act, 1966. This has three parts—the needs element, the resources element and the domestic element. The needs element is the successor to the General Grant of 1958; the resources element replaces the Rate Deficiency Grant; the domestic element is entirely new and designed to cover the cost of reducing rate poundages for domestic ratepayers. The Rate Support Grant now constitutes about 90 per cent of the total of central aid to local government.

The third leg of the tripod, the domestic element, gave residential occupiers a fivepenny (approximately 2.1 new pence) reduction in 1967-8. The size of the reduction has increased steadily and in 1977 was 18.5p in England and 36p in Wales. Initially the domestic element was intended as a temporary palliative to minimise the harshness of the rating system until a more radical reform of local government finance could be undertaken. In 1976–77 the domestic element cost £644 million, a dramatic increase over the total of £30 million in 1967–68.

Complex annual discussions are held to determine the size of the rate support grant. Representatives of central government, and of local government, the latter nominated by the associations of local authorities, examine estimates of future expenditure in great detail. Since 1975 these discussions have been placed on a more formal level by the establishment of a Consultative Council on Local Government Finance which provides a useful forum for an exchange of views between Ministers and leading councillors. However, the Government retains the whip hand in these discussions both because it is providing the money and because local expenditure is now so large that it must be made to conform with the economic policy of the Cabinet. In 1977–78 local rates had to bear a markedly increased proportion of local expenditure as a contribution towards solving our national economic difficulties.

At present, however, if some councils spend more than Ministers wish, financial discipline can be imposed only by reducing the total sum allocated to the RSG: when this is distributed according to formula, the councils which accepted the official guidelines suffer as well as the malefactors. The good boys are punished along with the bad. So in 1977 the Government proposed to replace the needs and resources elements of the RSG by a unitary grant to be calculated separately for each authority. The amount would be sufficient to bridge the gap between the cost of providing services comparable with those of similar authorities and the receipts from the local rate assuming it was fixed at a particular level specified by the central government. Thus Ministers would determine acceptable standards. Should a council wish to exceed these standards it could do so by increasing the local rate.

CAPITAL EXPENDITURE

Local authorities may borrow money to meet the cost of capital expenditure, subject to the consent of the Department of the Environment. Each loan has to be paid back over a period of years, the length of the period depending on the durability of the asset. The lifespan of capital assets is estimated on a conservative basis for this purpose; for example, loans for baths and wash-houses must be repaid over 30 years, for houses over 60 years, for housing land over 80 years. It follows that at the end of these periods the local authority will have a debt-free asset; it may achieve this position even earlier for no council is compelled to borrow for the maximum permissible period.

Inevitably, this raises the question—is it a good policy to borrow at all? An individual with an adequate income but no capital who seeks to buy a house has no alternative: he must try to borrow by raising a mortgage. But a local authority is not in the same situation. It has a flexible source of revenue and can increase its income by raising the rate poundage. Should ratepayers be forced to pay for capital assets immediately, without recourse to borrowing? This policy has one great advantage—cheapness. To raise a loan for a period as long as 60 years is extremely expensive. Interest rates are now very high. At the time of writing local authorities are having to pay 13 per cent. (Of course, if the rate of interest is below the rate of inflation, the lender stands to lose—quite apart from the tax that has to be paid on the interest received.) So local authorities can save money by paying for capital assets out of revenue, and a few councils did so in relation to at least part of their capital expenditure until the last war. Now the policy is out of favour for at least three reasons. Durable assets will be of benefit to the next generation of ratepayers, so why should the whole cost be met by the ratepayers of today? This is a powerful argument which is reinforced by the continuous tendency for the purchasing power of the pound to decline. A pound borrowed now will buy much more than it will when repaid in, say, fifty years time; admittedly this is only a prediction but all economic experience suggests it is a safe one! The faster the depreciation of currency, the greater the advantage to the debtor, the greater the loss to the creditor. The advantage to the debtor is offset by the interest that has to be paid but, unless interest rates are high, there is potential advantage in borrowing. At present interest rates are high, very high, and this encourages many authorities to charge small capital items to current revenue. To charge large capital sums to the rate fund would involve raising rate levels even more steeply and this would be politically unacceptable. If major capital schemes were financed from revenue, there is a danger that standards of provision would become not merely economical but parsimonious.

Ministerial control over local borrowing was firmly established by the end of the nineteenth century. The reasons for control of borrowing have changed over the years. Originally, the concern was to ensure that local authorities were not overstepping the limits of their financial resources by incurring unduly heavy commitments for the future repayment of debt. Such Gladstonian prudence has now gone. The central government was also concerned to ensure that engineering proposals by local authorities were technically sound: smaller authorities with inadequate specialist advice had to be protected from the possibility of expensive mistakes. Now the main task is to ensure that capital spending by local authorities is in conformity with the Government's overall economic programme and, indeed, is in conformity with Ministers' patterns of priorities. In any balance of payments crisis, the order is likely to come from Whitehall —no more town halls or swimming baths until the national economic situation improves: if the crucial problem is unemployment, then local authorities may be encouraged to spend more, e.g. on highway improvements.

Capital construction schemes are now allocated priorities two or three years in advance. To save administrative work loan sanction may be given not for individual projects but for a whole programme of construction. Once ministerial permission to borrow has been obtained, a local authority—and its Treasurer—are faced with two interrelated problems, how to obtain the loan and whether it is preferable to borrow on a short-term or long-term basis. The latter question involves attempting to forecast the future pattern of interest rates. If they are expected to rise, it is better to arrange a long-term loan with a fixed interest: if a fall is anticipated, it is better to arrange a short period loan so that the money can be reborrowed subsequently at a lower interest charge.

Various techniques of raising capital are available to a local authority. One is the Public Works Loan Board, established under an Act of 1875. The Board is financed by Government loans and the Treasury prescribes the interest rates to be charged. In recent years there have been a number of shifts of Government policy in relation to the PWLB. Originally the idea was that the Board should assist mainly the smaller authorities which lacked both the prestige and experience to raise funds easily in the money market. Then the post-war Labour Government decreed that all local borrowing, with some minor exceptions, should be through the PWLB. The theory behind this action appeared to be that competition for capital by local authorities would force up interest rates, and that higher charges might be at least partly avoided by a single co-ordinated borrowing programme for central and local government. In 1952 these restrictions were eased and local authorities were encouraged to find their own sources of capital. Some were reluctant to do so because the interest rates charged by the Board were often more advantageous than could be obtained elsewhere. So in 1955 the Government took firmer action to cut down the use of these facilities. Three years later the Radcliffe Report on the working of the monetary system urged that the PWLB channel of finance be widened to limit the amount of short-term borrowing by local authorities. This advice was not accepted immediately. However, an agreement between the Treasury and local authorities in 1963 provided that up to half of the capital requirements of a council could be arranged through the Board in return for an agreement by local authorities to restrict their temporary borrowing to 20 per cent of their total debt. The tendency is for the smaller authorities and those in less prosperous areas to make greatest use of the PWLB. The flow of capital through the Board remains well below the 50 per cent limit as some authorities find that they can borrow elsewhere on rather more favourable terms.

Other techniques of borrowing can be described briefly. Subject to Treasury consent, local authorities can issue stock. Relatively large sums of money can be obtained by this means for a long period and these advantages are important to large authorities when interest rates are not too high. The most common methods are to issue mort-gages or bonds. For technical reasons the bonds are simpler to administer and so are coming more into favour. Some capital is available from internal sources, e.g. superannuation funds. Short period and temporary loans are raised through the money market or from banks.

A general picture of local authority indebtedness can be obtained from the figures published by the Chartered Institute of Public Finance and Accountancy which show how capital debt has been utilised and the source of borrowing.

ANALYSIS OF LOCAL AUTHORITY DEBT, 1976

by service	£000,000	by form of debt	%
Housing:		Stock	6·2
Buildings, sites	13,182	Mortgages	12·0
Loans, improvement grants	3,269	Bonds	19·0
Education	2,839	PWLB	38·3
Highways	959	Temporary loans	12·0
Trading services	460	Internal advances	1·8
Town and Country Planning	621	Revenue balances	8·2
Amenity and Recreation	459	Other	2·5
Social Services	385		
Police and Fire	174		
Environmental Protection	145		
Other	588		
Total	23,081		

Source: CIPFA: Summary of Debt Outstanding

What role should the Government play in relation to local borrow-ing? Two views on this issue emerge in the local authority world. There is a general desire to remain as independent as possible of central control. There is also a feeling that, as most local loans are required to carry through national programmes, the Government should facilitate borrowing and perhaps offer favourable interest rates. Some advantages would accrue from the establishment of a central organisation to arrange a capital flow. The Institute of Municipal Treasurers and Accountants—now the Chartered Institute of Public Finance and Accountancy—has urged the establishment of such an agency which would have power to borrow on its own account, although it might be partly financed through the Consoli-dated Fund. This agency would not provide all loan capital required by local authorities which would continue to exercise initiative in fund raising. The scheme thus combines the attractions of local independence and central co-ordination. On the Government side there seems also to be two attitudes which ebb and flow. One stresses the need for a co-ordinated borrowing policy; the other wishes to avoid the strain on national borrowing facilities which would be imposed by an acceptance of full responsibility for local finance. There is no doubt that councils can tap funds from local sources that might not be available to the Government and many authorities can manage at present without making use of the PWLB. The problem is not lack of available capital, but high interest rates which are caused by national and international factors—not by the actions of local government.

RATES—INADEQUATE AND UNFAIR?

Rates probably cause more irritation than any other form of taxation. Before examining the causes of this discontent, it is well to look at the few advantages that can be claimed for the rates. The rating mechanism, in spite of complexities of detail, is traditional and is well understood. Now assessment has been nationalised, the valuations are generally just and, in any case, can be challenged by appeals. Since rates are payable on visible and immovable property, it is impossible to avoid paying. This means that the local authorities have a stable and reliable source of revenue. Rates are also a flexible tax in that it is easy to alter the level of the poundage. They are also economical to collect: according to the County Councils Association the collection cost is 1.2 per cent of the total revenue. Since rates are a tax on housing they act as a deterrent to under-occupation of property and may encourage people with excess accommodation to sub-let or move. And as the rates are imposed by local authorities they provide a degree of financial independence from the central government; without such independence, local councils would soon become mere agents of central departments spending from national funds. This last item in the catalogue is not an argument for rates *per se*, but it is an argument of basic importance for the retention by local authorities of an independent taxing capacity. So far no alternative to the rates has appeared to be politically or administratively acceptable; in these circumstances, the rates remain a bulwark of local autonomy.

Why then do rates provoke criticism? The first answer is psychological. Rates are a very obvious tax. Indirect taxes, for example those on tobacco, beer and petrol, are linked with the natural cost of the commodity: the public is generally aware that there is a substantial tax element in the total price, but the price is still accepted as the price *of the commodity*. Anyone entering a tobacconist's shop is not dominated by the thought that he is about to make a contribution to national revenue. Income tax, for the most part, is collected on a 'pay as you earn' basis, so the wage and salary earner comes to accept the net amount of his weekly or monthly pay-slip as his true income. The tax and insurance deductions are accepted, no doubt regretted, but ignored when it comes to planning personal expenditure. You do not miss what you have never had. In contrast to PAYE and indirect taxes, the rates are not hidden in any way. Money has to be extracted from disposable income and paid to the rates office. Since rates are usually payable on a half-yearly basis, the sum involved on each occasion is substantial: however, authorities are now less unwilling to collect by more frequent instalments. Yet it still remains true that ratepayers are more conscious of rates than of other forms of taxation. Other people may not share this awareness. And this is important because in 1945 when universal suffrage was extended to local government, a substantial gap developed between the number of people paying rates and those who can vote for councillors who impose rates. Those who suffer financial responsibility no longer correspond with those who exercise constitutional power. But this distinction should not be overstressed. Local authorities now obtain more revenue from grants than they do from the local rate and everyone is liable to contribute to national taxes. Further, adult members of a household normally contribute to its expenses and rent for furnished accommodation should contain a rate element.

There are many other objections. From the point of view of the local authority, the rates have an unsatisfactory tax base. Prices and costs rise ceaselessly; property values also rise but the quinquennial valuations are always postponed so that rateable values do not keep pace with the fall in the purchasing power of money. This means that rate poundages are forced up almost every year, thus creating annual discontent. It is also arguable that the reasonable rent basis of valuation for domestic property is largely spurious because, owing to the operation of rent restriction legislation, in many areas there is no free market in rented property. More equitable assessments might be achieved if capital values were used instead of hypothetical rental values. Householders may be deterred from expanding or improving their properties since to do so involves a bigger rate liability. There is also no connection between the use a ratepayer makes of local services and the extent of his rate bill. Whether this is a valid objection is a matter of opinion. Personal demands upon local services are either a matter of choice or need and, in so far as they result from need, the rate-supported services contribute to social equality. It is certain that areas in which the need for social welfare provision is greatest have the lowest rateable values per head; *vice versa* where needs are less, rateable values are high. This creates a situation in which it is easiest to raise rate revenue where it is least required as high rateable values tend to produce low rate poundages. The system of government grants is designed to assist the poorer areas, but they do not entirely eliminate disparities.

All this makes up a powerful case against rates. Yet the main criticism is that they fall unevenly on different classes of ratepayer. Those who are liable to pay in relation to shop, commercial and industrial premises can use their rate bill as an expense for which an allowance is made in relation to income tax liability. No such relief is available for the domestic ratepayer. Indeed, it is arguable that to give income tax relief for rate liability would be unfair since it would give no aid to those who need it most—those too poor to pay income-tax. In 1963 there was a great outcry about the unfairness of rating after the new valuation list had reassessed residential properties at current values. The storm of protest forced the Government to appoint a Committee to enquire into the impact of local rates on households. This Committee, under the chairmanship of Professor Allen, issued its report in 1965 and demonstrated clearly the regressive nature of local rates. Their incidence is quite different to income tax. A man with a large family enjoys substantial allowances in respect of his children when income tax is computed. He also needs to occupy more residential accommodation if he can afford it—and this will make him liable to pay more rates. A lodger pays no rates at all, at least directly. When the rating system was instituted on a national scale in 1601 it was broadly fair as between individuals since it was based on visible wealth, and the squire in the manor house could obviously afford to pay more than the tenant farmer or the yeoman. Today the size of a property is an unsure guide to the wealth of its occupants and their ability to contribute to the cost of local services.

However, the situation has altered dramatically since 1965. The Layfield Report showed that in 1975 households with a weekly income below £20 made no net contribution to the rates; above £20 a week the rates have a slowly increasing impact until a plateau is reached at income levels between £35 and £80 a week when the rates claimed between 2 per cent and 3 per cent of income; above £80 a week the rate demand consumes a diminishing proportion of income. So the regressive effect of local rates has been substantially diminished. Three factors have contributed to the change. More generous supplementary benefits have assisted low income groups to pay their rates. The Rating Act, 1966, provided for remission of rates for the poorest sections of the community, subject to a means test. The Local Government Act 1966, introduced a national subsidy to enable lower rates to be charged on all residential properties. This benefit is not subject to any income limitation and, as shown above, has been increased substantially over the years. Thus a great deal has been done to mitigate the hardships caused by the rating system but, because public memory is short, the extent of the improvement tends to be forgotten. Meanwhile, the policy of rate relief has one serious drawback—local government tends to become more financially dependent on the national Exchequer. And, inevitably, he who pays the piper calls the tune.

At present the rate of expansion of local government services is faster than the growth of the national economy. So rate revenue must increase not merely in monetary terms but as a proportion of the national product unless one of four other possibilities is adopted. These are a reduction in the scale of growth of local services; higher levels of central government grants; removal of some services from the ambit of local government; other sources of revenue for local authorities are developed. The first alternative slows down progress; the second implies loss of independence; the third weakens local government by limiting its scope. Clearly the fourth solution is the most acceptable to local authorities. In practice, it is the second and third alternatives that have been followed.

How could extra revenue be obtained for local councils in order to free them from suffocation by central subventions? Councils could impose more charges for the services they provide but this is open to social and political objections as illustrated by the reaction to higher charges for school meals and 'fair rents' for council houses. Various new forms of local taxation have also been suggested but all are open to some objection.

The rating system itself could be amended. The Government has accepted the Layfield Committee proposal that property be assessed on the basis of capital value rather than annual value. Another Layfield suggestion, to abolish agricultural derating, has been officially rejected. Such adjustments would strengthen the rating system but they do not really get to the heart of the problem. A satisfactory solution demands a new base for local taxation. Motor taxation duties might be transferred to local authorities. But if the *level* of charge were to be fixed locally, then it would be cheaper to register vehicles in some places than others: it might well become economic to garage large lorry fleets in areas with lower duties. Yet if the level of tax is not a matter for local decision, councils have no control over their income. A sales tax is more obviously capable of local adjustment, but it faces three major objections. Presumably it would be in addition to the national VAT and obviously would be a most unwelcome addition. Like the rates it would be regressive in that, unless restricted to luxury and semi-luxury goods, the burden would be heaviest on the poorest members of the community. Finally, people living in the countryside and in small towns spend money in bigger towns. To take the extreme case, London is almost a national shopping centre. So if the tax were collected by the present rating authorities on turnover in their own districts, rural areas would suffer badly. Were local government organised on a regional basis, this obstacle would partly disappear.

The idea of a local income tax has been widely canvassed for many years. It would add greatly to the financial independence of local government. As compared with a rate on property, it has the advantage that more people would be required to contribute to local revenues. The sums paid by individuals might also be more fairly related to their ability to pay; whether those with low incomes would benefit depends on the rules adopted for rate rebates and income tax relief. The Layfield Report, *Local Government Finance* (Cmnd 6453), published in 1976, suggested that local income tax should supplement local rates. It should be levied by local authorities that face the highest expenditure, the shire counties, the metropolitan districts and the London boroughs. However, the Layfield Report listed many practical difficulties to be faced. Expense is a serious obstacle. Rather than establish new local income tax offices, it would be cheaper to use the services of the Inland Revenue: however, the methods of the Revenue would need adjustment since income tax collection is based on the location of employers not on the residence of employees. Another problem is that at present national taxes are uniform; local income tax requires collection at varied levels. By the use of the Inland Revenue, Layfield estimated that administrative costs could be kept down to £100 million per annum at 1975 prices. Whether the advantages of the system justify such an amount is a matter of opinion, particularly when the trend of government policy is to restrict public expenditure.

Not surprisingly the Government's Green Paper issued in response to the Layfield Report (Cmnd 6813) rejected local income tax. The Treasury could be expected to resist any interference by local government with a key regulator of the economy. The Green Paper commented that local freedom 'to vary the LIT rate would have to be closely constrained so that it did not unduly complicate central government economic and financial management'. And if LIT were absorbed in PAYE deductions, the public would tend to lose sight of it; local accountability, so heavily emphasised by Layfield, would be lost.

It must be stressed that the Layfield support for local income tax was hedged by the stipulation that it should be linked with 'express moves towards giving greater power of decision to local authorities'.

So the proposed reform was specifically associated with the wider question of relations between central and local government. This aspect of the Layfield Report is considered in Chapter X.

Chapter VI

PERSONNEL AND PROCEDURE

A local authority, like any other piece of state mechanism, is governed by both law and practice. The conventions that develop within the formal structure of a local authority have a great effect on the way in which business is carried through and how decisions are made. No systematic description of the arrangements is possible since they vary between each authority. There is, however, one dominating factor—the extent to which a council is influenced by the political loyalties of elected members. The importance of political parties in framing the conventions of public life can scarely be exaggerated. The work of a local authority is based on the interrelationships of officials and elected representatives working together through a committee system. Especially in urban areas the outcome is substantially affected by party activity. To ignore the effect of politics on local government is unrealistic and misleading: a broad description of the political setting must be given before we move on to consider the respective roles of officers and councillors.

THE IMPACT OF POLITICS

It is often argued that politics should have no place in local government. Certainly, there are some grounds for this view. Where elections are held on a party basis, no candidate other than those sponsored by a party has a real chance of success. Where one party is dominant in a particular ward or district, nomination by that party is tantamount to election to the local council, for electors become accustomed to voting on party lines and do not know, or do not care about, the qualities of the individual candidate. Attachment to a political party thus becomes an essential pre-condition of election to a local council; in so far as this limits the field of recruitment, the quality of elected members may be reduced. There must be many men and women of high ability who would be willing to serve on local authorities but who are unwilling to give unswerving support to a party or who happen to belong to a political minority in their own locality. The other main causes of complaint are that where councillors organise themselves into political groups, decisions are taken by the majority group in private meetings, and that politics are allowed to affect details of local administration which are quite beyond the normal bounds of party controversy.

Equally, however, a strong case can be made in favour of party politics. Party activity does much to increase interest in local elections: party conflict tends to reduce the number of unopposed elections, and to raise the proportion of the electorate who vote in contested elections. Further, if a candidate is returned without a party label, it does not follow that he has no political affiliations but merely that he has not declared any he may have. To argue that politics should be taken out of local government is, in part, to mis-understand the nature of politics. In a democracy we argue freely about the proper aims and methods of public policy. This is political discussion. Inevitably, the major questions which confront local authorities, education, housing, planning, raise issues which are political in nature and attract the attention of political organisations. The idea that these matters should be left to 'the best man for the job' is fanciful since one cannot decide who is the best man unless the opinions of candidates are revealed. The charge that party groups should not have private 'caucus' meetings to settle policy is countered by showing that this is analogous to what happens in our national government; no one suggests it is wrong for Conservative and Labour MPs to hold separate private gatherings or that party leaders should not meet in conditions of secrecy at Cabinet or 'Shadow' Cabinet meetings. Party organisation in a democracy is essential for opinions to be organised into broad streams. The group or party representing the dominant stream of opinion becomes responsible for the conduct of public affairs for a limited time, and may be displaced from power at a subsequent election if it displeases the voters. It follows that where the business of a local authority is conducted on a party basis it is more likely to be planned and consistent than if it depends on unorganised and changing views of individual councillors.

Whatever view one takes of these theoretical considerations, it is vital to recognise that the impact of politics on local government is growing steadily. Even in rural areas, most local elections are now fought on a party basis. What does vary, however, and what is most difficult to determine, is how far party organisation affects the actual working of a local council. The variety of local arrangements is best illustrated by the description of extremes. In some councils, party loyalty matters little; members may be elected on a party basis but, once elected, tend to act as individuals; committee chairmen are chosen irrespective of politics and no group meetings are held. This is often the pattern in non-industrial areas. At the other extreme, party governs everything important. The majority group meets to determine policy on major issues; it secures a majority on all committees; it nominates the chairmen and vice-chairmen of all committees; the parties require complete obedience from their members, and any councillor who refuses to support a party decision is expelled from the group and will not get party support at the next election. Such extensive party influence is common in urban areas and other authorities dominated by the Labour Party. There are of course, many authorities which fall in between the patterns define above, where groups meet irregularly or committee chairmanship are not always distributed on a party basis. And sometimes when party loyalties are strong, the effect of politics is restricted becau no group has an overall majority of seats.

Against this background of an uneven degree of party activity, t work of elected members, officers and committees continues. Whe the party element is strong the ability of elected members to spe their minds freely in public is curtailed. On major issues the only free discussion may take place in the privacy of the party meet where party policy is decided, if necessary by a vote. An elec. member who finds himself in a minority among party colleagues required to bow to the necessity of political unity and vote again his opinion at committee and council meetings. Where strict par discipline operates, it follows that the policy adopted need n represent the will of the majority, but only the will of the majc of the majority—which may well be a minority of the whole. Furt the officers will have less influence on the direction of local af if party considerations govern policy and major decisions are ta at private meetings which officers do not attend. Even so, the pic must not be exaggerated. However intense party activity may t mass of minor matters remain to be settled by committee debate by consultation between chief officers and committee chairmen.

COUNCILLORS

Representative democracy in local government is secured by regular election of councillors. There are about 25,000 in Engla and Wales, excluding the minor authorities, the parish and commun councils. What type of people are they? The Government Soc Survey undertook a detailed investigation of councillors (a aldermen) in 1965 for the Maud Committee so that we have a fa picture of those who govern us locally. It is clear that they do n constitute a fair cross-section of society. Only 12 per cent of councillo were female. Their average age was 55: women councillors a county and rural district councillors had an even higher average age. A mere 5 per cent of male councillors were below 35. Twenty per cent

ere retired. Certain categories of occupation predominated,
nployers, managers, professional workers and farmers; this is
surprising since persons in such occupations are best able to adjust
ir hours of work to fit in with local authority business. Councillors
immobile; nearly two-thirds said that they had lived in the area
represent for at least 25 years. It is comforting that, judged by
st of examination successes, they were better educated than the
e of the total population: again it is unsurprising to learn that
ngest councillors were those who have obtained the most
c qualifications. Councillors were also among the most
rticipants in community affairs and had a high incidence
ership of political parties and other local bodies of all

survey is now out-of-date and it is possible that the intro-
on of payments to councillors (discussed below) may have
red their social composition a little. One hopes that a fresh survey
ll now be conducted. The abolition of aldermen should have
educed the average age of members of local authorities.

The Maud Committee on Management suggested that persons
er 70 should be disqualified from election, but this idea has not
en accepted. Already Justices of the Peace must retire from the
tive list at 75. The analogy is not exact because justices are nomin-
ted for life while councillors are subject to re-election. Is age
squalification justified? Certainly, the elderly are less likely to be
vigorous or alert as younger people. On the other hand, should
t the electors decide when an individual is unsuitable to represent
em? The ability to contest an election successfully is at least some
idence of energy, and many councillors over the age of 70 now
ve excellent service to local government. Yet younger councillors
could give even better service.

The 1972 reorganisation did cause a significant fall in the total
umber of councillors outside London. The reduction was approxi-
nately 11,600. And 4,400 aldermen also disappeared. Rural areas
uffered the greatest loss of representatives because here rural districts
and small urban authorities were joined together. In the largest
towns—the former county boroughs—there was often an increase in
councillors because these places now elect members to the county
council. Since the councillor/electorate ratio was lowest in large
towns and highest in country districts, the reorganisation tended to
moderate the disproportion. Even so, the variations are very considerable. A member of the Greater London Council represents about
80,000 people. A member of a large non-metropolitan county
represents at least 12,000 people. A district councillor is likely to
represent on average about 2,000 people. Areas which have third-tier

authorities also enjoy supplementary representation through pari
or community councillors. Overall it is still true that representati
is strongest, in constitutional terms, where population is relativ
sparse.

The reduction in the number of councillors implies that those
remain have even heavier duties. If councillors have heavy resp
bilities—should they be paid? The Local Government Act,
entitled members of local authorities to claim for loss of earni
the basis of a somewhat niggardly scale, but this did not c
payment. It was compensation rather than remuneration, a
mise that avoided paying a salary. The arguments against
the tradition of honorary public service in local governm
formidable. There was no wide demand that it should be
Indeed, the Social Survey report to the Maud Committee s
that both councillors and ex-councillors are generally hostile
idea: the report also showed that lack of time rather than fina
reasons was the main barrier to the recruitment of young, w
educated councillors. Payment introduces a new and unpleasan
question of motivation: all council candidates are open to the sne
that they wished to be elected to get easy money. Were this type
attitude to become prevalent, it is probable that many people wou
be deterred from standing and some present councillors might drop
out. Payment also increases the burden on the local rate and is thus
unlikely to be popular with ratepayers. There is also a difficul
question about how much should be paid. If the sums involved a
substantial and designed to attract people of ability, the operati
must be costly and there can be no guarantee that people of th
requisite calibre will come forward—or that they will be elected.
Large payments could well attract the wrong sort of person to council
work. On the other hand, if the amounts offered are too small,
councils may still be dominated by retired persons or those with
inadequate ability and experience.

The case for making payments is far stronger. Unless some
financial recompense is available for councillors, many people who
must spend the greater part of their time earning a living are perforce
unable to offer their services and the field of recruitment will be
limited to housewives, retired people, the self-employed and those
fortunate enough to have sympathetic employers willing to release
them for local government work. Elected representatives naturally
spend varying amounts of time on council work; their burden will
depend on their personal inclinations, the size of the authority and
their status within it. Leading councillors in the larger authorities,
including the chairmen of major committees, already devote a great
deal of time each week to public service. For some these duties become

virtually a full-time occupation. Why should we expect all this effort without significant financial cost to the community? If our councillors are to fairly represent all sections of the community, particularly if we want younger and able councillors, payment must be made. The loss of time allowance introduced in 1948 did little to ease the situation: the sums paid were inadequate to compensate most salary earners, especially as service on a council may well damage prospects of promotion. In addition, the scheme involved form-filling which was felt to be invidious and was difficult to apply to self-employed people.

The Local Government Act, 1972, authorises local authorities to fix the rate of an attendance allowance for councillors, subject to a maximum scale prescribed by the Secretary of State. In 1974 the maximum is £10 a day. The rate of payment is the same for all members but the amounts received by individual councillors vary with the time spent on council business. So while no special payments are made to committee chairmen, the likelihood is that many of them receive more than other councillors. The attendance allowance is taxable and is regarded as a net addition to income. People who serve on local authorities but who are not councillors, i.e. co-opted members of committees, get no attendance payment but may claim a financial loss allowance. Members of a local authority and its committees can claim travelling and subsistence allowances when engaged on council business more than three miles from their homes. Parish and community councillors receive no allowance of any kind for duties within the area covered by their own council. Chairmen and vice-chairmen of both county and district councils can also receive an allowance 'to meet the expenses of his office'. Finally, a local authority can insure its members against death or injury caused by accident while engaged on council business.

There has been some adverse comment about the size of the sums received by the more active councillors. One danger is that committee meetings will be multiplied in order to increase the income of members. Also there is still a little nostalgia for the ideal of unpaid public service. But a modern democracy cannot expect to operate a system of representative democracy without incurring cost. Without some financial recompense for councillors it is inevitable that those willing to stand for election would be restricted increasingly to the elderly, the wealthy and those people sufficiently fortunate to be able to adjust their hours of work.

There are many qualifications governing candidature at local elections. A councillor must be 21 years of age and a British subject. He must also be on the register of electors for the authority concerned, unless during the twelve months prior to the election he has been resident in the area, or it has been his principal place of work, or he has been the owner or tenant of land or buildings within it. For a parish or community councillor the residence qualification is more flexible: he must have lived within three miles of the area during the preceding year. People who satisfy these conditions may still be disqualified by any one of the following rules. An employee of a local authority cannot be an elected member of it. So a teacher employed by a metropolitan district can serve on the county council: a teacher employed for a county council can serve on his district council. Bankruptcy is a disqualification, so is a surcharge of £500 by the district auditor within five years of the election. Those convicted of corrupt practices at elections are barred as well as those convicted for any offence within the last five years for which the penalty imposed was imprisonment for three months or more without the option of a fine. Further, a councillor who is absent from council meetings for six months will vacate his seat unless the authority approves his reason for absence.

The barrier against local authority staff does limit the availability of prospective councillors. No doubt the disqualification is imposed because it is felt that an employee should not join his employing body, as this would produce a conflict of interest. Clearly, it would be inappropriate for an administrative officer to be elected to the council which it is his duty to advise and assist. Whether the ban should extend to all employees, in particular to manual workers, is a matter for argument. They would have to be prohibited from speaking or voting on any resolution affecting their own remuneration or conditions of service. Subject to this safeguard why should a manual worker not be eligible for election? There does seem an element of hypocrisy in a system which disqualifies a dustman from election to his district council because of some alleged conflict of interest but which does not take similar precautions in relation to estate agents, building contractors and surveyors. However the Redcliffe-Maud Committee on Conduct in Local Government recommended firmly that the present restriction on local authority staff should remain unaltered.

Perhaps the most intractable constitutional problem affecting councillors is the relationship between their public duties and their business interests. The law on this topic is now governed by Section 94 of the Local Government Act, 1972. In essence, the position is that a councillor who has a financial interest in any contract or other matter coming before his authority must disclose his interest and not vote or participate in discussion thereon. Failure to observe this rule renders the defaulter liable to a fine not exceeding £200 for each offence: any such prosecution must be initiated by the Director of Public Prosecutions. The details of the law are complex. Interests of a spouse are included in the ban provided the marriage partners are living together. Membership of a partnership or company is also included. But the disability is removed wherever an interest is so remote that it cannot reasonably be regarded as likely to influence a councillor's conduct. And shareholdings in a company do not disqualify where the nominal amount is below £1,000 or below one-hundredth of the issued share capital of the company, whichever is less. A councillor can make a general statement of his interests in writing to be available for inspection by other councillors; this will obviate the need for a specific declaration of interest on each item that is linked to his business concerns. Another escape route is that the Secretary of State can remove this disability from a council on any particular occasion when he feels the public interest so requires, perhaps because so many councillors would otherwise be disqualified. A district council has a similar power of dispensation in relation to a parish council.

Section 94 is decreasingly relevant to the situation. The original legislation, Section 76 of the Local Government Act, 1933, was designed to ensure that there should be no improper influence exercised by businessmen who might have contracts with their local authority. Today the threat to probity in local government is quite different. It is that elected members may use 'inside' information about probable future policy in relation to land use for their private advantage. If a member knows that his authority is likely to take certain action which will affect property values, he may make shrewd bargains before the intentions of the authority reach the stage of formal decisions and become public knowledge. Such behaviour is beyond the scope of Section 94. The problem is not that abuse is widespread but rather the virtual impossibility of formulating legislation that would effectively prevent it. To extend to local government some form of Official Secrets Act is at present beyond the bounds of possibility: it would certainly discourage recruitment of councillors. Many authorities have a Standing Order which decrees that committee business shall be treated as confidential until it is communicated to the council or the press, but such an instruction cannot be a water-tight safeguard against abuse. A council could decide to exclude from its planning committee any member with interests in business or property; the individual application of such a rule could be very unpleasant, it would deprive the planning committee of useful experience and would not necessarily stop the circulation of valuable information. The best safeguards seem to be the consciences of elected members and the pressure of public opinion.

Growing concern about the possible extent of corruption in local government, especially after the various cases connected with the architect John Poulson, led to the appointment of a committee to inquire into standards of conduct in local government. The chairman was Lord Redcliffe-Maud. The Report, published in 1974, concluded that local government was essentially honest but that corruption spreads unless it is stopped. So a number of additional precautions were proposed. The Committee recommended that the law on disclosure of interests be made tougher. Councillors should be required to disclose an interest orally and thereafter withdraw from the meeting while the relevant item was under discussion unless a dispensation had been received from the Secretary of State. Councillors should also be required to enter certain interests on a public register. A councillor should not be chairman of a committee whose affairs are linked to his personal interests; sometimes councillors should not even be members. The use of information received through membership of a local authority for private gain should be a criminal offence. The report argued that 'openness' in local administration was a valuable safeguard. It also recommended that the associations of local authorities draw up a national code of conduct for all councillors; this would define standards and have an important persuasive force.

The discussion of pecuniary interests raises the question of motive. Why do people continue to serve for long periods on local authorities? No authoritative answer to this question is possible. If elected members are asked why they serve, their replies will be highly subjective. Obviously they may be fired by political enthusiasm or be attracted by whatever prestige is associated with the word 'councillor'. It is probably true that most elected members feel that they are doing something useful for the community. A council and its committees become a sort of informal club which the retired members, in particular, find attractive. It is also possible that a few people join local councils out of the hope that financial advantage will be derived therefrom: certainly this is sometimes believed to be so by the general public. Should the idea spread that councillors are in local government for what they can get out of it, persons jealous of their reputation will avoid membership of local authorities. The 'club' would cease to be an attractive one. Here the problem is put bluntly, not because of any immediate prospect that this situation will occur but because it is a danger not to be overlooked. The maintenance of probity in local government is of the utmost importance from every point of view.

As a postscript to the discussion of councillors, something should be said about aldermen. Before the 1972 Act became operative county and borough councils had two categories of members— councillors and aldermen. The aldermen were chosen not by the electorate but by the councillors. Aldermen constituted one-quarter of a council except in the Greater London Council and the London Boroughs where the proportion was one-sixth. They were elected for a six-year term, and half were elected each third year: in counties the triennial aldermanic elections were held in the same year as the election of councillors. Aldermen were usually selected from among existing councillors, but not necessarily so: the legal requirement was that an alderman should be *qualified* to be a councillor on the local authority. Thus it was possible to give a council entirely fresh members through the aldermanic system.

The system was open not merely to objection but to abuse. It was introduced into the Municipal Corporations Act, 1835, at the insistence of the House of Lords, to try and strengthen the link between the reformed elected councils and the traditions of the ancient chartered corporations. The institution of aldermen was also supported as a device to secure some greater continuity of policy and personnel. Where triennial elections are held so that the whole body of councillors may be rejected by the voters, this argument has a little merit; it has no force at all in boroughs where the elections are annual. The dominant fact about aldermen was age; in 1965 over half were over 65. Once elected they tended to be re-elected, unless knocked out by a political convulsion on the council. They were often reluctant to resign in spite of advancing years and declining powers. Their selection was usually based either on seniority or party politics. Where politics dominated the loyalties of council members, aldermanic elections were settled in a party context: either the majority party took all, or nearly all, the aldermanic seats, or the parties came to an agreement to share aldermen proportionately with the number of their councillors. Not only was the method of indirect election essentially undemocratic in itself, it could also be used in the boroughs to frustrate the will of the electorate. Since aldermanic elections were held every third year, a party that gained a sweeping victory in a non-aldermanic year could obtain no extra aldermen even if a council followed the convention of allocating aldermen between party groups *pro rata* with councillors. Thus Party A might win a majority of popularly elected councillors while Party B retained control of the council through its aldermen. In boroughs that were politically marginal, this was not an uncommon occurrence. Sometimes the Conservative Party benefited and sometimes the Labour Party; always the cause of democracy suffered.

The Maud Committee on Management urged that the office of alderman be abolished. Subsequently both main political parties accepted this advice in spite of opposition from the Association of Municipal Corporations. The extinction of aldermen was due to four main reasons. Apart from the matters of senility and democracy, there were difficulties about payment and the size of councils. The introduction of attendance allowances for councillors raised the question whether they should be paid to aldermen: there were obvious objections to making payments to people for carrying out a representative function when they had not been directly elected. There was also general agreement that the number of members on a local council should not be so large as to make it unwieldy: the Maud Committee had suggested a maximum of 75 members. As the re-organisation of local government ensured that an authority should cover a large population, each councillor was likely to serve a large electorate. Retention of aldermen would have meant either that councils were bigger in terms of their membership or that every councillor would have had to represent even more people.

As originally drafted the 1972 Act retained the aldermanic system for London authorities. The Government subsequently accepted that there were insufficient reasons for creating such an anomaly. So the legislation was amended and aldermen disappear from the Greater London Council in 1976 and from London Boroughs in 1977.

COUNCIL CHAIRMEN AND MAYORS

The first business at the annual meeting of a local authority is to elect the chairman. It is difficult to make generalisations about the role of a council chairman because it has varied so much between authority and authority. A chairman may be the most influential member of his council, keeping in regular touch with senior officials about policy developments and giving general direction to affairs. Alternatively, at least during his year of office, he may stand aside from controversial matters and perceive his main duty to be the impartial control of council meetings. Other chairmen may follow a style of behaviour in between these extremes. These matters do not depend simply on the choice of an individual chairman; largely they are dictated by the traditions of the local authority. Since reorganisation of structure produces new authorities, it also creates new conventions that will grow into local traditions. The method of filling the office is a good guide to how it is used. If a new chairman is elected each year, possibly on the basis of seniority or as a result of agreement between political groups, then he is likely to exercise minimum influence. But if a chairman is re-elected time and time again, one suspects that he is an important force in council affairs.

The essential difference between a Mayor and a chairman is that the latter does not have such an intense social programme. District and county chairmen will make some appearances on public occasions and may wear a chain of office, but their status is not so high. Yet a Mayor has dignity rather than power. In some other countries the title 'Mayor' describes an official who has substantial personal responsibilities for the proper conduct of local administration. The French *maire* is in this position. In the United States the situation is complicated because there are many forms of town government and the traditional Mayor and council pattern has often been replaced by other systems thought to be more efficient or to provide firmer safeguards against corruption, but where the Mayor survives he generally has substantial personal responsibilities, analogous to those of the President in relation to the federal government. The British Mayor has a quite different position. His executive tasks are minimal. His main formal duty is to preside at council meetings and ensure that these are conducted properly in accordance with the rules of council procedure. But Mayors are always busy people. They are expected to undertake a formidable programme of appearances at various public occasions, to entertain distinguished visitors who come to their borough, to attend civic, cultural and charitable events, school speechdays and to visit local hospitals, especially on Christmas Day. This whirl of social activity is punctuated by speeches of welcome and votes of thanks. The Mayor becomes the embodiment of the community of the borough. By statute he has precedence over all other persons save a direct representative of the Crown such as the Lord-Lieutenant of the county. The Mayoralty is held in deep respect, but the respect belongs to the office and not to the man who holds it. This respect demands that the Mayor abstain from controversial activities—in the same way as the Speaker of the House of Commons: the general pattern is that the Mayor takes no part in political events during his period of office. It follows that he does not concern himself with the details of local administration. He does not direct or supervise borough officers. If important decisions have to be taken between committee meetings, the responsibility falls on the appropriate committee chairman rather than the Mayor. The normal position is that the Mayor will exercise initiative only in unusual circumstances and then in a non-controversial manner. Thus if there is a local disaster the Mayor may open a relief fund; by acting in this way he is not so much providing leadership as expressing the conscience of the community. The Mayoralty, then, is of much civic significance but does not bestow great influence over local affairs.

OFFICERS

The term 'local government officer' creates a mind-picture of people who work at desks in the local town hall or county hall. In fact, office-workers form but a fraction of the total employees of local authorities. Not only do local councils need the services of a large 'outdoor' manual staff concerned largely with cleansing operations and construction work, but a wide variety of skills are also required, e.g. teachers, policemen, welfare workers, if all local government duties are to be carried out effectively. But the administrative and clerical staff in the local offices are at the heart of the administrative system and for this reason demand our special attention.

The days when the parish, as the most important unit of local government, could rely on the services of part-time unpaid officers are long past. Elected members have neither the time nor the range of professional expertise necessary to direct all the business of a local authority. Parliament therefore insisted that certain officers be appointed. Each county, borough and district had to have a clerk, treasurer and medical officer of health; all, except a rural district, had to have a surveyor; all, except a county, had to have a public health inspector. These legal provisions have historical significance in that they recall some unwillingness in the nineteenth century to make certain appointments, notably in relation to health. They also helped to create a uniformity in the pattern of local authority departments. Today there are fewer specific requirements in relation to the appointment of staff. The provisions mentioned above have all been swept away. However, the 1972 Act retained ten categories of officials whose employment by local authorities is compulsory: they are police officers, members of fire brigades, chief education officers, directors of social services, public analysts, agricultural analysts, weights and measures inspectors, accountants to inspect the books of pools promoters, accountants and 'experienced mechanicians' to supervise totalisator operations and the Greater London Council must appoint district surveyors. The first four items in this list are the most significant because they imply that local authorities responsible for police, fire brigades, education and social services must organise them in separate departments.

Local authorities appoint a Chief Executive with overall responsibility for the efficiency of the whole organisation. No specific qualifications are required for this post. Yet the choices made by the new councils in 1973 were very conservative; nearly always a Clerk or Deputy Clerk was chosen. A few Treasurers were appointed and Birmingham selected a Chief Planning Officer. Somerset was more adventurous and appointed a Chief Executive from outside the local government field; the sequel is mentioned below. A Chief Executive is in a strong position to exert influence. He is expected to co-ordinate the work of the separate departments and through the Management Team is kept in touch with all major issues of policy. Yet much depends on the personality of the individual. If he is respected because of his ability and other personal qualities, he will be consulted willingly by other chief officers and possibly by committee chairmen. If he is disliked or feared, his influence may be less and certainly will be achieved less happily. The most successful top administrators recognise that their main duty is to interpret the mind of their local authority rather than to mould it.

According to the Local Government Act 1972 a local authority appoints staff 'on such reasonable terms and conditions, including conditions as to remuneration' as the authority sees fit. In fact, conditions of employment are negotiated through Whitley Councils consisting of representatives of employers and employees. Often government policy has an important influence on these negotiations, particularly in regard to teachers' salaries. Officers are protected from arbitrary dismissal both by their conditions of service and by the strength of trade unionism in local government. Policemen have additional safeguards. A chief constable cannot be dismissed without Home Office consent. Any policeman who is dismissed or required to resign can appeal to the Home Secretary. One other safeguard was repealed by the Local Government Act 1972—the stipulation that the Clerk of a county council could be dismissed only with ministerial consent. In 1974 the Somerset County Council proceeded to dismiss their Chief Executive who had held office for only a few months. This incident caused great concern to SOLACE, the Society of Local Authorities' Chief Executives, which felt that some type of appeal or conciliation machinery should be established to deal with any future similar cases. However, a council cannot be expected to retain the services of a chief officer if it has no faith in his judgement or personal suitability to hold a post of great responsibility. The way out of these difficulties is to pay compensation for loss of office.

Ministerial control over appointments is also used in a few cases to prevent the selection of anyone felt to be unsuitable. The Home Secretary must approve the nomination of chief constables; there have been cases where this approval has been withheld because it was proposed to fill a vacancy by internal promotion within the local force. Similarly, he must approve the appointment of chief fire officers. The DHSS has to approve the qualifications of Directors of Social Services. Whether controls of this nature are necessary or desirable is a matter of controversy. If a local authority is regarded by Parliament as being fully capable of choosing a Chief Executive or Treasurer—why is it not capable of choosing a chief fire officer?

There has been some reduction in central controls over local staff selection. No longer does the Secretary of State have to approve the appointment of a chief education officer. No longer do firemen have to be British subjects or citizens of the Republic of Ireland. But the minimum chest measurements of firemen are still prescribed by statutory instrument. The major safeguard against bad appointments is the requirement that officers in positions of responsibility should have appropriate professional qualifications. Sometimes this stipulation has a statutory basis, otherwise it is conventional or included in the schedule of agreements made through the Whitley machinery governing pay and conditions of service for local government officers. This demand for professional qualifications has certain effects on the recruitment of staff which are discussed in Chapter VII, but they are valuable in that they ensure a minimum quality of proficiency and obviate much of the possibility of corruption in making appointments. Another feature of the local government service is that promotion is obtained through moving from place to place, gaining wider experience of different conditions.

Officers of a local authority must now declare their interest in any contract involving their authority. The principle is the same as that applied to councillors. The declaration is to be in writing. Conscious failure to observe this rule renders the offender liable to a fine not exceeding £200. Whereas the prosecution of a councillor for this type of offence must be undertaken by the Director of Public Prosecutions, no such limitation is placed upon the prosecution of an official. The Redcliffe-Maud Committee on Conduct in Local Government recommended that officers should make oral disclosures of interests at meetings in the same way as councillors. It also proposed that a register of officers interests be kept which would be open to inspection by councillors. Further, senior and professional staff should be required to agree not to take up other employment in their authority's area, without the authority's consent, for a period of two years after leaving local government service.

The central issue which affects senior local government officers is the nature of their relationship with their employing authority—how far can officers persuade elected members to accede to their views? In law, there is no problem. A council decides policy and instructs its officers to carry out its wishes; officers, as servants of the council, must obey. However, in conformity with the general law of master and servant, a local government officer cannot escape the consequences of an illegal act by pleading that he was acting under the instructions of his council. In a notable application of this principle the courts have held (*Attorney General* v. *De Winton*, 1906) that a Borough Treasurer must disobey an order from his Council that calls for an illegal payment: the argument here is that a Borough Treasurer is not a mere servant of his council but has a fiduciary responsibility to the burgesses as a whole. If a Treasurer refused to carry out an instruction from his council because of doubts about its legality, it would still be open to the council, at least in theory, to dismiss their Treasurer. If ever a dispute threatened to reach this stage, public opinion would be aroused and play a large part in deciding the issue. There is no parallel ruling governing the position of a Clerk if faced with what he feels to be an illegal instruction. All that can be said is that if a Clerk wishes to secure his position against possible action by the District Auditor, he must at least ensure that the dubious instruction is given by the council as a whole and not merely by an influential member or group of members (*Re Hurle-Hobbs ex parte Riley and another*, 1944).

The inferior status of officers is symbolised by some authorities through the seating arrangements in their council chamber, for the Chief Executive sits immediately below the dais where the chairman (or Mayor) presides over council meetings. This layout is extremely inconvenient whenever the chairman wishes to consult the Chief Executive. Elsewhere the Chief Executive is permitted to sit on the left hand side of the Chair; this makes it easy, perhaps too easy, for the Chief Executive to offer advice. Most officials are unhappy about proffering advice at a public council meeting except on matters of procedure where the need may be simply to remind the council of its own standing orders. They prefer to advise in the privacy of committee meetings. Necessarily the officers have a store of information which elected members would be foolish to ignore. Officers can draw upon a lifetime of professional experience and will know, or should know, not merely the legal, financial and technical complications of matters that come before committees, but the various ministerial rulings and advice as set out in Departmental Circulars and other official publications. Obviously, an official may present factual information in such a way as to lead elected members towards the policy he thinks best. But advice must always be presented tactfully. A committee resents an official who appears overbearing or impatient. A wise officer knows that a committee should always feel that it has itself made the decisions. The influence of officers tends to be greatest where an authority meets least frequently and where it is not tightly controlled by a political group: these conditions apply in some county councils. Officers view the advent of party politics in local government with mixed feelings. On the one hand, it reduces the impact they can make on policy; on the other, it probably assists continuity and certainty of policy, for once the dominant group has decided upon a course of action it is loath to retract. The party element also strengthens the need for local government officers, like civil servants, to be non-political. Where one party has controlled an authority for many years there is a danger that chief officers will be identified with the ruling party—a situation that can cause great difficulty should the party control change hands. It follows that aspiring politicians should not seek to become local administrators. Local government employees, other than teachers, rarely gain political prominence.

STANDING ORDERS

Methods of procedure in local government are necessarily more complex, some would say clumsy, than the administrative processes in industry or commerce. Since local authorities spend public money they have a special duty to see that it is properly spent: risks which are commonly taken by private enterprise are less acceptable in public administration. The other difference is that local councils reach decisions after discussion, much of which is held in public, because in a democracy the public have a right to know how public business is being conducted. So to ensure that their affairs are conducted in a regular and orderly manner, local authorities draw up Standing Orders to regulate their own conduct. These are in addition to the statutory controls in the law of local government and they must not, of course, transgress statutory provisions.

Standing Orders are mainly concerned with laying down rules of debate and with the procedure for using the council seal and for dealing with tenders and contracts. The form of Standing Orders varies very much between authorities so that no detailed description would have general application. However, they will always govern the order of business at council meetings and how various types of motion or amendments may be moved. Some councils impose a time limit on speeches. This raises a number of issues: how much time should each member be given; how much preferential treatment, if any, should be given to the chairman of a committee or the mover of a motion; how far should there be a right of reply? It is much better to avoid any time limits, but this may not be possible in large authorities or where debates are animated by political differences. The major item of business at a normal council meeting is the consideration of minutes or reports from committees. Again, this can be organised in various ways. Committee chairmen may present their minutes or reports in turn and any questions or arguments about committee proposals may be allowed when the council is asked to approve them paragraph by paragraph. The danger of this method is that the council may spend an excessive amount of time on the affairs of those committees which happen to come early on the agenda. To try to obviate this imbalance of attention, Standing Orders may lay down an alternative procedure. This often takes the form of requiring the Clerk to read through the numbers of the paragraphs of each committee report: a member may interrupt to ask a committee chairman a question on the contents of a paragraph, but if he wishes to start an argument and challenge policy, he will say simply 'Object'. Then when the Clerk has finished reading through the paragraph numbers, the council proceeds to discuss the items to which objection has been taken. In this way members can get a conspectus of the total amount of contentious business before them and this may help them to use debating time more sparingly and effectively. Standing Orders can also guard against another danger—that a council will be rushed into hasty decisions without adequate prior consideration. There is a statutory rule that a county or district council cannot consider any business unless it has been specified in a notice summoning the meeting sent out three days in advance. This rule may be modified by local Standing Orders which may also extend the principle to committees. They also contain provisions to support the authority of the Chair in moments of disorder, may provide for the reception of petitions and deputations, and govern relationships between a council and its committees.

A main concern of Standing Orders is to maintain probity in local administration. They may incorporate rules about the declaration of interests by both councillors and officials. They will prescribe how tenders shall be invited and the form of submission. A general instruction is that the amount of a tender shall be treated as confidential in order to secure genuine competition among contractors. Conditions may be laid down to require compliance with specifications issued by the British Standards Institution. There is some feeling that Standing Orders may be unduly restrictive and inhibit the development of efficient purchasing procedures. They also define the extent and the circumstances under which the authority's powers may be delegated.

Standing Orders are a vital element in the constitution of a local authority. They help to ensure harmonious operation and financial regularity. It is, of course, essential that they are understood both by elected members and by officers in positions of responsibility. Officers must observe the detailed regulations covering contracts and financial management; elected members will not be able to play a full part in discussion unless they know when and how they may intervene.

Chapter VII

THE QUEST FOR EFFICIENCY

The development of ideas on the best way to organise the business of local authorities has been greatly stimulated by three official reports. In 1964 the Minister of Housing and Local Government appointed two committees of enquiry at the request of the main associations of local authorities. One Committee, with Sir George Mallaby as chairman, was required to investigate the staffing of local government. The other had wider terms of reference: 'to consider in the light of modern conditions how local government might best continue to attract and retain people (both elected representatives and principal officers) of the calibre necessary to ensure its maximum effectiveness'. Under the guidance of its chairman Sir John Maud (now Lord Redcliffe-Maud) this Committee undertook a far-reaching investigation into the management of local authorities. Both Committees reported in 1967 and these important documents will be discussed more fully below. The mere fact that these two enquiries were set in motion did indicate a widespread malaise about local government: indeed, the terms of reference clearly imply concern about the quality of the people in local government. No great institution can be efficient if those who work for it have limited ability or poor morale and if the public 'image' of the institution deters other more suitable persons from coming forward to help with the work. The Maud Committee proposed fundamental reforms in the internal organisation of local authorities because it felt that if councillors and officials were frustrated by petty and time-wasting methods of doing business, then able people would be less willing to concern themselves with the management of local public affairs.

The third report came from a Committee set up in 1971 as a joint venture by the DOE and the four local authority associations to advise upon management arrangements for the new authorities to be created in the major reform of structure then in prospect. A steering committee was formed under the chairmanship of Sir Frank Marshall and consisted largely of representatives of the associations: the detailed recommendations were produced by a working group headed by Mr Bains, Clerk of the Kent County Council. This latter body, with a single exception, was made up of senior local government officers. The document they produced will be referred to below as the Bains Report. But the main difference between the Bains Committee and the earlier Maud and Mallaby enquiries was that it had an immediate and precise task—to try and discover how the imminent changes could be made to work to the best advantage. Maud and Mallaby, operating with a more flexible time-scale, had to try to educate local government opinion on the need for change in the traditional *modus operandi*.

Apart from new ideas on management and establishment work, local administration has been greatly affected by the onward march of technology. Sophisticated equipment replaces men and women. Much routine office work is taken over by computers. The staff are called upon to learn fresh skills. New concepts in accountancy and new applications of mathematics are used to produce material which forms a better base for making decisions. This chapter outlines the various approaches to the task of making local government more efficient.

PERSONNEL MANAGEMENT

The officers of local authorities do not constitute a single body, such as the Civil Service, employed by one master. Each authority determines its own establishment of staff and appoints its own officials. Except in the few instances where appointment or dismissal is subject to ministerial consent, and in the few cases in which there is some central prescription of qualifications, each authority is free to recruit its own officers in its own way, and to impose what qualifications it desires. Nevertheless, the whole body of local government officers possesses many uniform characteristics and in recent years has conformed increasingly to standards and uniformities introduced into pay, service conditions, entry and promotion tests, and other elements in the officer's contract of service with his employing authority. These developments are due, partly to trade union organisation among the staffs themselves, and partly to joint organisation of both the staffs and the local authorities in Whitley machinery for collective bargaining. The local government officers trade union NALGO persuaded Parliament to pass legislation in 1937 to establish a unified superannuation scheme for local government. This facilitated the movement of officers between authorities, opened up better promotion prospects and enabled officers to acquire a wider range of experience. In the inter-war period NALGO also struggled hard to establish Whitley machinery, i.e. to create joint consultation with employers over questions of pay and conditions of service. While such consultation was operative in some areas, it was not until 1944 that a National Joint Council was established with the agreement of the associations of local authorities. The National Joint Council is supplemented by Provincial Councils which deal with local problems. In 1946 the NJC approved a national scheme of salaries and service conditions, known as 'the charter', providing a framework of scales for the grading of posts. This is now operative throughout the country and it has been supplemented by agreements for standard gradings among certain classes of officer. Other negotiating committees have agreed upon scales of pay and standard conditions of service for the Chief Officers of local authorities.

The Whitley machinery also became responsible for settling standards of recruitment, training and qualification. It enlisted the help of university staff, the governing bodies of the professions and the various occupational groups of the service in deciding the standards to be enforced. This policy was implemented by the NJC through the establishment, under its auspices, of a Local Government Examinations Board. This Board had advisory functions on questions of education, qualifications and training and also organised examinations, the syllabuses for which concentrated on government and administration. Success at these examinations (or in obtaining equivalent qualifications offered by professional bodies) became a prerequisite, but not a guarantee, of advancing beyond certain grades in the local government hierarchy. Local government is now open to the criticism that it is examination ridden. Yet this emphasis on paper qualifications has ensured a high level of professional competence among officials. It has also done much to eliminate canvassing or corruption in the making of local appointments.

These arrangements for recruitment and training worked tolerably well until the nineteen-sixties presented local authorities with a fresh kind of staffing problem—their ability to attract and retain staff of adequate calibre. In earlier years this had presented no difficulty. Boys from the grammar schools had been keen to enter local government because it offered both security and prospects of promotion to positions of respect in society. After entry, young men studied for various professional examinations and obtained promotion by moving round from one authority to another, and in due course the most able of them became chief officials. (Directors of Education were exceptions to this pattern as they are required to have university training.) Thus the local authorities had no worries about the quality of their staff as the grammar schools provided a steady flow of excellent recruits. Now this source of supply is less fruitful since an increasing proportion of young people with good GCE results leave school to follow various kinds of further education—at universities, colleges of technology, teacher training colleges, etc. Few are left for local government. This problem faced other professions that have traditionally recruited school-leavers. But local authorities did appear to be in greater difficulty, perhaps because their 'image' seems dull and uninspiring. This is not to assert that local government is dull and uninspiring. Like beauty, the image of local government is in the eye of the beholder.

Essentially this is the situation that faced the Mallaby Committee. Its central recommendations were predictable. Local authorities should improve their liaison arrangements with schools to show school-leavers that local administration offers an attractive and worthwhile career. Also they must recruit more university graduates and make the best possible use of the abilities of their staff. So the Mallaby Committee proposed various developments in post-entry training for staff, ranging from induction training for junior entrants to management training for senior staff. At the local level the Clerk of the authority should have an overall responsibility for establishment work including training; at the national level the Committee proposed the creation of a Local Government Training Board which should both exercise some general supervision over the nature of training and also provide a central organisation which would enable local authorities to pool the cost. The smaller, poorer authorities, and those in remote areas, found it difficult or impossible to provide adequate facilities for young officers who wished to obtain qualifications; such authorities could not recruit ambitious young people. To pool the cost of training on a national basis would help the poorer authorities and thus ease the problem. The associations of local authorities accepted this recommendation immediately. The Local Government Training Board was established in 1968 and also incorporated the work of the Local Government Examinations Board.

One of the Mallaby recommendations was undeniably controversial—that local authorities should provide a career structure for lay administrative officers which would take them up to the second or third tier position in a local authority department. The use of the term 'lay administrative officer' is curious and potentially misleading; in normal usage, a 'lay' member of a local authority is thought to be an elected representative. The Mallaby Committee thought of a 'lay' officer as one who had not obtained a specialised professional qualification but who, instead, had obtained a broad education at a university or had studied for the LGEB qualification, the Diploma in Municipal Administration. There is a clear analogy here with the general administrators who occupy the most senior posts in the Civil Service. The 1972 Bains Report took a different view. It asserted that local government could obtain staff through the professions who would provide the necessary leadership in management. Yet this Report also recognised the value of wider horizons by suggesting that able young officers be encouraged to make 'horizontal' moves from one department to another within an authority. This could mean a move into a post where an officer's qualifications were not immediately relevant to his work. The idea is attractive but it presents obvious difficulties.

These conflicting proposals raise the long-standing argument over the value of general education as opposed to specialised qualifications. Does a training confined to law, accountancy, engineering or medicine narrow the mind and so render men less able to carry out managerial functions? Is the man lacking specialised knowledge so much in the hands of specialists when dealing with practical problems as to be unable to provide effective leadership? The arguments are familiar. However, it is too often overlooked that the ability to administer, to make people work together as a team, to know when to use initiative and when to be cautious, to carry responsibility squarely but not too heavily—all these are functions of aptitude and personality, the development of which is perhaps but slightly affected by the subjects a person studies. If our senior Civil Servants are excellent administrators, is this because of the nature of their academic studies at Oxbridge or because they gained great benefit from the Oxbridge environment in their formative years?

The Mallaby Report did not have any great effect on the recruitment and promotion policies of local authorities. Indeed, the tendency has been to develop management services rather than personnel services. No doubt this is because management services appear to make a direct contribution to efficiency and cost reduction while career development policies increase expenditure and the benefits are not so immediate or so obvious. The Bains Committee urged that the status of personnel work in local government should be raised; that it should be kept separate from the development of management services with co-ordination exercised at a high level; that the word 'establishment' be dropped in favour of 'personnel management'.

The Local Government Training Board adjusted its regulations for the Diploma in Municipal Administration in 1972 in response to the Mallaby view that the status of the general administrator in local government should be enhanced. The intention is that the DMA shall more closely equal the final examinations of other professional bodies so that the career prospects of those who hold the DMA are improved. Whether the tactic will succeed is doubtful. No official figures are available but it is certain that an increasing flow of graduates is entering local government and that most of the graduates hold qualifications related to the various specialised professions that serve local government. There seems no reason why these people should not fill all, or virtually all, the more senior posts in the local government service since the various professional associations are becoming more concerned about post-qualification training, especially in the fields of administration and management. The new generation of specialised graduate entrants will thus be better equipped to undertake higher administrative duties. In these circumstances the outlook for the lay administrative officer is not bright.

The 1974 remapping of areas cannot fail to have some impact on the prospects of local government officers. Fewer authorities with larger departments must reduce the chances of an individual reaching the level of chief officer or a deputy. Again, if there are fewer separate employers, the opportunities to move from one authority to another must be diminished. If departments are larger there may be a greater tendency for middle-ranking posts to be filled by internal promotion. And as authorities become more uniform in size the possibilities for a knight's move type of promotion will disappear: no longer can the Town Clerk of a smaller borough become Deputy Town Clerk of a much larger county borough. The barriers between the two tiers of councils may become even more difficult to traverse, with county officials remaining with counties and district officials with districts. Further, this does involve divisions within a profession, e.g. district planners being separate from county planners. A tendency to split local government officers into competing cadres depending on the status of their employers existed before the reorganisation. The pity is that this situation is likely to be aggravated. Perhaps the most important long-term effect of reorganisation on staffing was to encourage the early retirement of a large number of chief officers and their deputies. A greater number of senior posts are now held by relatively young men so for the next decade the number of vacancies at the top of the tree will be relatively low. Able and ambitious officers at third- and fourth-tier rank are likely to experience growing frustration as the years go by.

To turn to the national level, no action has been taken to institute a Central Staffing Organisation as recommended by the Mallaby Committee. However, the Consultative Council on Local Government Finance is fully conscious of the need to promote the efficient use of staff and the local authority associations are alert to the manpower implications of the development of services. Meanwhile there are three national bodies concerned in various ways with local government staff—the LGTB (Local Government Training Board), LACSAB (Local Authorities Conditions of Service Advisory Board) and LAMSAC (Local Authorities Management Services Advisory Committee). There would be a simplification of machinery if these bodies could be united into one. Yet there are great obstacles in the way. In particular, the unions have a different role in each of these organisations. They nominate members to LGTB; they negotiate with LACSAB; they are held at arm's length by LAMSAC. And as long as local authorities jealously maintain the status of independent and individual employers it will be impossible to move far with the development of national personnel policies.

Training is essentially the responsibility of each local authority. It covers, or should cover, all classes of employee—not only clerical and administrative staff. The role of the Local Government Training Board is to identify and assess training needs, advise councils on how best these needs can be met, and provide a service to support the efforts of the local authorities. Where necessary, the Board produces training material, arranges courses and offers a limited advisory service. Acting with educational institutions, the Board also organises courses in areas such as management education, whereby valuable resources at both universities and polytechnics are developed to meet the special needs of local government; this work also has an experimental aspect in that new courses can be developed for future provision on a wider scale. It also mounts a research programme aimed primarily at developing training methods and material and evaluating the training provided. Originally the Board was financed by a voluntary levy paid by local authorities and, in return, the Board made grants to help local authorities to pay for their training programmes. However, this system ran into difficulties. Some councillors questioned whether the benefit was worth the cost. Some smaller authorities never joined the scheme at all. So the levy/grant principle was ended. Now the Board is financed by receiving a sum from the Rate Support Grant and the amount of this allocation is agreed by the associations of local authorities. The Board is still able to provide a limited financial incentive by way of grants to local authorities to stimulate new types of training; at the present time these 'pump-priming' arrangements are used to stimulate instruction programmes for manual workers and the local training officers themselves.

CO-ORDINATION OF POLICY AND ADMINISTRATION

The final section of Chapter III explained the crying need for co-ordination within the framework of a local authority. How is it to be achieved? The traditional answer has been through the Clerk of the council. A succession of official reports urged this solution in varying terms. The Royal Commission on Local Government recommended in 1929 that the Clerk was the most suitable officer to achieve co-ordination and suggested that his ability to perform this task would depend on his personality. It did not propose that the Clerk be put in a position to give instructions to other chief officers. In 1934 the Hadow Committee on the Recruitment, Training and Promotion of Local Government Officers thought that the essential qualification of a Clerk was administrative ability. This view naturally opens up the argument whether a Clerk should necessarily have legal qualifications. The Treasury O and M Report on Coventry in 1953 again laid heavy emphasis on the administrative role of the Clerk; he should give continual consideration to measures which would achieve economies and be responsible for establishment work and an organisation and methods service. This type of recommendation involves a very real difficulty. If the Clerk is to have an overall responsibility for the effective operation of all his council's activities, then he must be put in a position of seniority over other chief officers so that he is able, when necessary, to insist that they accept measures he feels requisite to improve efficiency. Naturally this involves some down-grading, some loss of independence, by other heads of departments and some change in the traditional practice that a chief officer is responsible to the council through his committee. Without some loss of departmental independence there can be no guarantee that a local authority's administration is an effective unity.

The Maud Report on *Management of Local Government*, leaning on the experience of foreign countries and of experiments at home at Newcastle and elsewhere, stressed more firmly than earlier official reports that the Clerk should be the undisputed head of the council's staff. Since the legal profession is not a unique source of leadership ability and managerial acumen, it accepted also that the Clerk need not be a lawyer.

The Committee produced a comprehensive plan to ensure co-ordination of both administration and policy in local authorities,

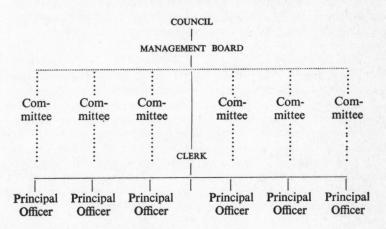

which involved a drastic reappraisal of the nature of committee work and the structure of local administration. A diagram illustrating the essence of the Maud proposals is given above. The core of this scheme was that each council should appoint a 'management board' consisting of between five and nine members of the council. The management board would formulate major policies and present them for approval to the council; it would have overall responsibility for the execution of these policies; it would take decisions on matters which exceeded the authority of chief officers; it would recommend proposals to the council on items which exceeded its own delegated powers. The Clerk would be responsible to the management board and through it to the council; he would also be the undisputed head of the whole of the staff. The heads of departments would be answerable to the Clerk and *not* to any committee. Obviously this plan provides unity and centralisation of decision-making achieved by down-grading all principal officers other than the Clerk and by down-grading all committees in relation to the management board. Thus in the diagram the unbroken lines indicate chains of command and the broken lines are channels of advice. The Maud Committee was specific about the new role of committees: 'Committees should not be directing or controlling bodies nor should they be concerned with routine administration.' What then are the committees to do? They would make recommendations to the management board on 'major objectives' and study how these could best be carried out. They would review progress in the sphere of the particular service that concerned them, consider reactions of the public and deal with any matters referred to them by the management board. Executive decisions would only be made in exceptional circumstances and when the management board required this to be done; the implication is that delegated authority would normally be given to officers rather than committees. The scheme also permitted a committee to consider any matter raised by its own members, but this seems to conflict with the principle noted above that committees would not consider routine administration.

The general effect would have been to transform each local government unit into a minor model of our system of national government. The council was Parliament, or perhaps the House of Commons; the management board was the Cabinet; the committees were to be analogous to the new specialist committees recently established in the Commons to exercise a general advisory function in a particular field. Just as the Commons is composed largely of backbenchers with a lesser number of Government Ministers, so local authorities would have two classes of members, those on the management board and the rank-and-file committee members.

Service on the management board would inevitably consume much time, so the Maud Committee proposed that its members receive part-time salaries. They urged that emphasis be placed on the collective responsibility of the management board in the same way, presumably, as we think of the collective responsibility of the Cabinet. To quote the Maud Report again, 'Individual members of the management board should have special spheres of interest and speak on them': this appears to mean that one member would become the local Chancellor of the Exchequer, another the local Minister of Education, another the local Minister of Transport and so on. Committee meetings would normally be open to the press: meetings of the management board would be private: most committee meetings in the Commons are public, but Cabinet meetings are not! The parallels are remarkably close.

Inevitably this Report aroused much criticism, a lot of which was defensive and came from those who wished to retain established positions. And before reviewing the objections one should also stress that they are themselves a tribute to the quality of the Report. If a scheme contains little that is new, if its proposals can easily be condemned, then it merits a minimum of attention. Because the Maud Report raised fundamental issues about our local government institutions and illuminated serious shortcomings in their practical operation, it stimulated a great debate.

To force local government to move towards our system of national government is to introduce the deficiencies of Parliament into local government. Thus MPs have insufficient information to act as a check on government departments. Under the Maud plan would councillors have enough information to be able to challenge the management board? The Maud scheme called for fewer committees and a maximum committee membership of 15 to include co-opted members; this implied that the backbench councillor would sit on one, or at the most two committees. Would not the backbench councillor know less of the operations of his authority than at present? Certainly he would be separated from financial administration. In this situation could a council be expected to scrutinise effectively the decisions of its management board?

Possibly the gravest criticism is contained in the Report itself in a note of dissent by one of the members of the Maud Committee, Sir Andrew Wheatley. While accepting the concept of the management board, Sir Andrew argued that committees must be given wider scope than that allowed to them in the Committee's plan. He feared that the management board might become too autocratic and remote from other members of a council and that this would damage the essential democratic quality of our local government.

He also argued that if backbench members of a local council were limited to a minor advisory role there would not be a sufficient incentive for able people to come forward and offer themselves as candidates at local elections. To serve on a committee without executive responsibilities is a sure prescription for frustration. As an alternative, therefore, Sir Andrew proposed that committees be given some executive powers; while they should always consult with the management board they should, in case of disagreement, report direct to the council. This view has much to commend it, but such disagreement would be highly unlikely in any authority run on strict party lines: it is relevant also that party influence is increasing steadily and will become more pronounced now that local authorities are fewer and larger.

The Maud Committee gave very full consideration to the impact of party politics in local government. On one matter they wished to depart from the national government model because they argued that minority parties should be represented on the management board. The Leader of the Opposition is not a member of the Cabinet! Ideally, members on a local council from all parties should be able to contribute to the good management of public affairs. Much of local administration is, or ought to be, essentially non-political in character. And unless minority supporters could have an opportunity to serve on the management board, there would be a break in continuity and a lack of experience whenever the party majority on a council changed. Even so, it is difficult to see how a local political 'cabinet' can effectively discuss controversial matters if their leading opponents are always present. There was no suggestion that the management board should be a 'coalition government'. Minority representation also implies that the management board as a whole would not be responsible for the conduct of affairs but solely those members who belong to the local majority party.

Not one local authority accepted the Maud scheme *in toto*. Yet many were stimulated to streamline their committee structures and to nominate one or more major co-ordinating committees. If the idea of the management board went beyond what was currently acceptable in local government circles, it also had an important educational effect and helped to pave the way for the rather less radical Bains Report of 1972. Largely because of Maud, the Bains Committee worked within a situation where the need for reform in administrative methods was already widely accepted.

The Bains Report was more flexible in its approach to management structures: it agreed that there was no ideal model on which a local authority should operate. It argued that the functions of councillors and officials were not separable into watertight compartments and that the nature of a councillor's interest in administration also varied between individuals. Some were mainly attracted to welfare work; others to restricting expenditure; others to management, often on commercial lines; others in general service to the community. The Report added 'Other categories can no doubt be identified', but was too tactful to proceed further. It follows from this analysis that councillors will want to fill different roles in their public duties. Some are keen to be involved in major questions of policy, resource allocation and management. Others are content to be occupied with more detailed committee work.

The Report followed what has become normal doctrine in urging that a local authority should have a senior or central committee, advised by a Chief Executive, to formulate policy on major issues and generally oversee all the authority's activities. Unlike the Maud management board, the Bains central policy committee was not to have a monopoly of policy-making because some decisions were to be left with functional committees. A central policy committee should frame a comprehensive plan to govern priorities in expenditure which should be revised regularly. It was important that previous decisions should not be regarded as immutable. The Report stressed that more attention should be paid to the effectiveness of local government services: in the past tools of measurement had concentrated on expenditure, on input into a service, rather than its output. This prescription is splendid in theory. Yet how can it be applied in practice? Education is the most expensive local function: here is the greatest opportunity to check efficiency by improving output. But how do you measure output of a school or college—by examination results? Any attempt to proceed on these lines would be reminiscent of the eighteen-sixties: it would invoke overwhelming opposition from educationalists. Output of clerical and manual employees engaged on mainly routine tasks can be subjected to some form of measurement, but to apply similar checks to professional and managerial staffs cannot adequately assess, and would probably damage, the *quality* of their work. The Bains Committee did not really face up to these problems. Its keenness to promote efficiency at the very highest levels of administration is still praiseworthy. There was to be no soft or quiet life for those in top jobs. It doubted whether every chief officer needed a deputy. And it produced the radical notion that chief officials should be subject to an annual appraisal of their performance by a sub-committee of the policy committee advised by the Chief Executive; the latter should be similarly appraised by the policy committee itself.

A central Policy and Resources Committee was the main feature of the Bains model for local authority management. Four sub-committees were also recommended to deal with finance, staff, land and a general review of performance in relation to objectives. It was emphasised that these sub-committees should not concern themselves with trivial questions of expenditure but should think in broad terms about major issues. The Policy Committee should not consist solely of chairmen of other committees; it should include 'backbench' councillors and some drawn from political minorities. So it would not be so much of a Cabinet as the Maud-style management board. There would be a less sharp distinction between inner-group councillors who serve on the Policy Committee and those who do not. The pattern of other committees should be related to the objectives of a council rather than to the organisation of particular services: thus committee structure need not follow departmental structure. When major decisions have to be made, committees should consider alternative means of reaching their objectives. Not surprisingly the Bains Report saw no virtue in area sub-committees operating within a scheme of delegated authority, for such bodies do not assist managerial efficiency. However, where an authority covers a wide area of countryside, there is likely to be pressure, not merely for decentralised access to services, but also for decentralised decisions so that county administration can become more sensitive to local needs and opinion. The Report did accept that, in some cases, services would have to operate through local offices and it recommended that such offices should cover areas which corresponded with district council boundaries.

The Bains Committee saw no need to insist that the Chief Executive should have any specific qualification: this recommendation leaves the field for recruitment wide open. Nor, the Bains Report argued, should he have an official deputy—a proposal that invites an awkward hiatus if the Chief Executive should become ill, die, resign or otherwise disappear. The intention was that the Chief Executive should have no specific departmental responsibilities so that his desk and his mind should be left clear to deal with major items of policy. The Bains proposal was that the traditional legal and administrative duties of the Clerk be transferred to a new type of chief officer—the Secretary of a local authority. Not all councils have adopted the view that their Chief Executive should be spared departmental cares. It can be argued that if the top administrator sits apart in semi-isolation he will find it more difficult to keep in touch with contemporary problems; that without a department to support him he lacks eyes and ears to tell him what is taking place throughout the whole organisation. A remedy for the threatened isolation is to give the Chief Executive a small personal staff and research staff. Of course, such appointments involve added expense and there is still a

tendency in local government to think of research as an unnecessary luxury. The real danger of a central research unit is that it
may be given work better undertaken within the specialised departments.

The Bains theory was that the Chief Executive would promote
co-ordinated decision-making through the assistance of a management team, a kind of Cabinet of officials, formed from the more
important chief officers. The existence of the management team
should be formally recognised by the council. Inter-disciplinary
teams of officials should be formed to advise the various committees.
This suggestion and the parallel recommendation that committee
responsibilities should not be allocated on a simple functional basis
were both designed to check the tendency for local administration to
develop separate departmental empires and loyalties based on the
provision of particular services. To put the matter in the more
formal language used in the Report—there should be a corporate
approach to management rather than a departmental approach.

It may be useful to bring these ideas together, as far as possible,
in diagrammatic form. Below is illustrated the Bains model for the
committee structure of a non-metropolitan county. The crucial issue
is the relationship between the Policy Committee and the other
main committees. It appears that the task of the Policy Committee
was to be less than control. It was to advise the council on the merits
of programmes submitted by other committees: the Bains scheme
mentions concurrent reports to the full council. The idea was that
the Policy Committee should co-ordinate rather than command.
The practice, no doubt, will vary from place to place. Where political
organisation is strong a Policy Committee must reflect the views of
(the leaders of) the majority group, and it can be assumed that other
committees and sub-committees will adjust themselves to carry out
the political programme of the majority party.

Alternative patterns for departmental structure were suggested by
the Bains Report. The simpler arrangement was that each chief
officer would organise his own department and be independent,
subject to co-ordination by the management team—of which he
might not be a member—and by the Chief Executive and, of course,
the ultimate control of the local council. The other pattern grouped
certain departments together under a Director. One such grouping
could be education, libraries and amenities and recreation. Another
could be planning, transport, engineering, architecture, valuation
and estates all placed under a Director of Technical Services. Multi-
departmental directors would belong to the management team but
would be subject to co-ordination in the same way as other chief
officers.

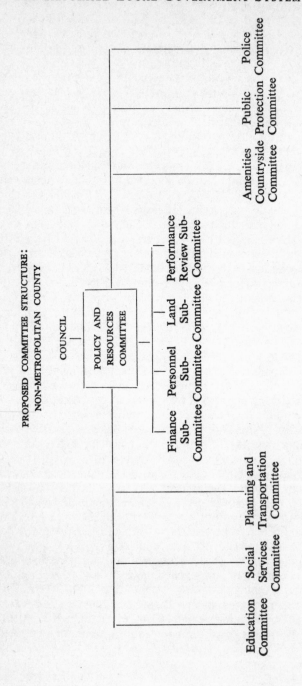

PROPOSED COMMITTEE STRUCTURE:
NON-METROPOLITAN COUNTY

Models based on similar principles can easily be constructed for non-metropolitan districts and the metropolitan authorities. The Bains Report suggested that the smaller districts might have as few as three functional committees dealing with housing, development and leisure services, and environment health. In such places all chief officers would belong to the management team.

It has been shown in Chapter II that the ideas formulated by the Bains Committee were highly influential; partly this was because they reflected concepts already adopted by many of the more vigorous and forward looking authorities. One criticism is that they ignored the element of party politics in local government. But would it have been inappropriate for a group of officials to make recommendations about political organisation? Again, the style of local political conventions is so diverse that an attempt to prescribe a single mould for them would be both unrealistic and undesirable. A great advantage of the Bains proposals is that they are not too precise and can readily be adapted to meet local situations. But the real difficulty may not be to persuade councillors to adopt an organisational structure that meets management desiderata: rather the problem may be to see their own role in sufficiently broad terms. Can they get accustomed to thinking in terms of objectives, priorities and programme review? How easy will it be for them to work with the sort of information that is an essential preliminary to taking decisions of this type? Councillors, especially new councillors, feel frustrated by the long-term nature of major local government programmes; they feel hemmed in by what has been decided in the past and often decided by central government rather than the local council. Programme reviews may moderate this mood but it is difficult to stop projects already under way and only a little less difficult to change their scope or direction. The Maud Committee demonstrated that many councillors feel more comfortable with the relatively trivial agenda items because they were easier to comprehend. This problem will remain with the reformed structure.

Some councillors resent the concept of corporate management and the existence of a Management Team of chief officers. They feel it increases the influence of officials to an undesirable extent. There can be no doubt that if senior staff work together to produce co-ordinated advice, then that advice will be very persuasive. The less able councillors may come to feel that the bureaucracy are controlling policy. In practice, the influence of the Management Team will vary in its extent. Where a council has a party political majority, and the majority group has effective leaders, then council opinion will remain powerful. Some chief officers feel that corporate management undermines their personal responsibility for their own department.

Management teams work differently; many aspects of their activities are unclear. What is the relationship between the Chief Executive and the other members of a Management Team? Is the Chief Executive the equivalent of a President of the United States in that he can overrule all the advisers in his Cabinet? Or is the Chief Executive to act more in the mould of a British Prime Minister who, while having great influence, can ultimately be overborne by his Cabinet colleagues? What is the strength of a decision by a Management Team? Is it collectively binding on the members or can they go away and give confidential advice, say, to their committee chairman, in opposition to the corporate decision? Can the interests of a department not directly or permanently represented on the Management Team be fully safeguarded? If a chief officer presents proposals or information to the Management Team will his committee chairman know what he is doing? All these items are potentially delicate issues. There is no uniformity in the manner in which they are resolved. In many councils a lot of the questions are never asked, at least in public.

MODERN TECHNIQUES OF MANAGEMENT

There is a third broad aspect of the quest for efficiency in local government which covers the various techniques that have been developed to improve and monitor the output of office and outdoor staff. They involve investigation combined with an element of numerical analysis. Processes of this type can also be used to organise information to aid decision making of the kind discussed above. The following paragraphs give an outline of these methods, their uses and their limitations.

The concept of work-study originated in industry. It is concerned with the examination of productive processes to improve efficiency, and developed a number of aspects including the design of machines and equipment, the lay-outs of working areas, and the pattern of labour organisation. The introduction of any bonus incentive payment usually involves some element of work measurement in order to define a norm that must be exceeded if additional payment is to be made; such measurement is another function of the work-study expert. Organisation and methods work is rather more recent in origin and developed in the Civil Service during the last war in response to the need to save manpower and limit administrative expenditure. It concentrated on the use of office machines, the design and simplification of forms and, in general, re-examined the need for traditional administrative practices. It also looked into the distribution of functions between government departments. O and M work, as it is popularly called, has thus a similar purpose to work-study, and the distinction between the two is increasingly blurred.

In local government interest in O and M activity developed in the nineteen-fifties. Elected members of local authorities welcomed it as a possible means of cutting expenditure fairly painlessly and so reducing the demand on the ratepayer. Some of the younger and more ambitious local government officers saw O and M as providing a new and stimulating career opportunity. Many of the larger local authorities have appointed their own O and M officers and the second-tier London Boroughs combined to establish a joint O and M unit. Elsewhere local authorities called in the services of business efficiency consultants, who normally are engaged by private firms to advise how their organisation and profitability could be improved. The use of consultants in local government did not always have happy results. Since their fees were high it was apparent that money would be wasted, not saved, unless their reports showed the way to significant economies. Other difficulties were caused because sometimes they were unfamiliar with local government law, traditions and practice. And whether or not business consultants are used for this work, it is generally true that there has been more resistance in local government to O and M activity than in the Civil Service. This is not surprising. The Civil Service is such a vast organisation that it is unlikely that any single O and M report will significantly affect career prospects of established staff and any redundancies can be smoothed over by moving people on to other duties or by dismissing temporary staff. Local authorities, being much smaller administrative units, do not provide such good opportunities for redeployment of staff. But resistance to O and M activity arises for other reasons. A crucial issue is how far-reaching should an O and M investigation be? Should it be limited to the pattern of office processes—or should it extend to the committee structure of an authority, to the division of responsibility between departments of a local authority, to the relations between committees and officers and, in particular, to how far decisions should be delegated by elected representatives to paid officials? These are fundamental questions which some councillors and some officials would prefer to avoid. Yet any management survey is emasculated if a local authority regards its *modus operandi* as being beyond reproach. Just occasionally friction has also arisen over the question of how much publicity should be given to O and M reports. Some councillors put the argument like this: if public money is spent to enquire into the efficiency of our authority, then the public are entitled to know the full results of the enquiry. But it is generally accepted that establishment matters, as they affect individuals, should remain confidential. Of course, should an O and M report suggest a basic reorganisation of departments or a reshaping of committees, then some public discussion must take place.

Operational research involves the study of routine tasks by specialists skilled in scientific observation who are usually expert statisticians. The idea is that an essentially mathematical investigation can provide valuable information that will act as a guide towards making the best possible decisions. A few examples will help to demonstrate the kind of problems that can be submitted to this type of examination. Invoices are normally checked to ensure that they are correct both in terms of arithmetic and as a record of goods received. But checking invoices costs money. How far would it be economical in any office to save the cost of checking and bear the risk of loss through inaccuracies going undetected? In any store, whether of materials needed in construction or in a store of office materials, the problem arises of how large an order to place for any item in regular demand. Infrequent ordering of large quantities saves time and trouble and may offer discounts for purchase in bulk, but large stocks demand larger storage space and involve spending money before it is absolutely necessary. What point on the scale between infrequent big orders and many small orders will give the best results? A proportion of outside staff employed on refuse collection is always absent from work for sickness or other reasons; if a refuse collection service is to be constantly regular some surplus labour will have to be employed to make up for the absentees. How much surplus labour is necessary to give a guarantee of regular collection? These are the type of questions to which operational research is applied. It is not possible, of course, within the confines of a short book on local government to explain the mathematical techniques which are used in the solution of such problems.

This sort of research is not an infallible magic that can always lead the way to the best possible decision. Major decisions usually involve judgements which may be of a political nature or simply raise the issue of how much people are prepared to pay to achieve a certain quality of service. Let us revert to the example of refuse collection. A piece of operational research might show that if 20 per cent more dustmen are employed above the number required if all men were always on duty, then the chances of maintaining regular collection are about 99 per cent. But a council might well take the view that they were prepared to face a higher risk of irregular collection rather than bear the cost of the additional labour involved. Or to revert to the case of invoice checking, a council might not be willing to reduce standards of internal auditing because of the visitations of the District Auditor. But operational research can provide a firm basis of information on which decisions can be made. Without such impersonal investigation decisions on administrative methods will be made on the basis of hopes, hunches or traditions, i.e. a problem is dealt with in a particular way simply because it was handled like that in the past when, quite possibly, conditions of scale or cost were quite different.

Cost-benefit analysis is another technique that has been developed to aid decision-making. This is more usually applied to projected future capital developments. If there are alternative schemes for highway development, the more expensive providing for freer, faster and perhaps safer traffic flow, which should be chosen? The idea of cost-benefit analysis, put simply, is to estimate the costs and benefits of alternative plans and to demonstrate their relative advantages. Here again there are substantial difficulties. Any estimate of future benefit must be hypothetical to some degree. Some benefits cannot be quantified or translated into monetary terms, e.g. a design for a road or a building may be aesthetically more pleasing than a cheaper design, but one cannot make a scientific estimate of the benefit to be derived from beauty. And when an analysis is completed there remains the basic value judgement of how much we are prepared to contribute now to benefit the next generation. This can be illustrated again in terms of highway development. Given certain expectations of the growth of motor traffic, a relatively modest scheme of highway improvement may be thought adequate to meet the needs of the next decade while a more elaborate scheme would be adequate for a much longer period. Which scheme should be adopted? Cost-benefit analysis cannot answer this problem. It can provide material upon which a more informed judgement can be made in that people can be made aware of the probable consequences of any decision.

This new emphasis on research and quantification as a preliminary to the taking of decisions has increased the need to carry out complex calculations with speed and accuracy. The growth of local authority administration also demands that routine office work be mechanised as far as possible. Together these requirements have produced a rapid increase in the use of computers in local government; many large councils have installed their own machine and often arrange to share their use with neighbouring authorities. A computer is a highly sophisticated piece of electronic technology. Only a limited number of specialists understand fully how they work. But it will be necessary for an increasing number of administrators to know what computers can do to help their work and, indeed, to know how to give instructions to the machines. Hence the very great interest in systems analysis and computer programming. Applications of the new technology are developing steadily: some of their most common uses are for regular payments of all kinds, e.g. wages and interest charges, the preparation of election registers, data storage and the analysis of expenditure and income, of costing, and of statistics relating to planning applications, traffic flows, housing lists and education.

The growth of interest among local authorities in management techniques has led them to appoint specialised staff to develop their applications. In addition, with the encouragement of financial help from the central government, a national agency has been formed to give assistance to local councils. This body is LAMSAC, Local Authorities Management Services Advisory Committee; it issues advice to authorities based on detailed research and also provides a confidential consultancy service for individual authorities. Problems dealt with include the desirability of installing a computer, changing an existing computer, or how to introduce job evaluation on incentive bonus schemes. LAMSAC has established groups to investigate some management aspect of every major local function. All this work obtains little publicity. It also faces the obstacle that if improved administrative methods reduce workload then the contentious issue of redundancy emerges. Economies may be achieved by not filling vacancies and by redeployment. But, in a period of high unemployment, there is less labour mobility so there is less possibility of cutting staffing costs painlessly. A major attraction of management studies has been that they promised to reduce expenditure. However, because of understandable trade union pressure, this promise may not be fulfilled.

Meanwhile, there is a widespread public belief that local authorities are not as efficient as they could or should be. A management expert based within an organisation may well hesitate to bring forward suggestions that are unpalatable to his colleagues. To have bite, a management review must come from outside. For this reason, as noted in the following chapter, the Layfield Report urged that local audit be reorganised.

LOCAL GOVERNMENT AND SOCIETY

THE PATTERN OF PRESSURES

It is important to visualise local government in the context of the sum total of its social relationships. This can be assisted by means of a diagram. The chart on the next page is a sort of map which shows how a local authority fits in with the public, with central government, with political parties and other voluntary organisations. It shows the flow of pressure and experience between these parts of the social system—the channels through which demands are made upon a local council, how the council itself may try to exert influence, how the council's services may arouse public reaction and how central government agencies help to supervise local services. Inevitably the diagram involves much simplification. It omits some links which are not immediately significant for the individual local authority. A chart cannot demonstrate the complex relationship within the council organisation between elected members and officers. But it does show the essential circularity of local administration—how people make demands on local authorities and subsequently react to how their demands are met. The chart is also able to distinguish those formal relationships which are enshrined in law. Statutory relationships are indicated by a continuous line and informal ones by a broken line. Most of these links operate on a two way basis, e.g. the local authority associations have an effect on Government policy but the Government also has an impact on the attitudes of the associations. It may sometimes be a matter of doubt which is having the greater influence on the other. Thus while local opinion may conceivably take note of the speeches of councillors acting as local opinion leaders, the constitutional position is that the voters choose councillors to represent local opinion.

It should be remembered that the diagram is purely *descriptive*. It does nothing to explain what sort of decision a council will make in any given set of circumstances. This is because it is not possible to quantify pressures or to assess precisely the effect of influences pulling in opposite directions. The diagram is merely an aid to understanding the social situation within which local government must work. In particular it illustrates how various voluntary organisations can have an impact on local administration. The churches are

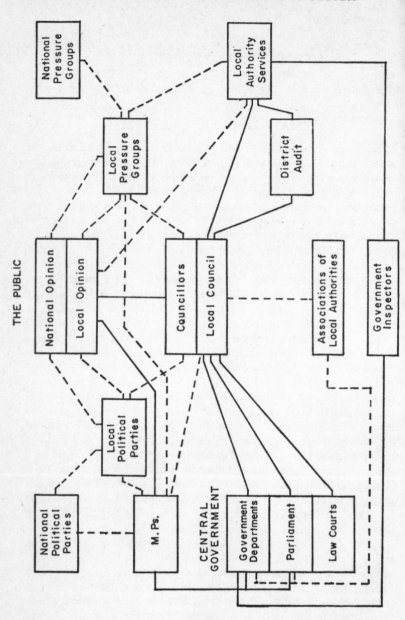

among the most important of these bodies; in the past they had a dominating position in relation to education. The Lord's Day Observance Society may be stung into action if a local authority arranges or permits some activity on a Sunday. Tenants associations are today among the most vigorous local groups and may organise protests if council house rents are increased. And there are a mass of other bodies urging a wide variety of policies on local authorities: progress in education, anti-fluoridation, rural preservation and so on. The interest of voluntary organisations in local government appears to be growing. They are a peculiarly valuable element in maintaining a spirit of local democracy as they frequently promote causes that cut across the lines of political party policies.

At least two other aspects of the chart demand comment. It shows that the local council decides policy in relation to local services, but it must not be forgotten that the experience of being a member of a local authority and gaining knowledge about local government functions may itself influence members of local councils. A new councillor may think that better standards of service should be provided; after some months on the council he may change his view as he comes to appreciate the financial and other difficulties. Alternatively, a new councillor may be critical of policies he feels to be extravagant; on a fuller acquaintance with the benefits derived from these policies he may come to accept that they are justified. The chart also implies that local experience of local services has an influence on behaviour at elections; if voters are satisfied with the services they will be content to keep the same councillors—otherwise they will seek to make changes. This is the way in which local democracy is supposed to work. In earlier years the theory may have had some connection with practice. Now wherever politics dominates local elections, voters react on party lines according to their views on the performance of the national government. So there may be a big change in the membership and political balance of a local authority, not because of dissatisfaction with the policies or the quality of its administration but because of reactions to Government activity.

VIRES AND DISTRICT AUDIT

The basic legal constraint on local authorities is the doctrine of *ultra vires* which requires them to be able to provide specific legal authorisation for all their actions. The principle was not imposed on local government by a deliberate act of national policy; it evolved from judicial decisions which limited the activities of railway companies to business directly connected with the running of a

railway. The argument was that railways were authorised by Acts
of Parliament and, as statutory corporations, they must be restricted
to the purposes for which they were created. Local authorities were
immediately involved because they are all statutory corporations,
apart from boroughs outside London. Whether provincial boroughs
were also governed by the *ultra vires* rule has become a wholly
academic question since, under the 1972 Act, all local authorities
are statutory authorities. So local government is fettered by a legal
rule that has not received specific authorisation from Parliament:
it is, moreover, a rule that the Courts have interpreted very
strictly.

There can, of course, be two views on the desirability of the *ultra
vires* principle. Certainly, it inhibits enterprise and experiment; it also
removes opportunities for extravagance and folly. Were councils
freed from this restraint they would still be subject to the ballot-box
and if electors were not satisfied by the reasons offered for inflated
rate-demands a change of councillors and council policy would
become highly likely. A few adventures or misadventures by local
authorities could rapidly reduce public apathy about their activities.
One has the feeling, however, that the *ultra vires* principle is now
widely accepted by Ministers, Parliament, local officials and councillors with a certain sense of relief in that it prevents unorthodoxy and
fresh difficulties. Optional activities are normally those which cause
.the greatest friction, partly because they provide obvious targets in
any economy drive and partly because their continuation depends
wholly on the will of the local council, and there is no possibility of
pushing off responsibility on to the central government. Some local
disputes about cultural expenditure have attracted widespread
publicity. In the nineteen-twenties Labour Members of Parliament
supported a Local Authorities (Enabling) Bill which sought to give
larger local authorities discretionary powers to promote trading and
cultural activities. Yet subsequent Labour Governments have shown
no enthusiasm whatever for this sort of legislation. The issue seemed
to be dead. However, the 1972 Act allows a local authority, other
than a parish meeting, to incur expenditure up to a rate of two new
pence for any purpose which in its opinion would benefit its area,
provided that such activity is not subject to other statutory provisions.
This element of freedom should be further extended by the 1973
property revaluation and the increase of rateable values. Especially
for parish and community councils, now treated for this purpose
equally with other authorities, the restraint of *ultra vires* has been
greatly weakened.

The Maud Committee suggested that a further relaxation be
allowed so that local authorities be given a 'general competence' to do

whatever they feel to be in the interests of their areas, subject to not encroaching on the spheres of other public bodies and to 'appropriate safeguards for the protection of public and private interests'. The proposal appeared radical but was also extremely vague. The idea of safeguarding private interests could inhibit any scheme to undertake commercial activities; even cultural and recreational provision could conflict with existing business interests. There would also be widespread objection to any right to subsidise local political or religious organisations. However, some foreign countries do have 'general competence' clauses. The idea has obvious attractions and could do much to enliven local government. But there are great difficulties in the way of giving this plan a precise legal form.

Although the 1972 Act did not include a general competence clause, it did limit substantially the scope of district audit. The traditional objection to this system was that it empowered a government official—albeit one independent of Ministers and exercising a quasi-judicial function—to impose penalties on elected representatives for using their judgement on how best to serve the interests of their electors. And surcharges were not merely on illegal expenditure but on expenditure held to be unreasonable. Under the 1972 Act district audit is concerned only with legality, not with reasonableness. Further, it no longer imposes penalties for presumed illegality; it has to ask a court of law to do so. Local authorities outside London can manage to avoid district audit by opting to employ professional audit, subject to the right of the Secretary of State to order district audit to make a special investigation into particular accounts. The objection now to the audit system is not that it is anti-democratic, but that it may involve much delay in settling a local controversy. Thus if a professional auditor issues a critical report on some items of local expenditure and this leads to further investigation by district audit which leads to a legal action, the time taken to dispose of the affair will be very considerable.

Today the district auditor seems much less of an ogre. The hostility from fifty years ago has gone. This is well illustrated by the relatively small number of councils which in 1974 chose to evade his attentions by resort to professional audit. Perhaps the district auditor is less sinister because there is less need for him to be so. Local authorities are now conditioned to accept central directions through a wide range of administrative controls, and so are less likely to engage in unorthodox spending. Political conflicts over local government expenditure are not so acute as in the nineteen-twenties —except perhaps in relation to council house rents. Also, instead of initiating legal action, he may give a private warning that certain expenditure is questionable and should not be repeated. He is required to report to authorities on any discrepancies found in the accounts. He can still criticise publicly the financial policy of a council. Such a report might provoke a ratepayer to initiate legal action against a council on the grounds that certain actions were *ultra vires*. To anyone who complains that the reduced role of district audit removes a potent check on local councils it seems fair to reply that there is more danger of local government being choked by too many controls than there is of it running riot through lack of restraints.

The Layfield Committee sought to strengthen the audit service, not in the context of checking *ultra vires* activities but as an aid to efficiency. At present the auditor is required to look for 'loss arising from waste, extravagance, inefficient financial administration, poor value for money, mistake or other cause'. The Layfield Report felt that this instruction was not fully carried out because the auditors were more concerned with the accounts than the realities, in particular the methods of management, that lay behind the accounts. So the Report proposed that the audit should be reorganised as a service independent of central or local government which would report either to a parliamentary committee or to a body representative of local authorities as a whole. Such a reform could bring a new and more dynamic scrutiny into local administration and implies the elimination of professional audit. It would offer a new form of accountability to the public.

CENTRAL-LOCAL RELATIONS

There is no generally accepted theory of central-local relationships. Two contrasting patterns are regularly promoted. One is a partnership of colleagues in a joint enterprise; the other is a principal/agent arrangement in which local authorities act at the behest of their national masters. Both patterns illustrate an aspect of the truth. Local services are organised by the local councils; without their co-operation the central government could not ensure the smooth running of these services, at least in the short run. Again, Ministers are usually willing to listen to advice from local authorities because of their practical experience and knowledge of local conditions. On the other hand, local councils depend for their powers on national legislation and some local government law is certainly shaped on the principal and agent framework, notably the provisions for education and the social services. Ministers tend to speak in terms of partnership when they want to be tactful and in terms of principal and agent whenever they wish to enforce a particular policy.

The development of political controversy in relation to local affairs has also tended to link central and local government more closely together. This is not simply a matter of national parties contesting local elections or of the control of a council's policy by the 'caucus' of the local majority party. It is also the case that Ministers often claim political credit for the activities of local authorities, especially in connection with building houses and schools, in spite of the fact that a large part of this construction has been carried out by councils dominated by their political opponents. Ministers also press the development of certain policies that affect the way local authorities carry out their responsibilities, e.g. green belt preservation, council house rents, the sale of council houses and, not least, comprehensive secondary education.

It is often argued that such ministerial influence is undemocratic in that the wishes of locally elected representatives can be overridden by the edict of a remote organisation in Whitehall. Yet this argument is not easy to sustain. If democracy is defined as the acceptance of majority opinion, it would seem to be as democratic to follow the will of the Minister who represents the national majority as it is to follow the wishes of those who represent but a local majority. If democracy is defined in terms of paying attention to local opinion, then the smaller the unit of opinion the more attention should be paid to its desires. Should a parish council be allowed to override a county council? Should the representatives of a ward be entitled to insist that a different policy be applied to their ward as opposed to the other wards in the borough? Financial considerations apart, claims of this sort are a prescription for anarchy. Here is a dilemma. A healthy democracy needs strong, vigorous and independent-minded local government genuinely able to exercise initiative and judgement. At the same time local authorities get massive monetary aid from the Treasury and are expected to assist in promoting national social purposes.

The independence of local authorities has been deeply under-mined by their reliance on financial help from the central government. The rating system is now under such severe attack that its continued existence is uncertain. There is no doubt that local rates are a most unsatisfactory form of taxation for there is no certain corre-lation, as there is with income tax, between the amount an indivi-dual has to pay and his capacity to pay. Resistance to paying higher rates, aggravated by the unfairness of the system, has effectively reduced the taxing capacity of local councils and has led to incessant demands for more state subsidies. It is widely argued that education —easily the most expensive local government service—is a national service and, as such, should be financed entirely by the national Exchequer. Yet how far would it continue to be a local government service if education authorities had no financial responsibility save to the Secretary of State for Education? Meanwhile, local control of administration and expenditure, albeit constrained by Whitehall, does preserve an element of community responsibility, pride and satisfaction. Services provided by the central government do not inspire similar attitudes. Compare the health service to local welfare services. There is general dissatisfaction with the hospital service— not necessarily with the individual contributions of doctors, nurses and hospital administrators—but with the scale of provision as a whole. There is a feeling that 'they', the anonymous, abstract and unknown controllers of the system, ought to effect various improvements. Controllers of the local welfare services are not unknown; if there are serious complaints, they will soon hear of them. Where cost is the obstacle to meeting the complaint, the difficulty is more readily appreciated. 'To improve the welfare services means putting the rate up' is a statement which carries a more meaningful choice than 'To improve hospitals means an increase in taxation.' It is not merely that the national purse may appear bottomless, it is also the case that any successful local claim on national resources has a net benefit to the local community. So long as cost is linked to a local tax, the cost-benefit relationship is realistic. Whenever the Government takes over a local service it puts a premium on grumbling by destroying local financial responsibility. Further, the nineteenth-century desire to achieve minimum standards throughout the country in relation to vital services such as poor relief and education has tended to develop into the imposition of maximum standards and, indeed, to an overall regime of uniformity. As local authorities receive so much financial aid this equality of provision is easily justified on grounds of fair distribution of the national taxpayer's money.

Lack of revenue is not the sole economic cause of greater central supervision. As a major public consumer of labour and capital resources, local government is required to keep in step with the changing face of the Government's economic policy. Wages and salary levels of local authorities will be influenced by any national incomes policy: the nature and extent of capital expenditure on local schools, housing, roads, swimming baths, etc. will have to fit broadly into a national scheme of priorities. All public bodies are expected to co-operate in freezes and squeezes or any other general measures that Ministers feel necessary to promote the national economic interest.

Whenever there is pressure to reduce spending, the tendency is to cut capital projects rather than current expenditure. This is a natural reaction because new construction implies some improvement of service while a cut in current expenditure normally means a lowering of existing standards. If the choice is between fresh ventures and the preservation of what has .already been achieved, then the latter may seem the more prudent course of action. Yet the axe falls on capital schemes also because this alternative avoids redundancy for local authority staff and thus avoids trouble with trade unions. The result is some lack of flexibility of local policy which may prevent the optimum use of resources. New needs can be sacrificed for past needs that are no longer as strong as they once were.

Further, the concept that the flow of capital works can be turned off and on like a tap—to suit the contemporary economic climate— suffers from serious limitations. Construction plans take time to prepare—planning enquiries and compulsory purchase orders may be involved. Construction works take time to complete. So it is impossible to commence projects that are not yet ready to start: it is wasteful to slow down or stop projects that are nearing completion. Capital programmes are now worked out two or three years in advance and acquire a momentum of their own. Indeed, a political party that gains a majority at Westminster or in a local council chamber will find that the rigidity imposed by capital schemes, already in hand or about to commence, can be so great as to frustrate the introduction of new policies which involve construction work.

The status of local government has been eroded in this century both by local weakness and by the development of a highly centralised form of public administration. Local weakness is financial and also a matter of organisation and personnel. The traditional committee system was better designed for promoting discussion than for promoting leadership. The reformed structure and streamlined committee organisation will make for improvement but they also impose a heavy burden on many councillors, especially committee chairmen. Some chairmen have the necessary time, ability and vigour to take full command of the business of their committees. Others—probably a majority—lack one or more of these essential qualities. With chief officers increasingly conditioned to think in terms of efficient management rather than adventurous policies, it is almost inevitable that, with exceptions, local councils conform to a national trend and do not take exciting initiatives. Meanwhile the advantage of the central government is the product of powerful interlocking factors: a country that is densely populated but relatively small in area; the cultural, financial and political supremacy of London; the firmly entrenched two-party system that gives the Cabinet a secure parliamentary majority; the acceptance by both parties of welfare policies which they are determined to control nationally.

The Maud Report on *Management of Local Government* accepted this centralised pattern and proposed to strengthen it still further.

The Government was recommended to see if it were possible to nominate a single Minister to be responsible for co-ordinating its policy in relation to local authorities. The establishment of the Department of the Environment in 1970 went a long way towards meeting this request. The Maud Committee also wanted the establishment of a Local Government Central Office to promote research, operate a central staffing organisation and conduct negotiations with the central government. Such an office would take over a large part of the present functions of the local authority associations. These proposals are a logical step ahead in the further unification of public administration. Yet there is a danger to the creation of a main official channel of communication. It may well be more efficient; it may also become rather remote from the individual local authority. And any agreement reached in this central channel would be difficult to overturn in Parliament or anywhere else.

There is a case for urging that these centripetal forces should be resisted. Strong reasons can be advanced against national intervention in local affairs, notably on matters of detail. Every increase in central control requires more staff in national offices to check what local authorities are doing. Not merely does this cost money but it adds to delay. Each new item in the catalogue of supervision means a further loss of local responsibility. Both councillors and local government officers can plead with some justification that it is not their fault if something goes amiss since they are acting under central direction. Distant control must be frustrating. It can develop a feeling among vigorous and able people that service in local government as elected representatives or salaried officers is not worthwhile. The claim for clear—if limited—independence for local government was stated by the Local Government Manpower Committee in 1950, '. . . local authorities are responsible bodies competent to discharge their own functions and though they may be statutory bodies through which Government policy is given effect and operate to a large extent with Government money, they exercise their responsibilities in their own right, not ordinarily as agents for Government Departments. It follows that the object should be to leave as much as possible . . . to the local authority and to concentrate the Department's control at key points where it can most effectively discharge its responsibilities for Government policy and financial administration.' This type of sentiment attracts some support from politicians, especially when in opposition. In terms of law and practice, the recommendation of the Manpower Committee has been ignored. To take just one example: Section 8 of the Public Libraries and Museums Act, 1964, permits the Secretary of State for Education and Science to decide the scale of fines for books overdue from a public library. It is impossible to provide adequate justification for a control of such a petty nature.

The Town and Country Planning Act, 1968, did constitute a distinct check to the centralising tendency. There is now less detailed Ministry supervision over local development plans and the inspectors who hold planning appeals are empowered to take minor decisions themselves instead of merely preparing recommendations for ministerial consideration. At the same time more emphasis is being placed on the need for local planners to consult local opinion. Why were these changes made? Is it that national administration has greater faith in the wisdom of local authorities? The more realistic explanation is that the highly centralised system of approvals and appeal decisions began to break down through the sheer volume of work. Delays in obtaining Ministry decisions lengthened so greatly that some simplification of the system became inevitable.

The Local Government Act, 1972, removed further detailed controls especially in regard to requirements to appoint certain committees and obtain ministerial approval for certain appointments. This is very welcome. Yet it is important not to be misled about the trend of future central-local relationships. Petty, irritating controls can be removed because other more basic legal and financial restraints are ever-present.

Members of the Layfield Committee on Local Government Finance were acutely aware of the effect on central/local relationships caused by the financial weakness of local councils. They were concerned about the confusion caused by a clear lack of accountability for local authority expenditure. Most local spending is directly related to some statutory obligation imposed by central government. The whole Layfield Report is based on the theme of accountability: it argued that those responsible for causing expenditure should accept the onus of finding the money to meet the bills. If present trends continued this would require central government to accept responsibility for the bulk of local expenditure. Ministers would have to determine broadly how much local authorities should spend and for what purpose. Ministers would provide grants and would also indicate the rate poundage necessary to finance appropriate standards of local service. Some local discretion would still remain. Thus local authorities could provide a better standard of service than that required by central government; for this purpose the local rate would be raised above the level required by central government. Councillors would be responsible for the discretionary element in the rate levy to the local electorate; they would be accountable to the Minister for the efficient conduct of the non-discretionary expenditure.

The Layfield Committee were not happy with the prospect of such developments. They preferred an alternative in which local councils would be free to make their own spending and taxing decisions. Even so, it was admitted that central government would need, in the interests of national economic management, to supervise the total of local spending. (Whether this could be done without interference on matters of detail is questionable.) Certainly, local councils could not attain such financial autonomy without fresh taxing powers. To give them such independence, the Layfield Report proposed the introduction of a local income tax.

Contrasting models for the future development of local government are set out in the two preceding paragraphs; these are sometimes described as the 'centralist' or 'localist' alternatives. Without doubt, the pressure of events is tending to push local government towards the former. Professor Day, in a note of reservation to the Layfield Report, proposed a third alternative or a middle way. His suggestion was that national government should define *minimum* standards for local services and pay for the cost of providing them. Local councils would decide how far they wished to go beyond the national minima and should pay, through local taxation, for whatever they decided to spend. However, local freedom would not be absolute: councils would have to restrict spending within a ceiling imposed by central government in the interests of national economic management. This system would differ from the 'centralist' arrangement because that implied Ministers would determine what the nation could afford: under Professor Day's plan, Ministers would decide upon an acceptable minimum. The Layfield Committee rejected this middle way because it felt there would be grave difficulties in fixing minimum standards and costing them.

How did the Callaghan Government respond to the alternatives posed by the Layfield Committee? Tactfully it stood aside from the localism/centralism conflict and commended the middle way. The Green Paper *Local Government Finance* then argued that the 'middle way' suggestions made by Professor Day were impractical. It followed the familiar theme that the relationship between local and central government must be a partnership, the nature of which would develop over time as conditions change. In fact, the whole force of the Green Paper was to press the centralist case. Ministers, it was argued, must exert greater influence over total local expenditure and sometimes would need extra financial weapons to ensure local adoption of particular policies. This philosophy formed the basis of a scheme described above (p. 106) to reshape the Rate Support Grant in a way which would enable Whitehall to put greater pressure on individual councils to adopt spending programmes agreeable to

Ministers. So the Layfield Report is unlikely to lead to a new dawn of local freedom for initiative. Indeed, local independence is likely to be increasingly throttled by the requirements of macro-economic planning.

COMPLAINTS MACHINERY

The growth of public services has provided much wider facilities for everyone. It has also made life more complicated. How are people to know what their rights are? How are they to discover what opportunities are available? How can they feel reasonably certain that their claims and applications have been handled fairly by public officials?

There are two separate problems here. One is an aspect of the general need for wide dissemination of information about local government: this is discussed in the following section. The other problem is to ensure that the administration of public policy is efficient and fair as between individuals. Whether policy itself is fair can be a matter for political judgement and argument, to be decided by public debate and the ballot-box. The task for public administration is to ensure that current policy is effectively and impartially carried out. National government has felt obliged to appoint a Parliamentary Commissioner or Ombudsman to look into complaints. (Strictly speaking, the use of the word Ombudsman is inappropriate. The Scandinavian Ombudsman, on which our system is based, can initiate legal action against defaulting officials; our Parliamentary Commissioner for Administration does not have this power.) The complaints must be about administration—not policy— and must be forwarded to the Commissioner by Members of Parliament. This machinery was an attempt to overcome an evil of mass society, that the shortcomings of bureaucracy may not always be held in check by the traditional means of parliamentary question and debate. But it was also argued that many matters on which the sense of personal grievance may be greatest, concerning planning, housing, education and welfare provisions, come within the ambit of local government rather than national government. If national civil servants are liable to be investigated by an independent official acting in response to a complaint from an aggrieved person, it seems natural that this practice be extended to local authorities.

Local government already suffers so many checks and restraints that it must be asked whether an extra one is needed. The parallel with central government is far from exact. Local authority administration is on a much smaller scale than national administration and the chance that serious mistakes will go uncorrected should be substantially less. At Westminster the Member of Parliament is physically remote from civil servants; he will not know them personally except by rarest chance; he will scarcely if ever meet them. Traditionally, Members have sent in complaints to Ministers who will have a political, if not a personal, motive for asserting that the administrative processes of their departments are tantamount to perfection. Virtually none of this applies to local government. Councillors know their chief officials and take complaints to them direct. They are, indeed, concerned with the details of administration through their committee work. Do local authorities need Ombudsmen since, in a sense, they have plenty already through the presence of elected representatives? But it is not clear that a councillor can always fill the role of an Ombudsman. If a complaint concerns a decision reached in one of his committees he may be asked to investigate one of his own actions or the consequences thereof. If a councillor does not belong to the relevant committee he may know nothing of the basis on which a decision is made and so is not well placed to make critical enquiries. Further, the time councillors can devote to complaints from the public must be limited by their other commitments. The problem of 'constituency' duties is now more fully recognised. The Bains Report proposed that councillors be provided with secretarial services to help them to carry out this function. Certainly, a councillor should be a first link between an aggrieved individual and local administration—but he may not always provide full protection.

It is vital for democracy that the claims and grievances of citizens be dealt with equitably. This cannot mean that all grievances should be satisfied and all claims accepted. It does require that complaints be reviewed impartially and that where one claim is given preference over another real justification can be found for the decision. Thus if a council house is allocated to Brown rather than to Smith, it must be because Brown has greater need of accommodation, because he has been evicted or is living under more crowded conditions or some similar reason—not because Brown has a friend or relative on the council or because he has bribed an official. In Britain these principles are understood and accepted. There is a tendency to feel that administrative abuses are so rare as not to constitute a problem. While corruption and other patent abuse is infrequent, there are still many cases of administrative error, failure of communication and lack of understanding. Local government does show concern and respect for individuals and is well placed to set an example for central government in these matters because of the smaller, more intimate scale of its operations. However, the reform of local government structure has now given us fewer but larger units of local administration and fewer councillors. The councillor, like the MP, is becoming divorced from administration. All these factors greatly strengthen the case for local Ombudsmen. But five years of discussion and negotiation were required before positive action was taken. The arguments over the form of the new organisation raised important issues.

The Prime Minister, Harold Wilson, accepted the need for such complaints machinery in a statement to the Commons in July 1969. But what form should this machinery take? JUSTICE (the organisation which popularised the Ombudsman idea in relation to central government) subsequently issued detailed proposals. It suggested that Commissioners of Local Administration should be appointed by the Lord Chancellor; that their salaries should be charged to the national Exchequer and that they should work through a single centralised office. Complaints of maladministration would be made to the Commissioners directly by members of the public. A report on each investigation would be sent to the person who initiated the complaint and to the local authority concerned: an Annual Report of the work of the Local Administration Commissioners would be presented to Parliament. It would be for the local authority to decide what action, if any, to take upon an adverse report from the Commissioners. The Labour Government's own proposals were somewhat different: the 1970 White Paper *Reform of Local Government in England* (Cmnd 4276) stressed that the function of local Ombudsmen would be to help councillors to ensure high standards of administration. Complaints would be made via councillors and the Commissioners would report to local councils and not to Parliament. The scheme was to be administered through a body representative of local government and costs would be met from local funds. Thus the complaints machinery would be separated from central government and would not be another facet of central control.

The scheme now in operation was introduced by the Conservatives through the Local Government Act, 1974. It follows in broad outline the earlier Labour proposals. A complaint need not necessarily be made through a councillor but it must have been submitted to the responsible authority which must have had a reasonable chance to investigate and reply to the complaint. England is divided up between the Commissioners, each of whom is responsible for complaints from a particular area. Wales has a separate Commission. Matters excluded from their attention embrace the conduct of schools; personnel matters; anything that took place before 1 April 1974; anything that could be the subject of appeal to a minister or an administrative tribunal; anything for which a remedy could be obtained from a court of law; anything connected with the commercial activities of a local authority or with criminal investigations. The Commissions report on the pattern of their work to national bodies representing local authorities. Investigations into complaints are held in private. Reports on each case are to be made to the parties concerned; these reports mention no names of individuals, but must be available for public inspection. Where a grievance is found to be justified it is for the local authority to decide what remedies should be offered. Any remedy should be notified to the Commissioner who, if not satisfied, could issue a further report. Thus the Commission has no power over the local council: the essence of this safeguard is impartial investigation followed by publicity. But a council that does not respond to criticism by a Local Commissioner could expect a considerable public outcry.

This machinery creates fresh problems. What limits should be placed on matters to be investigated? The Local Commissioners are to enquire, not into policy, but into maladministration. But what exactly is maladministration? One answer is the so-called Crossman catalogue produced by Mr Crossman when introducing to the House of Commons the legislation which authorised the establishment of the national Ombudsman. The catalogue is bias, neglect, inattention, delay, incompetence, ineptitude, perversity, turpitude, arbitrariness. Put more simply, maladministration would seem to cover any situation in which a local official's action has been improper or seriously inadequate. But maladministration does not include the exercise of discretion. For example, if a local authority is empowered to give or to withhold some benefit, a disappointed applicant cannot claim maladministration unless he can demonstrate some fault in the way in which the decision was made.

Local government officers may be worried lest unjustified complaints damage the reputation and career prospects of an innocent party. Will allegations be made by cranks or embittered and malicious people? This possibility is more serious in local government than in central government for the Civil Service is remote and anonymous. Anyone who alleges maladministration against the Civil Service will only rarely know which official is responsible. A local complaint is more likely to have a personal element. The first safeguard for the local official is the law of defamation. A councillor who forwards a complaint to a Local Commissioner and any report by the Commissioner are both privileged, i.e. they cannot be the subject of a libel action. But this protection does not extend to whoever makes the initial complaint. Another safeguard is that Local Commissioners will be fully aware that allegations that come to them may be wholly ill-founded and malevolent: they will take no action in such cases. Even so, some local officials may feel a little nervous. The danger is that they will become more cautious and less helpful to the public lest additional explanation or kindly advice become a source of complaint.

The system has a quiet and undramatic start. In the first full year of operation ending 31 March, 1976 the English Commissioners received 2,499 complaints of which 1,749 were not investigated, either because they contained no indication of maladministration or because they raised issues outside the jurisdiction of the Commissioners. Only 52 complaints resulted in a finding of maladministration. Planning, housing and education were the subjects that stimulated most concern. There were relatively few complaints about social services which may be a reflection of the relative inability of the clients or consumers to formulate their dissatisfaction. To present effectively a case against a public authority requires literary or verbal skills that not everyone possesses. As noted above, the Commissioners cannot force a local council to offer a remedy where a complaint is found to be justified. However, in the great majority of such cases local councils have taken steps to minimise the grievance. Occasionally, to remedy maladministration would be to cause injustice to someone else. Where planning permission has been given after inadequate scrutiny of the consequences of the proposed development, it would be unreasonable to require the demolition of building carried out with the consent of the local authority. A major shortcoming of the local Ombudsman system is that anyone who secures a finding of maladministration cannot, as a result, seek damages through a county court action. It is arguable that this rule should be altered. A council may offer an *ex gratia* payment as a recompense, but that is inadequate protection. Meanwhile, the administrative competence of the Local Commissioners is open to challenge: the average time taken to complete an investigation is eight months. Surely that is excessive.

PEOPLE AND LOCAL GOVERNMENT

It is a commonplace that we live in a mass society. All major units of social organisation, with the family as the main exception, tend to increase in size. Employers are fewer in number and operate on a larger scale; trade unions are fewer and larger; towns, schools, hospitals, even universities, get bigger. Government departments and local authorities also grow larger. Taken together, all this must have a great psychological impact on the individual. There can be a

tendency to feel lost in the crowd, to experience a sense of helpless-
ness in face of major social pressures, to lose interest in community
problems, indeed, perhaps to lose part of a sense of responsibility
for one's own actions. In a word, a dangerous possibility can
develop—some would say has developed—for the individual to
become alienated from society as a whole. The public support given
to youth organisations and other cultural, social and recreational
activities is in some measure a recognition of this danger and an
attempt to counteract it.

Local government, as the smallest and most approachable unit
in our system of public administration, should be able to play a major
role in breaking down the invisible barriers between the individual
and society. It is easier to make an impact on local decisions than it
is to affect national decisions. An essential aspect of the deterrent
which is inherent in the Ombudsman concept is the publicity which
will accompany the ultimate report on any case. Publicity could have
a greater impact in a local context than it has on Civil Service
administration. It could help to lessen the widespread indifference
to local government. This apathy was fully demonstrated by the
research undertaken by the Government Social Survey for the
Maud Committee. Over a quarter of those interviewed by the Survey
were unable to name *any* service provided by their borough or district
council: in county areas, the position was worse as nearly half the
interviewees apparently knew nothing of the county's services.
People in London Boroughs and rural districts were the worst
informed: in the metropolis men and women are lost in the mass
society and in the countryside the county council is not so much
impersonal as remote. Under one-fifth of those interviewed by the
Social Survey remembered having approached a councillor for
advice. This picture of indifference is not surprising. Life is short and
the potential range of human endeavour and interest is vast. It is
not unreasonable to feel that there are other and better things to do
than to concern oneself with the problems of local government.
Apathy can be a measure of contentment. If people are satisfied with
social conditions why should they bother about them?

But apathy may be caused by alienation and ignorance rather
than contentment. The nature of possible improvements may be
unknown; when produced they may be warmly appreciated although
not widely demanded in advance. If local government is to flourish
it must take some trouble to educate those of the public willing to
listen. Why not circulate to all households after each election the
names and addresses of council members, together with a note of
their committee assignments? Anyone who calls in at a council
office in search of this information will not always find it is easy to

obtain. Under the 1972 Act press and public have a right to attend council and committee meetings unless excluded on a specific occasion. There are personal matters relating to staff and financial details of land and property transactions which should be kept confidential. Access to meetings, however, is not enough. Attempts should be made to explain the major decisions facing a council to the public at large, possibly by issuing local White Papers on the analogy of Government White Papers. Of course, where an issue becomes political it is often better tactics to reach a decision quickly rather than stimulate public argument. Local and regional radio and television stations could do more to provoke interest in council activities. Yet councillors and local government officers often treat the mass communications media with reserve. The press, in particular, are sometimes accused of inadequate and inaccurate reporting or of seeking out trivial but apparently sensational news items. Councillors are sensitive about publicity. Perhaps this is due to a desire to avoid controversy; perhaps it is because misleading information can easily create embarrassment for them and may cause needless anxiety for some members of the public.

Some local authorities have appointed public relations officers. The Bains Report urged that the larger authorities should establish a public relations and information unit; it also recommended that authorities should consider producing an annual report containing not merely a factual record of the authority's services and use of resources but also a statement of plans to cope with present problems. All this should promote public understanding of local government and is to be welcomed. But public relations work can raise delicate issues. If a council is divided on party lines, a public relations officer who secures publicity for council policy can be accused of implicitly supporting the policy of the majority group. This challenge may be most difficult to avoid in relation to the exposition of plans for the future. Should public funds be spent on the dissemination of controversial matter? Some such spending is justified otherwise the public cannot know the details of the controversy—and many burning local issues depend not on general principles but their detailed application.

Zealous public relations work has its dangers. The alternative danger, apathy, is at least equally serious. If unchecked it may lead to deterioration of standards of services and permit the erosion of democratic safeguards. One old saying is worth requoting: the secret of liberty is eternal vigilance. A test that should always be applied to any scheme to improve local services is whether it will increase or reduce links with the public. To give local authorities greater freedom of action in the form of general competence powers or to allow them wider discretion in other ways is to increase their impact on society and should arouse more interest. This is not to argue that the 'democracy' test can be the sole or dominant criterion of policy, but it is an aspect of decision-making that may be given too little weight in face of considerations of administrative convenience.

Recently, the fashionable cure for apathy has been to stress the need for participation in local affairs. The Skeffington Report, *People and Planning*, issued in 1969 urged that local planners should do more to take the public into their confidence. Meetings and exhibitions should be held at an early stage of any major planning exercise at which comments and suggestions would be invited from organised groups and individual members of the public. Subsequent meetings should explain the final form of the planning proposals. There is no doubt that local bodies such as Chambers of Trade, residents' associations and amenity associations can play a useful role in this kind of process. Whether the average man in the street can make an impact on the complex and professionalised task of planning is dubious. How far is it meaningful to think of individual participation in local government? A parent can play a useful and vigorous part in a parent-teacher association that is raising money to build a swimming-pool. But this is merely to assist with others in the implementation of accepted policy. To 'participate' alone to try and influence policy is likely to be unsuccessful and frustrating. It is inevitable that participation arrangements always have something of a public relations flavour: if the planners encourage participation then people may be less unwilling to accept the consequences of planning.

Concern about the numbing effects of centralisation, apathy and the feeling that the quality of our democracy is in decline were all reflected in the report of the Royal Commission on the Constitution (Cmnd 5460) published in October 1973. The origin of this inquiry was the growth of nationalist sentiment in Scotland and Wales; much of the report deals with the problems that arise from arranging wider devolution of powers for these areas. Nevertheless, it also raised allied questions about devolution to regions within England which might have an impact on local government. Of course, this is not a new topic. Since 1965 England has been divided into eight regions for the purposes of economic planning. Each region has an Economic Planning Board composed of civil servants from the regional offices of government departments; each region has also an advisory Economic Planning Council with representatives of various interests including employers, trade unions and local authorities. When these bodies were first mooted there was some objection from the world of local government since it was feared they might diminish the status and powers of elected local councils. It was argued that more bureaucratic government would detract from the freedom of local authorities. They might also lose the right of access to Whitehall. Members of Parliament might be less able to influence or speed up decisions that were made at regional centres. To abate these fears the original titles 'regional planning boards' and 'regional planning councils' were changed to *economic* planning boards and councils to emphasise their link with industrial development.

The Commission on the Constitution envisaged a growth of regional institutions as a limited parallel to more extensive devolution in Scotland and Wales. Its proposals were neither precise nor unanimous. The general idea was for regional councils nominated by local authorities; they would provide advice for government departments which would be organised on a more decentralised basis. The Memorandum of Dissent from two members of the Commission was more explicit. Regional Assemblies were suggested, one each for Scotland and Wales together with five for England. They would take over the responsibilities of existing *ad hoc* regional bodies, particularly the Health and Water Authorities, and would also have some supervisory powers over the regional gas and electricity undertakings. The guiding principle of this Memorandum was that the outposts of central administration should be brought under democratic control.

The Scotland and Wales Bill, debated in 1977, raised fundamental constitutional issues that range far beyond the scope of this book. As far as Wales was concerned the central proposal was to establish a Welsh Assembly in Cardiff which would inherit many of the powers now possessed by central government departments to supervise local administration in Wales. This power extends to the issue of Statutory Instruments. However, the pattern was complex with some crucial matters reserved still for decision at the Whitehall level. Welsh local authorities were thus faced with a dual system of central control, part of which would be located at home within the Principality. No change was suggested for the actual functions of local authorities, but the very existence of the Welsh Assembly nevertheless poses a threat that it may, in future, take full charge of some activites now locally administered.

What implications are there for England in the policy of devolution for Scotland and Wales? If devolution has advantages, why should England be left out? To meet this challenge the Labour Government produced a consultative document, *Devolution: The English Dimension,* which consists, in essence, of a summary of objections to further change. The idea of an English Assembly, on the lines of the Welsh model, is rejected as being totally disruptive of our system of parliamentary government. A similar objection is made against the creation of a number of regionally elected bodies with powers inherited from central government. If these regional bodies were given some local authority powers, then this would involve a basic re-examination of local government structure when the new system had been in operation for a short time. The consultation document does mention the possibility of limited adjustments within the two-tier structure. Yet this idea has no connection at all with the basic issues raised by devolution. Even such restricted change would cause a storm of argument within local government circles. Public enthusiasm for further upheavals is scarce. The prospect of any action must be dim. Disenchantment with the 1974 reorganisation has left a weary sense that reforms are expensive and that the benefits thereof are often overestimated.

One should not conclude on a note of pessimism. The reformed local government system provides an opportunity to supply higher standards of service to the community. Its performance will be hampered by economic restraints. There are also stronger doubts about whether bigger units are necessarily more efficient in terms of cost per unit of output. But it is still important to stress that the educational role of local government is a major support for our whole democratic system. As people come to understand the intricacies of local problems they are better equipped to understand the tasks of national government. The limited but still substantial number of men and women elected to take local government decisions have a fuller appreciation of the responsibilities of Ministers, MPs, judges and senior Civil Servants. Ability to join in the process of government at local level may stir unfortunate feelings of pride and prestige, but it also enhances knowledge and judgement and provides a channel of communication between government and governed without which no democracy can flourish.

Appendix A

SIZE OF LOCAL AUTHORITIES: ENGLAND

(i) London

The Greater London Council serves a population of 7,167,000 a figure which is steadily declining. Its rateable value is approximately £1,900 million. The 32 London Boroughs vary in size from Croydon with a population of 329,000 down to Kingston-on-Thames with 136,000 people. Rateable values in London Boroughs range from £311 million in the City of Westminster to £26 million at Sutton. The City of London remains a unique authority in terms of its constitution and powers but it has only 5,300 residents.

(ii) Metropolitan Counties

Name of County	Population (000s)	Rateable Value £MN
Greater Manchester	2,709	300
Merseyside	1,588	188
South Yorkshire	1,317	124
Tyne and Wear	1,193	116
West Midlands	2,777	386
West Yorkshire	2,083	189

(iii) Metropolitan Districts

Metropolitan County	Number of districts	Population range (000s)	Rateable Value range (£MN)	Largest district
Greater Manchester	10	180–656	18–70	Manchester
Merseyside	5	193–561	20–71	Liverpool
South Yorkshire	4	224–561	16–61	Sheffield
Tyne and Wear	5	171–297	15–37	Newcastle
West Midlands	7	199–1,086	25–155	Birmingham
West Yorkshire	5	194–738	15–78	Leeds

(iv) Non-Metropolitan Counties

English County	Population (000s)	Rateable Value (£MN)	Number of districts
Avon	920	109	6
Bedfordshire	489	71	4
Berkshire	658	106	6
Buckinghamshire	502	81	5

English County	Population (000s)	Rateable Value (£MN)	Number of districts
Cambridgeshire	551	63	6
Cheshire	911	116	8
Cleveland	565	69	4
Cornwall	401	39	6
Cumbria	474	42	6
Derbyshire	887	91	9
Devon	937	100	10
Dorset	573	74	8
Durham	608	51	8
East Sussex	657	89	7
Essex	1,411	205	14
Gloucestershire	488	56	6
Hampshire	1,450	177	13
Hereford and Worcester	586	71	9
Hertfordshire	938	152	10
Humberside	848	88	9
Isle of Wight	111	12	2
Kent	1,445	160	14
Lancashire	1,369	130	14
Leicestershire	836	96	9
Lincolnshire	521	51	7
Norfolk	659	74	7
North Yorkshire	636	60	8
Northamptonshire	505	87	7
Northumberland	287	26	6
Nottingham	983	107	8
Oxfordshire	535	70	5
Salop	355	37	6
Somerset	402	43	5
Staffordshire	995	110	9
Suffolk	570	66	7
Surrey	998	158	11
Warwickshire	472	59	5
West Sussex	623	83	7
Wiltshire	512	52	5

Welsh County	Population (000s)	Rateable Value (£MN)	Number of districts
Clwyd	373	36	6
Dyfed	320	27	6
Gwent	440	41	5
Gwynedd	224	20	5
Mid Glamorgan	540	34	6
Powys	101	8	3
South Glamorgan	392	45	2
West Glamorgan	372	36	4

(v) Non-Metropolitan Districts

The English non-metropolitan districts differ from the other new county and district authorities in that their boundaries were not defined by the Local Government Act, 1972. Instead their boundaries were proposed by the Local Government Boundary Commission for England in their First Report (Cmnd 5148). These proposals were accepted by the Secretary of State and incorporated in Orders submitted for parliamentary approval.

In carrying out its task the Commission had extensive consultations with existing local authorities in order to try and find local solutions that were generally acceptable. It also had to work within the framework of a set of guidelines from the Secretary of State. The guidelines were as follows:

POPULATION, THE COUNTY PATTERNS OF DISTRICTS AND THE IDENTITY OF TOWNS

1. The Boundary Commission should recommend a pattern of districts for the non-metropolitan counties ranging upwards in population from 40,000. Only very exceptionally should a district be proposed with a population under 40,000.
2. Except in sparsely populated areas the aim should be to define districts with current populations generally within the range of about 75,000–100,000. These figures are in no sense absolute limits; some districts will be larger or smaller, according to local circumstances; but regard should be had to the desirability of producing in each county a pattern of districts which are broadly comparable in population and conducive to effective and convenient local government throughout the county as a whole.
3. The identity of large towns should be maintained. The whole designated area of a new town, or the whole of an area defined for town development, should ordinarily fall within one new district.
4. Normally it will be necessary to take only current population levels into account in considering the size of district to be proposed. Account should be taken of a town's engagement in an approved programme of rapid expansion, e.g. under the New Towns Act or Town Development Act, but even in these cases regard must also be had to the population level needed to sustain efficient services in the meantime.

Definition of new districts

5. Wherever reasonably practicable a new district should comprise the whole of one or more existing county boroughs or county districts. Where this is not practicable, the new district should

comprise whole parishes or wards. Because of the need to concentrate on the main pattern of the new districts, new boundaries which do not follow the boundary of an existing local government unit or electoral area should be proposed only in special circumstances. Once the new authorities have taken over, the Commission will be invited to carry out a thorough review of proposals for detailed adjustment of boundaries, including those of the counties and metropolitan districts.

General considerations

6. In formulating their recommendations the Commission should weigh all relevant considerations in the light of the general objectives of local government reorganisation as set out in the Government's White Paper, Cmnd 4584. Among other things they should have particular regard to the wishes of the local inhabitants, the pattern of community life, and the effective operation of local government services.

7. The Commission will also wish to take note of the pattern of Parliamentary constituencies in each county.

Population criteria provided the more important guidelines. However, the Commission ultimately proposed the establishment of 14 districts below the projected minimum of 40,000. Most of these authorities are in sparsely populated areas where the creation of larger authorities would have meant that the district councils were unduly remote. One exception to this rule is Christchurch in Dorset. The original intention here was that Christchurch should be combined with Lymington to form a district council of average size. However, at a very late stage in the parliamentary discussion of the Bill, the House of Lords successfully insisted that Lymington remain in Hampshire, so Christchurch was left to form a district on its own with a population of 33,000. A quite different type of special case is provided by the county of Cleveland where the Government issued a special instruction to the Commission requiring it to divide up the existing county borough of Teesside. This was felt to be essential as otherwise Teesside would have provided two-thirds of the population of the county.

Appendix B

ALLOCATION OF MAIN FUNCTIONS

Non-Metropolitan Counties

Social Services

Education and Related Services
  Education
  Libraries
  Museums and Art Galleries (c)

Housing and Town Development
  Certain reserve powers, e.g. over-
    spill
  Town Development

Town and Country Planning and
    Related Matters
  Structure Plans
  Local Plans (in special cases)
  Development Control (strategic
    and reserved decisions)
  Acquisition and Disposal of Land
  Clearance of Derelict Land (c)
  National Parks (subject to exist-
    ence of boards)
  Country Parks (c)
  Footpaths and Bridleways
  Commons—registration
  Caravan Sites—provision (c)
  Gipsy Sites—provision
  Smallholdings and Cottage Hold-
    ings

Highways and Related Subjects
  Transport Planning
  Highways
  Traffic
  Parking
  Public Transport (co-ordination)
  Road Safety
  Street Lighting

Non-Metropolitan Districts

Education and Related Services
  Museums and Art Galleries (c)

Housing and Town Development
  Housing
  Town Development

Town and Country Planning and
    Related Matters
  Local Plans (most)
  Development Control (most)
  Acquisition and Disposal of Land
  Clearance of Derelict Land (c)
  Country Parks (c)
  Footpaths and Bridleways
  Caravan Sites—provision (c) lic-
    ensing and management
  Gipsy Sites—management
  Allotments

Highways and Related Subjects
  Highways—can claim powers
    over unclassified roads in urban
    areas
  Public Transport—operation

Environmental Health
Food Safety and Hygiene
  Control of Communicable Disease
  Control of Office, Shop and Factory Premises

Consumer Protection
  Weights and Measures
  Food and Drugs
  Trade Descriptions
  Consumer Protection

Other Environmental Services
  Land Drainage
  Refuse Disposal
  Health Education (c)

Other Environmental Services
  Local Sewers
  Land Drainage
  Refuse Collection
  Litter
  Coast Protection
  Clean Air
  Building Regulations
  Street Cleansing
  Nuisances
  Cemeteries and Crematoria
  Markets
  Offensive Trades
  Health Education (c)

Police and Fire
  Police (subject to amalgamation)
  Fire

Recreation and Tourism
  Swimming Baths (c)
  Parks and Open Spaces (c)
  Physical Training and Recreation (c)

Recreation and Tourism
  Swimming Baths (c)
  Parks and Open Spaces (c)
  Physical Training and Recreation (c)
  Publicity for Tourist Attractions

Licensing and Registration Functions
  Births, Deaths and Marriages
  Adoption Societies

Licensing and Registration Functions

Other Services
  Entertainments (c)
  Aerodromes (c)
  Natural Emergencies (c)

Other Services
  Entertainments (c)
  Aerodromes (c)
  Natural Emergencies (c)

c = concurrent functions

This table ignores minor variations which may exist in Wales

Metropolitan Counties	Metropolitan Districts
	Social Services
Education and Related Services Museums and Art Galleries (c)	Education and Related Services Education Libraries Museums and Art Galleries (c)
Housing and Town Development Certain reserve powers, e.g. over- spill Town Development	Housing and Town Development Housing Town Development
Town and Country Planning and Related Matters Structure Plans Local Plans (in special cases) Development Control (strategic and reserved decisions) Acquisition and Disposal of Land (c) Clearance of Derelict Land (c) National Parks (subject to exist- ence of boards) Country Parks (c) Footpaths and Bridleways Commons—registration Caravan Sites—provision (c) Gipsy Sites—provision Smallholdings and Cottage Hold- ings	Town and Country Planning and Related Matters Local Plans (most) Development Control (most) Acquisition and Disposal of Land (c) Clearance of Derelict Land (c) Country Parks (c) Footpaths and Bridleways Commons—management Caravan Sites—provision (c) lic- ensing and management Gipsy Sites—management
Highways and Related Subjects Transport Planning Highways Traffic Parking Passenger Transport Road Safety	Highways and Related Subjects Highways—can claim mainten- ance powers over unclassified roads in urban areas
	Environmental Health Food Safety and Hygiene Control of Communicable Dis- ease Control of Office, Shop and Factory Premises
Consumer Protection Weights and Measures Food and Drugs Trade Descriptions Consumer Protection	

Other Environmental Services
  Land Drainage
  Refuse Disposal
  Health Education (c)

Other Environmental Services
  Local Sewers
  Land Drainage
  Refuse Collection
  Litter
  Coast Protection
  Clean Air
  Building Regulations
  Nuisances
  Cemeteries and Crematoria
  Markets
  Offensive Trades
  Health Education (c)

Police and Fire
  Police (subject to amalgamation)
  Fire

Recreation and Tourism
  Swimming Baths (c)
  Parks and Open Spaces (c)
  Physical Training and Recreation
    (c)

Recreation and Tourism
  Swimming Baths (c)
  Parks and Open Spaces (c)
  Physical Training and Recreation
    (c)
  Publicity for Tourist Attractions

Licensing and Registration Functions

Other Services
  Entertainments (c)
  Aerodromes (c)
  Natural Emergencies (c)

Other Services
  Entertainments (c)
  Aerodromes (c)
    Natural Emergencies (c)

c = concurrent functions

FURTHER READING

THE HISTORICAL BACKGROUND

Dilys M. Hill, *Democratic Theory and Local Government* (Allen & Unwin, 1974).

Bryan Keith-Lucas and Peter G. Richards, *A History of Local Government In The Twentieth Century* (Allen & Unwin, 1978).

J. Redlich and F. W. Hirst, *The History of Local Government in England* edited by B. Keith-Lucas (Macmillan, 1958).

PREPARING THE NEW SYSTEM

Peter G. Richards, *The Local Government Act 1972: Problems of Implementation* (Allen & Unwin, 1975).

Bruce Wood, *The Process of Local Government Reform 1966–74* (Allen & Unwin, 1976).

Report of the Royal Commission (Chairman, Lord Redcliffe-Maud), Cmnd 4040, 3 Vols (HMSO, 1969).

THE LEGAL BACKGROUND

R. J. Buxton, *Local Government* (Penguin, 2nd edition, 1973).

W. O. Hart and J. F. Garner, *Local Government and Administration* (Butterworths, 9th edition, 1973).

CENTRAL-LOCAL RELATIONS

J. A. G. Griffith, *Central Departments and Local Authorities* (Allen & Unwin, 1966).

Evelyn Sharp, *The Ministry of Housing and Local Government* (Allen & Unwin, 1969).

PROBLEMS OF PARTICULAR FUNCTIONS

J. B. Cullingworth, *Housing and Local Government In England and Wales* (Allen & Unwin, 1966).

J. B. Cullingworth, *Town and Country Planning In Britain* (Allen & Unwin, 6th edition, 1976).

Maurice Kogan, *Educational Policy Making* (Allen & Unwin, 1975).

G. Marshall, *Police and Government* (Methuen, 2nd edition, 1967).

FINANCE

N. P. Hepworth, *The Finance of Local Government* (Allen & Unwin, 4th edition, 1978).

A. H. Marshall, *Financial Management in Local Government* (Allen & Unwin, 1974).

Report of the Layfield Committee, *Local Government Finance*, Cmnd 6453 (HMSO, 1976).

MANAGEMENT AND STAFFING

K. P. Poole, *The Local Government Service* in England and Wales (Allen & Unwin, 1978).

J. D. Stewart, *Management in Local Government* (Knight, 1971).

Report of the Maud Committee, *The Management of Local Government* (HMSO, 1967).

Report of the Mallaby Committee, *The Staffing of Local Government* (HMSO, 1967).

Report of the Bains Committee, *The New Local Authorities: Management and Structure* (HMSO, 1972).

LOCAL GOVERNMENT AND SOCIETY

W. Hampton, *Democracy and Community* (OUP, 1970).

Dilys M. Hill, *Participating in Local Affairs* (Penguin, 1970).

L. J. Sharpe (ed.), *Voting in Cities* (Macmillan, 1967).

Justice Report, *The Citizen and His Council* (Stevens, 1969).

Report of the Royal Commission on the Constitution, Cmnd 5460 (HMSO, 1973).

INDEX

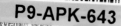

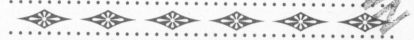

BACKYARD FARMING

➤ *Make your home a homestead* ➤

KEEPING HONEY BEES

"EXPERT ADVICE MADE EASY"

Kim Pezza

hatherleigh

𝕏 hatherleigh

Hatherleigh Press is committed to preserving and protecting the natural resources of the earth. Environmentally responsible and sustainable practices are embraced within the company's mission statement.

Visit us at www.hatherleighpress.com and register online for free offers, discounts, special events, and more.

Backyard Farming: Keeping Honey Bees
Text copyright © 2013 Hatherleigh Press

Library of Congress Cataloging-in-Publication Data is available upon request.
ISBN: 978-1-57826-452-0

Cover Design by DcDESIGN
Interior Design by Nick Macagnone

Printed in the United States
10 9 8 7 6 5 4 3 2 1

TABLE OF CONTENTS

. . . .

INTRODUCTION

The world of beekeeping is one full of mystery and intrigue for the common man. As they watch the beekeeper, carefully moving among their hives in their full protective suits, gathering honey from the unique little insects that make it, many people wonder what it must be like to keep bees themselves.

Also, now, with issues like colony collapse posing a major survival problem to the honeybee's world, more and more backyard farmers and homesteaders are becoming interested in beekeeping. Yet how do you know if beekeeping is really for you?

Adding hives and honeybees to your backyard farm requires a little more time, effort, and investment than planting a garden or raising chickens. Local restrictions and space requirements are even more important to consider. By deciding to keep honeybees, you are making a decision to install and maintain a small world run by your bees and watched over by you. If done correctly, however, keeping bees can be an enjoyable and incredibly rewarding experience.

Along with helpful hints and expert tips, this book touches on the basics of beekeeping: from obtaining bees and what the different varieties available to new beekeepers are to choosing the right environment for producing the right types of honey. In clear, easy-to-understand language, this book helps to teach you what to expect as a beekeeper, the pros and cons of the trade, and how the ways in which the bees are kept affect almost every stage of their lives.

Backyard Farming: Keeping Honey Bees will be an excellent go-to source for those who may be considering obtaining their own hives, but are not quite sure whether it is for them. With this book written with these excited new beekeepers in mind, even the most novice readers will find themselves ready to add beekeeping to their backyard farms.

Backyard Farming: Keeping Honey Bees is meant to be a source for those who are considering a start in the world of bees. Laying out the basics simply and clearly without a lot of complicated, in-depth information, it will give potential new beekeepers an idea of what they can expect when (or if) they decide to have a hive of their own or if it is a hobby or potential business that they even want to continue to pursue.

So sit back with your favorite beverage (perhaps with a little honey?) and begin your adventure with honeybees, honey, and all the magic that beekeepers cherish about their little charges.

MEET THE EXPERT

. . . .

Kim Pezza grew up among orchards and dairy and beef farms having lived most of her life in the Finger Lakes region of New York State. She has raised pigs, poultry and game birds, rabbits and goats, and is experienced in growing herbs and vegetables. In her spare time, Kim also teaches workshops in a variety of areas, from art and simple computers for seniors, to making herb butter, oils, and vinegars. She continues to learn new techniques and skills and is currently looking to turn her grandparents' 1800s farm into a small, working homestead.

CHAPTER 1

A SHORT HISTORY OF THE BEE AND ITS MAGIC

I t is a good bet that there are probably only a few people in the United States—or anywhere else for that matter—who have never seen a honeybee at least once in their lives. It is also well known how important these busy, buzzy little girls (yes, *girls*, but we'll cover that later) are to our own food supply. It has even entered the public consciousness that honeybees are now facing peril on a worldwide scale. However, what isn't well known is just how long and storied a history the honeybee has, dating back millions of years (around 60 million years in fact).

There is even evidence to suggest that a bee species native to North America lived approximately 14 million years ago, its existence proven through a worker-bee fossil found in Nevada in 2009. Unfortunately, those bees died out long ago, and the honeybee did not reappear on the North American continent again until about 1622, when European settlers brought their hives with them. Like many other species of wildlife that originated with the European settlers, it is thought that some bees left their captivity and set up shop in the untamed wilderness of North America.

Yet it isn't just prehistoric North America that has played host to honeybees. A 19 million-year-old giant honeybee fossil was found on Iki Island, Japan, and there is evidence of beekeeping going as far back as ancient Egypt, Greece, and Spain. Some of this evidence even includes excavations of preserved hives. In fact, the Egyptian *Papyrus Ebers*, the oldest known book of medicine, includes a number of recipes that utilize honey for its curative effects.

Despite being one of the oldest agricultural practices known to man, beekeeping continues to find popularity today, not only in rural fields, farms, and backyards, but in the urban landscape as well. Small city lots, suburban backyards, and building rooftops have all become home to hives, not only in the United States, but in other areas of the world as well. Ironically, as enthusiasm for bees and beekeeping continues to grow, the world's bee population continues to shrink. The decline of the honeybee population in the United States alone has resulted in a 50 percent decrease over the last fifty years. People are not only becoming involved in the plight of the honeybee and what humans stand to lose with the loss of the bees, but are getting involved with beekeeping themselves. By learning to keep bees, you are joining a proud tradition, which has existed and thrived for thousands of years, at one of the most important times in its history.

CHAPTER 2

WHAT DISTINGUISHES A HONEYBEE?

· ·

A bee is a bee, and all bees basically look alike, act alike, live alike, and make the same honey the same way for harvesting, right?

Wrong.

In general, there are over 20,000 species of bees in existence. Scientifically, the honeybee species is that of Apis. The class is Insecta, the order is Hymenoptera, and the family is Apidae. However, out of all of those, only seven species are recognized as honeybees.

They are:

- *Apis mellifera* (Western)
- *Apis nigrocincta*
- *Apis koschevnikovi*
- *Apis cerana* (Eastern Asiatic)
- *Apis andreniformig* (Black Dwarf)
- *Apis dorsata* (Giant Honeybee)
- *Apis florea* (Red Dwarf)

Along with the recognized species, there are 44 subspecies.

Common Bees in the United States

Although there are no longer any species of honeybee that are native to North America, there are six types of bees, imported throughout the decades (if not centuries), that are most commonly available in the United States.

They are (in no particular order of popularity):
- Italian Bee
- German Bee
- Carniolan Bee
- Caucasian Bee
- Buckfast Bee
- Russian Bee

A quick review of each of the six types of common honeybees in the United States is as follows:

Italian Bee: The Italian bee was first imported to the United States in 1859. For the beekeeper, the Italian bee has a gentle temperament, which makes handling it much easier. They are excellent honey producers, and their tendency to swarm is quite low, meaning that it is less likely that a keeper will have his bees leaving the hive in search of a new home. (The full story on swarming and why bees do it will be discussed later in Chapter 6.)

An Italian worker bee. Photo courtesy of Wikimedia Commons.

German Bee: Also known as the European Dark, the German bee is hardy in winter, a good flier in the cold, and is, therefore, a great choice for cold climates. Like the Italian bee, they have low swarm tendencies. The worker and queen can have good longevity if cared for properly. It should be noted, however, that hybrids/crossbreeds of the German bee may have aggressive tendencies, which could make handling the bees more difficult for the beekeeper.

Carniolan Bee: The Carniolan is a subspecies of the Western honeybee (Apis mellifera). Although this species is prone to swarming, can have problems in the heat, and the queen may be difficult to locate within the hive, the Carniolan is still a favorite due to the fact

A Carniolan bee. Photo courtesy of Wikimedia Commons.

that, although it will defend itself against other insects and insect intruders, it remains gentle to its handlers—even the queen remains gentle.

The Carniolan bee is also resistant to (at least some) diseases and parasites. They can be kept in populated areas (great for urban beekeepers), and adapt quickly to changes in the environment. They also do well in regions with long winters.

Caucasian Bee: Also a subspecies of the Western honeybee, the Caucasian is a gentle and calm bee, with strong colonies. However, they are not a good choice for those keepers in northern climates, as they do not winter well. The Caucasian may also drift away from a hive entered by a robber bee. (Robber bees will be covered later in Chapter 10, but it is almost exactly what it sounds like: a bee that steals from other hives.)

Buckfast Bee: The Buckfast bee is a crossbreed (in anything that I have found, it just states that this breed is a cross of many breeds, but, so far, nothing specific) that takes its name from Buckfast Abbey in Devon, the United Kingdom, from whence it originated.

It is popular among beekeepers due to the fact that they are gentle, good tempered, and calm, with low sting tendencies. They have a keen sense of smell, are hardy in the winter, and are good honey producers.

A Buckfast bee. Photo courtesy of Marc Andrighetti.

Russian Bee: The Russian bee originated in the Primorsky Krai region of Russia. They were imported into the United States by the USDA Honeybee Breeding, Genetics, and Physiology Lab in 1997. Although the species endures winters well, is resistant to some parasite mites, and is comprised of good honey producers, the Russian bee does tend to swarm, and its numbers tend to explode.

A Russian bee. Photo courtesy of Robert Engelhart.

Living

The honeybee is a social bee, meaning that it lives in an organized structure, working and living in constant cooperation with others. In contrast, the solitary bee has no social structure and will live and hunt alone.

It should be noted that it is precisely this social colony structure that allows the honeybee to survive for years, as it has the ability to huddle and eat its honey to survive the winter.

However, it would be inaccurate to assume that it is only the honeybee that produces honey. Solitary bees and the bumblebee are good examples of non-honeybee honey producers. Yet, although these bees will both produce and store honey, they do not produce anywhere near the quantity that honeybees do, making them unfit to use for honey harvesting.

The size of the typical honeybee colony can average 60,000 residents. This will break down into about half of the bees tending to the young and assisting the queen, while the rest go out and forage for nectar and pollen, both being food for the bees (though the bees will also need water). Along with the queen, you also have the worker and drone. All workers are female and work the hive in various roles. All drones are male and are only breeders. These roles will be covered in more detail a bit later.

Stages of the Bee

As do other insects, the honeybee goes through developmental, or life, stages. These stages are:

- Egg
- Larval
- Pupal
- Metamorphosis into Adult Bee

Eggs and larvae in their combs. Photo courtesy of Waugsberg.

Much like the butterfly, the honeybee will go through each one of these stages, eventually becoming the functioning worker, drone, or, in some cases, new queen.

The fertilized egg of the honeybee is laid within the wax chambers, or cell, of a honeycomb. The honeycomb that is used for laying eggs is called the brooder comb. Looking like little grains of rice, each egg stands on and within its own small cell. Within only three days of being laid, the eggs will hatch, beginning the next stage of development, which is the larval. The larva looks like a little white worm. At this stage, the larva does not have legs or eyes.

For the first few days, the larva will live on a diet of royal jelly, a substance rich in protein, vitamins, fats, and minerals. Starting at day three, the larvae's diet will be altered, according to the roles that it will play in the hive or colony. Those destined to be workers and drones will be switched to a honey, pollen, and water diet. Those that have the potential to become queens will continue on an exclusive diet of royal jelly. The larva will have five moltings

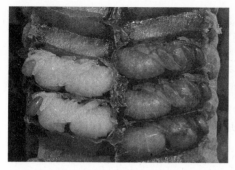

A drone pupa. Photo courtesy of Eugene Aufnahme.

during this period. Be they worker, drone, or queen, the care given to the larva by the workers is nonstop, providing it with at least ten thousand meals.

After a period of time (five and a half days for queen larvae, six days for worker larvae, and six and a half days for drone larvae), they will move on to the next stage: the pupal stage.

At the pupal stage, the larva goes through a complete body overhaul, totally changing its structure. As tissues reorganize, the body will change into the more familiar form of the bee. Normally this takes seven and a half days for a queen, fourteen and a half days for a drone, and twelve days for a worker. The final stage is the metamorphosis into the adult bee, thus completing the cycle within a 21-day time period.

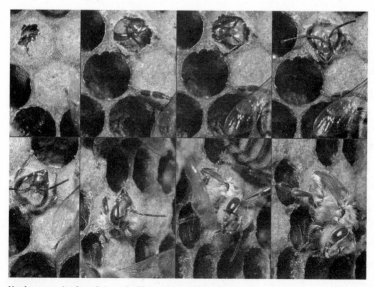

New bees emerging from their combs. Photo courtesy of Waugsberg.

Bee Anatomy

The anatomy of the adult bee is broken into three main parts:

- Head
- Thorax
- Abdomen

The Head

The head consists of the antennae, the eyes, the mandibles, and the proboscis. The eyes consist of two compound eyes as well as three simple eyes.

The compound eyes are basically light-sensitive cells that can understand color, light, and direction. The three simple eyes (or ocelli) are arranged in a triangle and determine light.

Antennae are used for sense of smell through hairs that cover them and, sometimes, are even able to figure out the direction that an odor is coming from. The antennae can also measure flight speed, as well as information about taste, temperature, and humidity. The antennae are also sensitive to vibration.

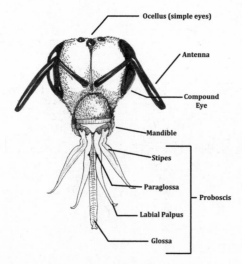

The parts of a bee's head. Illustration by Ariel Delacriox Dax.

The mandibles are, in basic terms, very strong jaws. They are used for eating pollen, cutting and shaping wax, feeding the young as well as the queen, cleaning the hive, grooming, and fighting.

The proboscis is the tubular part of the mouth used for feeding. It is also referred to as the glossa. Basically, it is like a tongue, but the bee will sip water nectar and honey through it as we would use a straw.

The Thorax

The thorax consists of the wings, legs, and movement muscles. The wings are in two parts: the forewing and hind wing. The forewing is the larger of the wings. It is used mainly for flight, but can also be used with the hind wing for cooling. The hind wing is used for flight and cooling the hive. The forewing and the hind wing may hook together to work in unison.

There are six legs that provide movement and the ability to

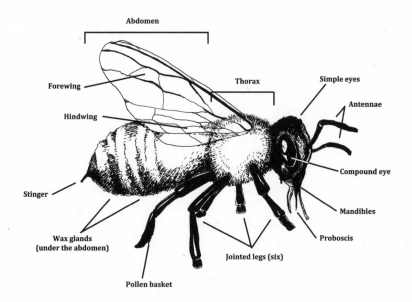

The anatomy of a honeybee. Illustration by Ariel Delacriox Dax.

manipulate and carry pollen. One set is structured to clean the antennae. Each front leg has two parts, with a notched spot that wraps around the antennae and pulls it through the notch, removing dust and other particulates that could interfere with the sensitivity of the antennae. This is called the antennae cleaner.

The middle leg, although not having a particular special purpose, helps to collect pollen off of the bee's body for deposit into the pollen basket.

Bee with filled pollen bucket. Photo courtesy of Wikimedia Commons.

The hind legs are home to the pollen baskets. The pollen basket is a small cavity surrounded by small hairs. The pollen goes into these hairs, getting pressed in and held in place between the small hairs. From there, the pollen goes to the pollen comb (also located on the hind leg), where it is pressed, compacted, and then transferred to the outside of the hind leg, where the pollen is secured by a single hair.

Each leg has a foot, and each foot a claw. The claw allows the honeybee to hold onto rough surfaces.

The Abdomen

The abdomen is in seven segments. In segments four through seven, wax is created and secreted. In the queen bee, the abdomen also contains the female reproduction organs, and, in the drone, the male reproduction organs.

The stinger is also found in the abdomen. The workers and the queen have stingers, which they use for defense; however, once a worker bee stings, it will die. This is due to the fact that, once the stinger, which is barbed, tries to pull away, the abdomen ruptures, causing the death of the bee.

Now that some of the basics have been discussed about the honeybee, let us explore a bit further as to some of the things that a potential beekeeper needs to know as you consider your future with the honeybee.

A Few More Facts on the Honeybee

As insects go, the honeybee is an interesting one, and one that has lots more little secrets surrounding them. Besides what has already been discussed, a few more tidbits of information are worth noting, if for no other reason than to show more of what these little powerhouses have behind them.

If you have ever seen a honeybee fly, you may have noticed that the wings are going so fast that you can hardly see them. This is because the honeybee's wings beat over eleven thousand times per minute. Also, that "buzz" that you hear is due to the flap of its wings.

While we are discussing wings, the honeybee flies at an average speed of between 12 and 15 miles per hour, usually keeping within a one to five-mile radius of its hive. (The closer the bee can stay to the hive, the better it likes it.)

Honeybees perform best between temperatures of 62°F and 105°F. However, they will slow down in winds of 15 miles per hour, and they will stop altogether in 25 mile-per-hour winds.

Vision wise, honeybees can see every color that a human being can see, with the exception of red, and is the only insect that produces food fit for human consumption.

CHAPTER 3

HIERARCHY OF BEES

Like all societies, honeybees have a definite social structure. From the queen, without whom the colony would not exist, to the drone who can be literally quite dispensable, the honeybee has a very interesting social ladder. So, for those of you who are not familiar with their social structure and way of life, once you have learned more, you may never look at honeybees the same again.

The honeybee has what would be considered an actual, functioning class system, where everyone knows its place, status, and job straight from the date it hatches. In a working colony or hive, there can be between 50,000 and 60,000 of which 99 percent of the hive will be female.

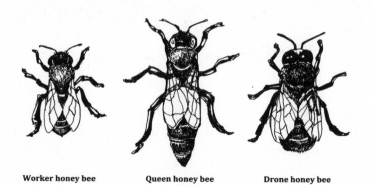

| Worker honey bee | Queen honey bee | Drone honey bee |

The three types of bees. Illustration by Ariel Delacriox Dax.

There are three "classes" within all honeybee colonies or hives:

- Queen
- Worker
- Drone

The Queen

There is only one queen in any hive or colony, and her one and only job is to produce eggs in order to populate the colony. She is the only fertile female within the colony. The queen is the largest bee in the colony. Her life span is up to five years, with approximately three of those years being productive (although some queens may need to be replaced sooner).

On her maiden flight, the queen will leave the hive, at which time drones will fertilize her. Although this will be her only mating, the process lasts several days, during which she will store the sperm within her body. The drones that fertilize her may not necessarily be from her hive or colony. She will then return to the hive, after which she will remain indoors for the rest of her life. (The only other time that the queen may leave is if the hive becomes overcrowded. If that happens, she may lead a swarm to a new location.)

The queen will begin her job of populating the hive as soon as she returns. She will average 1,000 to 1,500 eggs per day, with approximately 200,000 being laid in her lifetime. At some point, the queen will become infertile or perhaps even sick. When this happens, she is then replaced in a process called "supersedure." While beekeepers may do this themselves, it is equally viable for the colony itself to create a new queen to take over for the old.

Yet how can a colony actually create a queen? It all begins at the larval stage. The workers will first create queen cups. Queen cups are larger than the regular cells/cups, and they are vertical instead of horizontal. The existing queen will lay eggs within the cells, just as she would in the others. Unlike the others, though, the larvae that could be queens will be fed a diet made up entirely of royal jelly.

Royal jelly is secreted from the glands in the head of the worker bee, which, in this case, is the nurse bee. The jelly is rich in protein, vitamins, fats, and minerals. For the first three days of the larva's life, it is fed a diet strictly of royal jelly. After the third day, only the larva that is to be queen will continue on this exclusive diet, doing so during the entire larval stage.

A queen bee surrounded by drones. Photo courtesy of Wikimedia Commons.

Hatching time for the queen larva is 16 days. Although there are multiple queen larvae, it is the one that hatches first that becomes queen. Basically, it is all in the luck of the hatching. Once the new queen hatches, she will then "eliminate the competition" by going to each queen larva's cell and stinging the occupants to death. Then, if the old queen is still in the hive, she will meet the same fate. It should also be noted that a queen may safely (safely for her, anyway) sting multiple times; as her stinger is not barbed, it will not remain in the victim, nor will it pull away from her abdomen as she withdraws.

However, it can happen that the workers will kill the old queen before the new one can. "Cuddle death" is when the workers surround and press their bodies against the queen until she gets so overheated that she dies.

On a less solemn note, do not forget that a new queen does not always spell doom for the old queen. A hive may simply be lacking its queen because she left with a swarm to find a new residence.

Once the new queen has taken her place in the colony, the maiden-flight fertilization ritual begins again, and the entire cycle starts over.

The Workers

The next rung down on the caste ladder is the worker bee. When the term busy as a bee was coined, it was with the worker honeybee in mind.

Although they start out essentially much as the queen does (which ends at day three), when the larvae are taken off of the royal-jelly diet, they instead are fed a combination of honey and pollen, sometimes called "bee bread," which they will subsist on for the rest of their lives.

Soon after leaving their cocoon, the worker bees begin their job (remember that all the workers are female). For the first four days, however, the newly hatched workers will be cleaned and fed by the nurse bees until their bodies harden and their glands begin producing wax for combs.

The life span of the worker bee is about 40 days. However, as discussed earlier, in the wintertime, particularly in areas where temperatures are cold enough to slow the bees down, the worker may live a bit longer.

The life of the worker bee, in addition to being rather short, is not a particularly easy one. They live their lives in cycles. For the first 17 days of their productive lives (counting the first four days of their lives, during which they are completing their maturation), the worker bees will feed the larvae, process honey, manipulate wax, air-condition the hive when needed, and provide guard duty, amid a number of other jobs that need to be done for the colony or hive to survive.

The remaining days of their lives will be spent gathering pollen, nectar, and water. At the end of their life span, the workers simply leave the hive and go to die. This final journey of the cycle lasts approximately 20 days. The final 20 days include their gathering time.

The worker bees will attend to the larvae, the queen, and even the drones. Yet their work does not end there. In Chapter 4, we discuss the roles of the scout and the forager. However, the colony has many, many more jobs needing to be done. Let us look at some of the other work that goes on in the hive, keeping in mind that the worker bees can have more than one job during their lifetime.

A worker's job will usually change with its age, with each job having workers in the same approximate age range.

Nurse bees are the youngest of the matured workers. They will feed and care for the larvae and the queen, as well as feed the drones.

Sometimes, water needs to be brought to the hive to cool it down. It is the job of the water carriers to find and bring water back to the hive, carrying the water the same way as they do nectar. Once they find a good source, they will continue to use it for as long as they can.

After the water is brought back to the hive, the carriers will then sprinkle water on the fanning bees' backs and/or throughout the hive. As the fanning bees fan their wings, the water will add extra cooling to the hive. This is usually practiced only when the hive is in danger of overheating. It is basically natural air-conditioning.

The fanning bees are those workers whose job it is to keep the hive cool through the repeated fanning of their wings. Working like a living air conditioner, they are very important to the hive, especially in the hot weather. If the hive overheats, it can kill the colony. Although, when most bees die, they are outside of the hive, some will pass inside, as will some larvae.

As honeybees are very clean and tidy, it will fall to the mortuary bees to take care of the problem. Just as the name suggests, the mortuary bees take care of the remains of the dead larvae and bees that have died within the hive. It is up to them to remove the bodies and deposit them outside of the hive. Not only is this part of the bees' cleanliness routine, it can also free cells and help prevent disease when the foragers return with their nectar. Some of the workers within the hive will then take the nectar that the foragers have collected and begin the honey-making process. Workers are also responsible for cleaning the comb cells, as well as opening or sealing them as necessary.

Also, as we have discussed before, it is up to the workers to perform guard duty at the hive. Woe betides any poor trespasser, as these girls can pack quite a punch.

As you can see, the lives of the worker bees are hard, but predictable, as they work themselves quite literally to death.

Yet, on the other hand, workers can have quite a bit of a say in the hive as well. It is usually the worker that decides if it is time to swarm, although sometimes, as we have discussed before, a queen will also make that decision. It is also the workers that make the decision as to when it is time for any leftover drones to leave the hive for good and to throw them out. Finally, many times, it is the workers that decide when and if the queen needs replacing, to the point of sometimes killing her themselves, if need be, while creating the new queen to replace her.

The worker bee is the most fascinating and hard-working occupant of the hive. It can also be the most ruthless. As important as the queen is to populating the colony, none of it could function without the workers.

The Drones

At first blush, it seems like the drone has it pretty easy in the hive. After all, it is fed by the nurse bees, and its one and only job is to go out and fertilize any queen that it can find. In truth, though, it is the drone that really gets the short straw in the caste system of the bees.

In appearance, the drone is larger than the worker bee, yet smaller than the queen. Its eyes are twice the size of the workers and the queen, but, unlike them, it is unable to sting, as it lacks a stinger.

Drones are fed by the workers (usually the nurses) until they are ready to mate. Also, although their main reason for existing is to fertilize a queen, once they do mate, the drones will die. This is due to the fact that the drone and queen will meet in midair, and, when it does fertilize the queen, its genitalia ends up quite literally ripped from its body.

Drones and worker bees (drones in front with larger eyes). Photo courtesy of Wikimedia Commons.

If that is not bad enough for the poor drones, those that are still alive will most likely be kicked out of the hive in areas having harsh winter weather (also, they will be removed if the hive is running into other hard times in regard to nutrition) and left on their own to starve. This is done to be sure that there is enough stored food to keep the larvae, workers, and queen going during hard times. As the drones are considered replaceable and not as important to the colony, they are sent away for the good of the hive.

As you can see from this brief account, in the honeybee hive, everyone has its place and job. There is no room for slackers, and those that do not work for and on behalf of the survival of the hive are quickly taken care of. It is a very strange kind of existence to the human mind, with one side being organized to the point of fascinating, while the other side is brutal and unforgiving.

It is all part of the magic of the honeybee.

CHAPTER 4

EASE OF KEEPING

O ne of the first things you may need to think about when considering beekeeping is how easy they would be to keep. Do they need constant care? What are the disease risks for the bees? Will I have predator problems? What about weather and seasonal changes? Housing is another issue the potential beekeeper will have questions about; however, this will be covered in Chapter 6.

The truth is that honeybees are really no more complicated to keep than most other livestock. Feeding, disease and disease prevention, protection from predators, and general upkeep through the seasons and all types of weather are all concerns that apply to honeybees as much as cattle or fowl. Every animal or bird on the homestead or backyard farm will have some sort of work involved or idiosyncrasy to account for. Yet, to many, the world of the honeybee seems so mysterious and magical that they feel there *must* be some difficult secret involved in learning how to raise these little girls (and boys—what few there are).

As with all things, the trick is to take things a step at a time. The first issue we will cover is that of feeding honeybees.

Feeding the Hive

Honeybees eat nectar and pollen, and, of course, they drink water. In the wintertime, in regions where hives are unable to forage for themselves, they will survive on their stored honey and pollen. In addition to their own natural stockpiling, keepers may also provide supplemental nourishment both inside and outside of the hive. Depending on the climate you live in and are keeping your bees in, they may hunt seasonally, remaining bundled up in the hive in the winter, or they may hunt for most of the year.

In the world of the honeybee, it is the job of the worker bees to feed the hive. Those who "handle" the food detail are known as "scouts" and "foragers."

In the hive, 25 percent of the worker bees are "scouts." The primary job of the scout is to find various food locations. Once the scouts have located viable food sources for the hive, they will return to base to inform the foragers as to where to find these food sources. The foragers are the bees that will actually go out and bring the food back to the hive. They do so through the use of odor, direction, and distance.

Upon their return to the hive, the scouts will do a little dance that will actually convey information to the foragers about the distance and direction that the food is from the hive.

There is a different dance for different distances:

- Up to 50 meters: The dance only conveys direction, not distance.
- 50 to 75 meters: The "round dance" is performed on the comb surface, with literal dancing in circular movements.
- 150 meters or more: The "waggle dance" is performed.

The "waggle dance" has two parts. The first part tells the foragers the direction of the food, while part two, which conveys information through the speed with which the dance repeats, indicates the distance. Remember that the closer the food is, the better the bees like it.

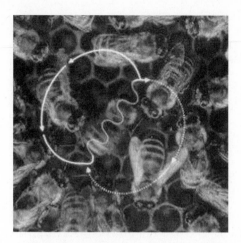

A diagram of a bee performing the waggle dance. Photo courtesy of Toutz, M. Kleinhenz.

The scouts also use odor to provide information to the foragers. It is thought that the scouts bring back the unique scent of the flowers that they have visited to the foragers. The foragers will then proceed to go after the food that the scouts located to bring back to the hive.

So what happens when the foragers bring the food back to the hive? Pollen intended for honey making will need to be stored right away. The reason is that, if the pollen is not stored correctly, it will spoil. To protect the pollen from spoiling, it must be kept in a honeycomb cell mixed with honey, which acts as a preservative. This will prevent the pollen from spoiling and allow the hive to safely store the pollen until it is needed.

Nectar that is gathered by the forager is divided between the bee's main stomach and the honey stomach. Although this will be covered further in Chapter 8, here it is briefly: the honey stomach is the bee's second stomach. It is here that the rest of the nectar is processed into honey. Upon returning to the hive, this processed nectar is placed within the individual cells of a honeycomb and sealed in as the food supply.

Before we go further, it should be noted that it is best for the bees if they are allowed to store their own food for winter. Although this can mean less honey for the keeper, it will mean a much better chance for the hive (or hives) to survive the winter.

However, sometimes the keeper may find it necessary to provide supplementary food to the hive to ensure its survival. Also, when the keeper does find the need, it must be done properly for the health of the colony.

A bee gathering nectar from a flower. Photo courtesy of Stan Shebs.

There are a number of reasons that a beekeeper may need to provide supplemental food to the hives. Some of these situations include:

- Increasing colony size
- Sustained colony development during unfavorable weather conditions
- Sustaining the ability to feed the young during unfavorable weather conditions
- Not enough honey produced for winter
- Providing backup during a pollen/nectar shortage

However, there are only a few situations in which supplemental feeding would be *necessary*. As stated, the colony's own honey is what is best for the survival of the hive, including during the winter. A single hive/colony should have 60-80 pounds of honey available to them and their hives in the fall to carry them through the winter.

Furthermore, if and when it becomes necessary to provide your hive (or hives) with supplemental food, there are three options available that will provide the necessary nutrients that your bees will need: dry mix, moist cake, and sugar syrup.

Dry mix compositions include brewer's yeast or soy flour. The dry mix can be fed inside the hive into the brood nest (where the larvae are) or outside of the hive in an open container such as a tub or tray. However, if placed outside of the hive in an open container, the dry mix must be sheltered from becoming damp due to rain and dew. This can be accomplished simply by the addition of some sort of little roof structure set up over the container.

One drawback with feeding dry mix outside is that other bees besides your own may find and feed on it, so keep in mind the environment that your hives exist in.

Another feeding option is moist cake. Moist cake is made up of pollen pellets, sugar, and soy flour. Moist cake may be fed to the bees inside the hive. The cakes should be placed close to the larvae so the nurse bees (worker bees that care for the larvae) can feed their charges. If more moist cakes are made or obtained than can be used at any one time, they can be frozen for several weeks without losing any nutritional value.

Sugar syrup is made from cane sugar, beet sugar, or isomerized corn syrup mixed with water. A carbohydrate substitute, sugar syrup may be fed outside the hive in any open container. However, there must be something for the bee to stand on in the container if using a tray or dish for the syrup. Some keepers will install their own jar feeders as well.

Sugar syrup may also be fed to the bees inside of the hive as well. Some of the ways that this may be achieved is through:
- Empty chamber combs: Sugar syrup is placed (usually squirted) into empty honeycomb chambers, where it can be

held for the bees to use.

- Division board feeder: A boxlike replacement for comb placed in the brood nest.
- Plastic bag feeder: A plastic bag encloses one or two frames in the lower edge of the nest. This will then hold the sugar syrup and allow the bees to feed.

It cannot be overstated that the bees' own honey is their best food; however, it can be comforting to know that there are alternatives that are healthy, safe, and nutritious if there is an emergency or a natural food shortage.

Keeping and caring for honeybees can seem a daunting task at first glance. One look at a beekeeping outfit can leave people feeling that the whole process is drawn out, complicated, difficult, and maybe a bit scary. Yet, in actuality, bees are industrious, organized little insects that are more than capable of taking care of themselves when correctly handled by their keeper. So, when approaching beekeeping, think of it more in the vein of caring for fruit-bearing trees than actual livestock, even though bees are (technically) considered livestock.

CHAPTER 5

EQUIPMENT

. . . .

The equipment that you will need for your honeybees and your hives will vary, depending on the size of your apiary, number of hives, and amount of honey being produced. However, there are certain basics that any beekeeper will need, whether you have one hive or fifty.

The basics you will need are:

- Hive components (see Chapter 6)
- Beekeeper's suit
- Smoker
- Hive tool
- Equipment for handling honey

Basic Equipment

As the components that make up a honeybee hive require a more in-depth explanation, hive components will be discussed in Chapter 6. In this chapter, we will be dealing primarily with the tools of beekeeping.

The beekeeper's suit covers the keeper from head to toe. It helps to protect the keeper from the threat of stings. The suit should be white or off-white. Even a cream color will work: not only is white difficult for the honeybee to see, but a dark suit may also end up causing a case of mistaken identity, with you being mistaken for a predator and being attacked.

The **beekeeper's suit** consists of a hat and veil, gloves, and a full-body one-piece suit that covers arms, legs, and torso with sleeves and pant legs that will have Velcro or zippers to keep them tight to the body so the bees cannot get into the suit. Some keepers may also choose to include a pair of work boots.

The veils are mesh and should allow total clear visibility. Those veils that have solid sides can end up obstructing the beekeeper's vision, possibly creating a dangerous situation.

The newer suits are made from a cotton/polyester-blend fabric. It is strong and, although not sting-proof, keeps the beekeeper safe from stings. For the most part, the gloves are made from the same fabric. Not all beekeepers wear gloves, however, as many find it difficult to perform delicate work with

A suited beekeeper at work. Photo courtesy of Wikimedia Commons.

them on. Yet, as a beginner, you may decide to wear the gloves until you learn how to handle your bees and are more comfortable doing so.

You might see pictures in which the beekeepers are wearing no suit at all. While this is entirely possible for an experienced keeper, new or novice beekeepers should wear a suit, at least until they learn their way around their bees, which includes learning proper handling of the bees to minimize stings.

One final thing to remember when wearing your suit is to make sure it fits properly: the arm and leg openings should be tight against the wrist and ankles, with boots over the pants and a well-fitting hat and veil. Again, this is because you do not want bees getting into your sleeves, leggings, and veil areas.

A **smoker** is used to calm the bees so the beekeeper can get in to inspect the hive or gather the honey. Although there is much more to it, basically, the smoke will interrupt the bees' defense response.

A smoker has three parts: the fire pot, the bellows, and a nozzle, which is used to direct the smoke in the right direction. In its most basic terms, think of it as sort of a coffeepot with the bellows attached to it.

The smoker is operated quite easily. Smoldering fuel is placed in the fire pot. The fuel may be pine

A smoker used in beekeeping. Photo courtesy of Robert Engelhardt.

needles, burlap, pulpwood, or corrugated cardboard, although commercial fuel may also be purchased. Bellows, attached to the side of the fire pot, force air through the pot, which, in turn, forces smoke to come out through the nozzle to be directed where the keeper needs. The smoke should not be hot.

There are also newer styles of smokers available, which use heated coils (propane) that produce a smoke fluid, which is said to be less noxious to the bees, as well as using food-grade ingredients. Instead of continual smoke, the beekeeper can even pump the smoke as needed. Which type of smoker is used is up to the beekeeper.

As an interesting aside, it is known that the ancient Egyptians used smokers with their bees. However, their smokers were simply a piece of broken pottery or even a shell holding smoldering cow dung. The beekeeper would then blow the smoke at the hive to where it was needed.

A **hive tool** is simply a little pry bar–type apparatus with a scraper on one end. The hive tool has multiple uses, including removing excess brace comb, scraping propolis from hive parts, loosening hive bodies and frames, and dismantling the hives.

There are many designs of hive tools; however, if the tool is made of stainless steel, it is easier both to clean and sterilize.

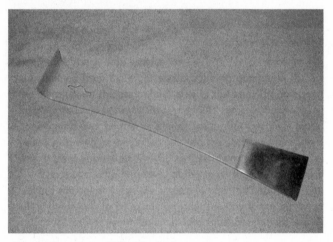

A hive tool. Photo courtesy of Richard Engelhardt.

Equipment for Handling Honey

Finally, we have the equipment for handling the liquid gold, the honey.

The common equipment needed here is:
- Extractor
- Uncapping knife
- Strainers

The **extractor** does just what the name says: it extracts the honey from the uncapped combs. Basically, the drum or bucket of the extractor holds a frame basket where the honey-filled frames sit. The drums spin, and, through centrifugal force, the honey is thrown from the comb. The comb remains in one piece on the frame and may be used again by the bees.

An extractor, with full frames waiting for extraction (in background). Photo courtesy of c-hahn.

There are different types and sizes of extractors, from home versions holding as few as two frames to commercial types holding up to one hundred frames or more. However, extractors can be expensive, so some backyard honeybee-keepers may opt to simply cut the comb out from the frame, and then crush or squeeze the comb to release the honey. Some even do this by hand, although it can be a sticky mess. Yet, on a shoestring budget, it works. The biggest problem with this method is that the comb is destroyed, leaving the bees to have to rebuild it.

It may be possible to borrow or rent an extractor. Check with other beekeepers, clubs, or local organizations, as they may either rent or loan one out themselves, or at least know who does.

An **uncapping knife** cuts the wax caps off the comb before you put the call in for extraction. Most keepers use either a cold knife or electric knife that can warm up. Some may simply use a serrated bread knife.

For ease of cutting, the knife needs to be warm. Electric knives have their own heating element. Otherwise, the knives are dipped into hot water first. However, you must be careful not to get water into the honey, so dry the knife first.

Removing the caps for honey extraction. Photo courtesy of Justin Nussbaum.

Last, but not least, is the **strainer.** You can use either a kitchen strainer or the stainless-steel types sold by beekeeping supply companies. An important piece of equipment, the strainers remove all the wax bits and other impurities that may be floating around in your honey before you package it.

So, in a nutshell, these are the basic pieces of equipment the new beekeeper will need to own or have access to. Of course, there is more to learn about the equipment, and it is certainly necessary to do your homework before making your selections and, ultimately, your purchases. There are wide ranges in cost, quality, and size. As a new beekeeper, you will need to figure out what will work best for you, your bees, and your budget.

CHAPTER 6

HIVES

. . . .

What is the hive? At its most basic level, the hive is a home and workplace for the honeybees, where they will live and raise their young. There are two types of hives: natural and artificial (or manmade).

Natural hives are those that occur naturally in structures where wild honeybees may live. Natural hives may be found in rock cavities and hollow trees. They may also be found in the walls of buildings, usually abandoned buildings. You might also find combs in abandoned cars or even on branches. However, those that are exposed to the elements will not survive in areas of harsh winters and cold temperatures.

Artificial hives are man-made structures, usually wooden-box type, which are designed and built to house honeybees, their young, and their stores of food and honey. At one time, man-made

A reproduction of an old-fashioned bee skep. Photo courtesy of Kim Pezza.

hives were simply round, tall structures made out of coils of straw called "skepts." Today, the artificial or man-made hive will most likely be made of wood and have several parts to it.

The parts are:
- Stand
- Bottom boards
- Hive bodies or supers
- Frame/comb
- Queen excluder
- Inner cover
- Outer cover

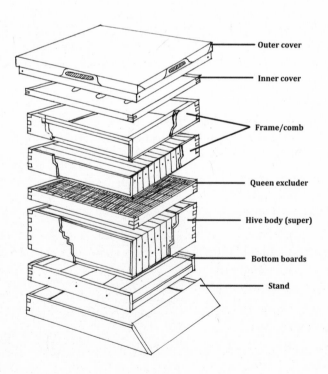

The hive and its parts. Illustration by Ariel Delacriox Dax.

Parts of a Hive

The **stand** is down at the very bottom of the hive. Although it is an optional piece of equipment and is not necessary to the hive, it does provide a landing board for the bees, making it easier for them to get into the hive.

A beehive. Photo courtesy of Imkerei Hartmann.

There are two styles of **bottom boards** to choose from: solid and screened. These are exactly as they sound. The solid bottom board has a solid bottom. You can use it to help keep the hive a bit warmer in areas where the winters may be harsh and cold. However, it does not allow dirt and debris to escape from the hive. Screen bottom boards are covered with a screen bottom instead of solid. These can aid in ventilation, especially in areas with hot summers or climates. You will need only one or the other in your hive. It is best to choose according to your honeybees' needs. Some beekeepers may use a screen bottom in the good weather and swap out to a solid bottom during cold winter months, but, again, it is your choice.

Hive bodies, or supers, are the large boxes that make up the body of the hive. There are two supers for each hive: the deep super and the honey super. The deep super is a large hive box that holds ten frames. The honey super is the box that holds the frames where the bees will store their honey. The deep super frames are made from either wood or plastic. The frames will usually have a wax foundation in the middle, and are used by the bees to build their own wax on. Honey super frames fit in the **honey super** and are also for the bees to use as a base to build on, as with deep super frames.

The super or hive body. Photo courtesy of Wikimedia Commons.

Frames are simply the pieces that slide into the super to allow the bees to build their combs. Think about a really, really simple wooden picture frame, but with a wax sheet where the glass would

Bees resting on one of their frames. Photo courtesy of Wikimedia Commons.

go, and you have the basic idea. Because they slide in and out, it makes for easier removal and allows the beekeeper to check the hives periodically without harming the honeycomb.

The **queen excluder** is a flat rack that has holes large enough for workers to get in and out, but small enough not to allow the queen to get out. Usually made of metal or plastic, it is used to prevent the queen from getting into

Beehive frames. Photo courtesy of Axel HH.

the honey super and lay her eggs in the honey. Although it is not absolutely necessary to have an excluder in your hive, many keepers find it quite helpful.

The **inner cover** of the hive is made of wood angles on the super at the top of the stack. It has two entrance holes: one in the middle, and one to the outside, as well as a winter side and a side for the rest of the year. Basically, it is rim-side down for the winter and rim-side up for the rest of the year.

There are many types of outer covers to choose from, but one of the most popular has a galvanized metal top attached to it. Outer covers are basically ones that go over the inner covers with sides that hang over, providing a snug fit and protection from the weather.

There are also a few other options to consider for your hive. One is an entrance reducer. Entrance reducers are small pieces of wood that fit between the bottom board and first deep super. They make entrance holes smaller, keeping your hive safe from robber bees and controlling the traffic in and out, as well as helping with ventilation and temperature control.

The **slanted wrap**, another option for the hive, helps ventilation and congestion by providing warm room between the entrance and the brood area.

Honeybees at the entrance to a hive. Photo courtesy of Wikimedia Commons.

Besides the standard hive type, which as its name suggests is the most common type of hive that you will probably see both in use and for sale, there are a few other styles/types of beehives. They are not overly common (at least in the United States), so I am just touching on them so you are aware of other hive options. Some beekeepers believe that these are a more natural and bee friendly way to keep their bees.

The alternative hive styles are:
- Warré
- Delon
- Top Bar

Let us now take a brief look at each of the three styles.

Warré

The **Warré** hive was developed in the early 1900s by French monk, Abbé Émile Warré, who was also the author of L'Spiculture Pour Tous ("Beekeeping for All"), a book that is still available today.

The basic concept for the Warré is boxes, but with bars instead of frames (for the bees to build their combs), with the bars having a started strip attached, which allow the honeybees to build their combs. With the Warré, the hive is usually opened only at honey harvest time. This is due to the bees building their comb downward from the top bar. Being that there is no frame, the comb can and, many times, is damaged during opening.

The Warré was initially used in France, Switzerland, and Belgium, with it coming to use in the United States around 2008.

Delon

The **Delon** hive is also known as the Stable-Climate hive. Developed by Roger Delon, who was a commercial beekeeper in France and Switzerland, the hive basically reconfigures a Warré and is based on a hollow tree.

Top Bar

The **Top Bar** hive is a very basic hive style (probably one of the most basic). The box is in the shape of an inverted triangle with legs and a cover (looking like a wooden feed trough). There are bars running across the top, allowing the bees to attach and hang their combs (again, no frames). It should be noted that this style is best suited for tropical and temperate climates.

The early Top Bars of Ancient Greece are thought to have had

Ancient Greek Top Bar beehive. Photo courtesy of Wikimedia Commons.

an even more basic setup: baskets with bars across the top. The concept is thought to be thousands of years old.

As the Top Bar hives have no frames, the honey cannot be removed from the comb with an extruder (this would apply to the Warré and Delon as well). However, the nonbrooder combs (which we discussed in Chapter 3) may be used as cut-comb honey (basically, a cut honeycomb), which can be highly prized, or you can actually squeeze the honey from the comb with your hands.

So, in a nutshell, these are the three other alternatives that you have available to hive you bees. If you are seriously considering one of these hives, it is strongly advisable to do your homework before you jump in. If you are able to, go online and find beekeepers that actually use or have used the style that you are interested in. If you cannot get online, the local extension office should be able to tell you about beekeepers in your area, as well as beekeeping organizations in your area, region, or state. Ask about the pros and cons, areas that the hive is best used in, ease of use, safety issues (for both you and your bees), and any honey-production issues. (Remember that, even if you are not harvesting honey, your bees still need it to sustain themselves.)

You may be able to purchase these three hives, but you can build them as well. (I have included websites that have plans for building your own hives in the "Resources" section.) Keep in mind that, whatever style/type of hive that you decide to use, make sure that it is the best one for both you and your bees.

Setting Up Your Hive

Whatever you choose for your hive, it is important to keep your hive up off the ground. This is easily done by setting the hive on cinder blocks with boards running across them (to stabilize the hive on the block).

Another important step in hive construction is to give the hive's wood extra protection from the elements. Most keepers will paint them. Make sure to only paint the exposed outside areas, however. The bees will take care of the inside by covering it with a plant, sap, and wax mixture of their own making called propolis.

Finally, when the hive is done, you need to find the right spot for it. It should be away from roads or pathways when possible. This will help to prevent your bees from being bothered by too much human and pet foot traffic, which would result in them becoming grumpy and on the defensive.

The ideal placement should also feature limited exposure to wind, have a water source nearby for the bees, and be in an area of good drainage. It should be level, have some sort of wind block (especially if you are in an area of cold and snowy winters), and have a good balance of sun and shade. More sun is preferable than more shade if you cannot find the "perfect" spot, as your bees will slow down if it is too cool and shady.

Do not worry if you cannot account for all of these conditions when placing your hive. Yet do remember one thing: be sure to allow easy access for yourself. For the other steps, do what you can, but things like sun and a dry area are important to your hive, as is the water source (which you may have to create yourself if there are no natural sources nearby).

Establishing a Colony

Now that you have built and placed your hive, it is time to establish a colony in it. There are a few ways to obtain a colony: buy one, have one given to you, or catch a swarm and establish it in your hive. It is most likely that you will purchase your first colony.

If you would rather not purchase your first colony, the other common option is to attract a natural swarm. Swarming is when a group of bees will leave the hive due to it becoming too crowded. Sometimes, the swarm is started by the queen, but it is usually a decision of the workers. The swarm is actually the formation of a new colony, breaking off from the old.

Although intimidating in appearance, honeybee swarms are usually quite docile during this initial period, due mainly to the fact that they are concentrating on finding a new home and having no young to protect. Even so, should a swarm feel threatened or endangered, it may become aggressive.

Swarms can usually be seen hanging off of a tree branch. The honeybees may remain there for a few days until they find their new home. **Swarming** can leave honeybees quite vulnerable, since the only food that they have is what they were able to bring with them in their stomachs, and, if a suitable home is not found quickly, the bees will starve. Again, it is up to the scout to find the perfect location and persuade the rest of the colony to follow.

Some experienced beekeepers see a swarm as an opportunity to add another hive to their apiary. In fact, a successful capture of a swarm is fairly commonplace.

Swarms may be caught by simply capturing them in a box called a nuc. Swarm traps are also available, or the swarm may be sprayed with a sugar solution, and then shaken off its branch onto a white sheet with the nuc sitting on it. The bees will see the nuc opening and walk in. This works best on a sunny day. Some keepers will also collect swarms using suction pumps.

Due to the fact that it is best for only experienced beekeepers to catch swarms, capture methods have been touched on here only briefly. Should you find a swarm that you want to start a hive with, you should have an experienced person with you to do the capture. This is not only for your safety, but for the bees' safety as well.

A swarm of bees. Photo courtesy of Wikimedia Commons.

For the beginning beekeeper, it is best to purchase your bees from a reputable dealer or keeper in your area, some of whom may have a hive available for purchase. The best way to deal with your purchased bees and get them into the hive would be to follow the directions that *should* have been sent with the bees. If you believe that you will still have a problem, it could help to contact another beekeeper who would be able to either transfer the bees into the hive for you or guide you through the process yourself. Although you may be charged for the assistance you are being given, remember that a few dollars out of pocket at the outset beats losing all your bees because you did not do it properly.

CHAPTER 7

POLLINATION

· ·

Honeybees are important pollinators. They are responsible for pollinating approximately 80 percent of the crops in the United States, a value of anywhere between $10 billion and $15 billion a year.

So what exactly is pollination? Pollination is the movement of the pollen from the anther (male) to the stigma (female) of a plant or flower.

Pollination. Illustration by Ariel Delacriox Dax.

Plants need pollination for a variety of reasons. Some plants have separate male flowers and female flowers, so the pollen needs to go from flower to flower. Sometimes, a single flower can have both the stigma and anther, but it is unable to self-pollinate. Other times, pollen needs to go from an older plant to a younger one, as the stigma of the other plant is ready before its pollen is released. Still, other plants (or trees) have specific male and female plants, meaning the plant is either totally male or female. In all these cases, pollination from a bee, bird, or even a bat is necessary, as, unless the pollen is light and can travel on the wind or water, it needs help to do the job.

It is interesting to point out that some plants, such as blueberries and cherries, rely almost entirely on honeybees for pollination. Other plants, like almonds, do depend entirely on the honeybee for their pollination needs.

Although other insects and birds do pollinate, as do some bats, honeybees are the superior pollinators; unlike the others, which really happen to get into the pollen only while feeding on the nectar, which is what they really want, the honeybee looks for the pollen as well as the nectar, as it needs both in order to feed its larvae and itself. In other words, while other pollinators might find pollen, honeybees actively pursue it. They prefer plants that are close to the hive, but will travel.

Although the honeybee is the only pollinator used commercially for pollination (by transporting hives to orchards and crop areas all over the country), much of the pollination is still done naturally, meaning no hives on-site, with the bees just finding the spots on their own.

There is much more to pollination, and, as a serious beekeeper, you will need to learn more. Yet, for now, we are just stating the obvious. Honeybees are very important in the production of a large portion of our food.

CHAPTER 8

HONEY AND WAX HARVEST

· ·

We have been discussing the honeybee and the honey they produce throughout this book. Yet what exactly is honey? We have touched on it a bit, but there is much more to the story.

First, let us get a little history on honey.

Bees have been producing honey for 150 million years. In fact, during at least one period in history, honey had quite a value. During these times, honey was occasionally even more valuable than the currency of the time.

The ancient Egyptians, themselves innovative beekeepers, used honey for, among other things, embalming. The pharaohs even valued it to the point where honey was placed in their tombs. Many tombs also have drawings and paintings of the honeybee.

Honey was also an important food in ancient Greece, and Spain has cave paintings of bees and beekeeping from as far back as 7000 B.C.E., making them the earliest known records of beekeeping.

In Germany during the eleventh century, peasants paid their feudal lords in honey and beeswax, and, in much of Europe, it was not until the Renaissance (when sugar made its appearance) that honey lost its importance. By the late seventeenth century, honey was overtaken by sugar in use.

So what exactly is honey, this food that was so valuable in ancient times?

To quickly review the information touched on in Chapter 4, honey is produced when the forager bees gather nectar; the nectar goes into the bees' second stomachs, or honey stomachs, where it thickens. The foragers then return to the hive, where the thickened nectar is deposited into a cell. There, more water evaporation takes place, where it turns into the end product, honey.

The honey not only contains sugars, minerals, amino acids, vitamins, and antioxidants, but it is also the only food that includes everything necessary to sustain life, including water. It is the only food that never spoils, as bacteria cannot grow in honey. If stored, honey will crystallize (meaning it gets sugary looking); however, simply reheating it will restore it to its previous form. In fact, when some honey was discovered in the tombs of pharaohs, it was found to still be edible when tasted by archaeologists.

Yet remember that the honeybees are actually producing this incredible foodstuff for their own food stores. For them, their honey provides 80 percent of the sugars and 20 percent of the water, minerals, and other nutrients that are necessary for their survival. So, as a responsible beekeeper, you need to be very careful as to how much honey you remove from your hives each year.

Not to mention that it also takes a lot of work on the bees' part to create the honey. In fact, a single bee will produce only one twelfth of a teaspoon of honey in her brief, but busy lifetime; and it takes the pollen from about two million flowers to make a single pound of honey.

Types of Honey

There are many types of honey, and the type of honey you get depends on where your bees are getting their nectar from. In other words, if the bees feed on orange blossoms, you would have orange-blossom honey. If they are around clover fields, you get clover honey. If they feed from buckwheat fields, they will produce buckwheat honey, and so on. Wildflower honey would be honey made from various wildflower sources. In some honeys, these nectars and flavors may be blended as well. The color of the honey ranges from very light to very dark, with the flavor also depending on the nectar source.

Many consumers will ask if the honey is organic. While some areas do certify that their honey is organic, it is not the norm for the industry. It is very difficult to be sure that the honey that the bees produce is organic, for the simple reason that you do not know for sure where your bees have sourced their nectar and pollen. Even though you may have your hives in an organic orchard, for example, what if a few bees ventured away from the orchard to a neighbor's fruit tree in his yard? Or another orchard a mile away, which may or may not be organic itself? As a result, few organic-certification organizations will certify honey as organic.

As a consumer, there are a few different ways that you can purchase honey. There is liquid honey, which is the most common form of honey there is. Liquid honey is what you normally see for sale in jars or little squeeze bears. Then there is granulated or crystallized honey, which has a sugary look to it. Creamed honey is liquid honey with finely crystallized honey added to it, while cut-comb honey is pieces of honey-filled comb, usually cut and sold in squares and, occasionally, rounded shapes. Finally, there is chunk honey, which is simply chunks of comb in a container of honey.

Many commercial honeys found in grocery stores have had the pollen filtered out. That leaves only the nectar, and although it is all natural from the honeybee, it is not considered real honey. Also note that, unless your store-bought honey says 100-percent organic, raw, or natural, you risk having corn syrup or high-fructose corn syrup mixed in. (In fact, imported Chinese honey can be up to 40 percent corn syrup.)

Beeswax

When talking about honey, we cannot forget the all-important comb or beeswax. As discussed in Chapter 4, the wax is used to build the comb, and the combs are used to rear the young and store the honey and pollen. It takes about 10 pounds of honey to produce one pound of wax. Of course, the wax is produced by the worker bee. In brief, wax scales

Location of wax glands on bee's anatomy. Illustration by Ariel Delacriox Dax.

are secreted from the eight wax-producing glands on the inner side of the sternites on the abdominal area of the bee. The temperature in the hive needs to be between 91°F and 97°F for secretion to take place. The honeycomb wax begins as almost white, but becomes more and more yellow or brown as the pollen oils and the propolis incorporates with the wax. It takes approximately 1,000 scales to produce one gram of beeswax.

The wax can be harvested at the same time as the honey. If you are leaving the columns on the frames to use, the cappings that are cut to allow the honey to be extracted from the comb can be saved, cleaned, and processed. If using the crush-and-squeeze method, then the comb is rendered unusable to the bees, but the wax can still be saved and used by the beekeeper.

In brief, to claim the wax (but not the cell), separate the wax from the honey, but let the wax cool and harden. Re-melt and strain the wax of any impurities, and allow it to harden.

Although extraction was discussed in Chapter 5, some may decide that they want to harvest the entire comb instead of just the honey from the frame. This would be to produce cut-comb honey.

Cut-comb honey is just the comb taken from the frame, then cut into pieces (usually squares) and packaged. It is honey in its truest, most natural, and basic form, as there is no other processing involved.

Finally, there is one little tip that can help in the honey harvest. Simply put, raise gentle bees. Gentle bees are easier to work with, especially at harvest time. There is what is called a "gentleness test": basically, the gentleness test is how the bees react when the hive is opened and the brood nest is exposed. If the bees are "gentle," they should pretty much ignore the entire situation. An aggressive hive, on the other hand, may attack. In fact, the website, www.coloss.org, has a 1-4 gentleness scale chart, which may be helpful in determining where your particular colonies may stand.

You will probably find that your bees have better manners during certain times of the day or certain weather situations. For example, you may find them to be more defensive later in the day, but gentler when the weather is warmer. Just remember that the gentler your bees, the easier your job will be, whether it is during harvest time or just through general care and maintenance of your hives and colony.

CHAPTER 9

HONEY AND WAX USES AND STORAGE

oney has many varied uses, not only in the culinary world, but in the medicinal sphere as well. Let us look briefly at the medicinal side of honey first. Remember that, as you review, this is only a short outline. You should do your own in-depth research on honey for medicinal use and speak with a doctor or other medical professional as necessary.

Honey as Medicine

The medicinal use of honey dates back as far as the ancient Egyptians, who used it to dress wounds. Aristotle recommended using honey for a number of different ailments, and Hippocrates also touted the use of honey not only for wound dressing, but to ease sore throats as well. It is still considered a good remedy for soothing sore throats and coughs today.

Presently, a great number of people turn to honey as a medicine, as it is said to speed healing, combat infection (due to the fact that it can inhibit bacteria growth), stimulate skin regrowth (on a wound), and, as a result, reduce scarring, as well as help control stomach discomfort due to the ability to fight bacteria in the intestine.

In short, honey:

- Is an effective antibiotic
- Cleans infection
- Reduces pain, inflammation, and swelling
- Encourages fast healing, resulting in minimal scarring
- Prevents bandages from sticking to wounds
- Reduces pain from burns by acting as a barricade and protecting air from hitting the burned skin

It should also be noted that the darker the honey is, the better it will serve as an antioxidant and antibacterial remedy. The darker the honey, the less water it contains. Buckwheat honey, in particular, bears mention as being high in antioxidants.

It is also said that some diabetics may be able to use honey. However, this is still quite controversial and must be considered only upon consultation with a doctor.

Again, this has been only a brief look at honey as medicine. Although most of the uses have been tried and utilized for centuries, I have not included enough information for anyone to just start medicating themselves with honey. You will need to do your homework, as well as check with your doctor, before trying unfamiliar remedies.

Storing Honey

Storing honey is neither difficult nor time consuming, and it can be stored indefinitely if stored properly. Although it should be kept in a cool area for long-term storage, honey needs no refrigeration, and, in fact, should not be refrigerated.

Honey should be kept in a tightly capped container (as it can absorb moisture) at temperatures ranging from 65°F to 75°F (basically, room temperature), and should be kept away from stoves, ovens, and sunlight. Again, should the honey crystallize,

Royal Jelly

Royal jelly is another by-product of the bees. Used since ancient times for both medicinal and cosmetic purposes, royal jelly is rich in protein, vitamins, fats, and minerals. Today, it is sold as a dietary supplement, and, so far, cannot be made synthetically.

While the ancient Chinese used royal jelly as an aphrodisiac, the ancient Egyptian pharaohs believed that it would keep their bodies young and beautiful in both life and death. Like honey, royal jelly was also used in mummification. Today, royal jelly is used to treat a number of symptoms and ailments, including asthma, insomnia, hay fever, symptoms of menopause, and even some skin problems.

Royal jelly may be purchased in many forms, and is available commercially in tablets or capsules, powder, or freshly frozen in its natural state, with most agreeing that the latter is the best way to purchase whenever possible.

There are a number of ways to consume royal jelly; the "Resources" section of this book offers a link to an excellent website that suggests how to use royal jelly properly, written in a straightforward, easy-to-understand manner.

It must be said that royal jelly can be expensive, as it is so time-consuming to harvest. Also, unlike honey, royal jelly is perishable in its natural state, requiring immediate refrigeration or freezing upon harvest.

It is important to note too that some people may have an allergic reaction to royal jelly. You should be especially careful if you are already known to have an allergy to honey or bee stings. If ever in doubt, consult a doctor before consuming.

Although the benefits of royal jelly are questioned today, one has to wonder why, if it has no benefits, royal jelly has been in use since ancient times.

simply place the jar in a pot of water, gently heat, and stir. Do not overheat, as overheating may caramelize the sugar and even change the color and flavor of the honey. Why can you get crystallization in honey? A few reasons are cold temperatures as well as raw honey with a high pollen count.

So, if your bees present you with a lot of honey, or you have even purchased in bulk from a local apiary, do not worry. As you can see, honey is easy to keep.

Beeswax

Some keepers will also prepare and use the wax after the honey has been removed. Although it is a process, and some keepers choose either to allow the bees to keep their combs after the honey has been removed from the frames or simply give the wax away or discard it, others will clean it for later use.

Some beekeepers will melt the wax in a pot in a low-temperature oven. As the wax melts, the honey and debris will drop to the bottom, while the wax will rise to the top for skimming.

Another, more popular method is to drop the comb in a pot of water. The water is allowed to come to a boil, melting the wax. The wax will rise to the top, while any debris or bits of leftover honey will sink to the bottom.

The pot is then removed from the heat and allowed to cool just long enough so the wax may be handled without you getting burned. The wax is placed into a double boiler and remelted, at which time any remaining debris may be removed (some people will also put it through a strainer to catch more debris). The wax is then poured into a mold (usually a square or rectangular block mold), allowed to harden, removed from the mold, and stored in a cool, dry place until ready to use.

Beeswax may be used for cosmetics, crafts, ornaments, batik, and candles, and can even be rubbed onto thread to give it some strength. However, when using beeswax for cosmetics, check with the beekeeper (if not using wax from your own bees) to make sure that no chemicals were used with the bees, as these can sometimes get into the wax and may be harmful to humans.

Finally, when melting beeswax, no matter what you are melting it for, it should be noted that, while the beeswax will not boil, it can catch fire. This can be somewhat avoided by not melting the wax in a pan (unless it has water in it) or simply melting the wax in a double boiler.

As you can see, there are many different ways to utilize beeswax. Use your imagination and have fun trying out different uses for your very own farm-fresh beeswax.

CHAPTER 10

DISEASES AND DANGERS

L ike any animal or insect, honeybees can become ill through parasites and diseases. Even under the best circumstances, your hive is always at risk of diseases and parasites being introduced. There are a number of diseases and parasites that pose danger to honeybee colonies that anyone considering beekeeping should be aware of.

Robber Bees

We have discussed things that can affect the health of your hive: diseases, parasites, loss of the queen, starvation, and so on. However, one obstacle not mentioned is your hive being burglarized by the last people that you would expect: other honeybees.

The aptly named **robber bees** usually come about during hard times food-wise. Bees from one hive will come and steal the stores of another hive. A robber bee finds hives by scent and goes back to its colony. Then they get together and go back to steal the stores of the other colony.

After the scout robber finds a target hive, it will look for an unprotected entrance and weak spots among the guards. Once it has found that, it will return to its home and send others to come and steal the honey.

Sometimes, the worker bees will be able to fight off the robber bees. Other times, the robber bees can decimate a hive, as they will continue to return until the honey is gone. In fact, should the robber bees attack in groups, especially when a hive is weak, the invaders can overwhelm the entire colony, resulting in many deaths and, in extreme cases, even the killing of the queen. Robber bees will leave the victim hive or hives to starve to death.

Compounding the problem is the threat of foreign infection. Robber bees can also spread disease, and not only to the victim hives. If one of your hives turns robber (due to insufficient food stores) and goes to another hive in an apiary that has a disease problem, it will bring that disease back to the hive. Likewise, if your healthy hive is invaded by diseased robber bees from another apiary, they can spread the disease to your hive. At the same time, if your hive is diseased, the robber bee that invades it will take the disease back to their apiary and hive.

There are ways to protect your hives from robbers and prevent your own bees from becoming robbers. Keep the entrance to the hive small. Make sure that your hive/colony is strong and healthy. The stronger and healthier it is, the better your bees can defend themselves. Finally, to prevent your own bees from becoming robbers, make sure that your colonies always have enough food. In lean foraging times, this may mean providing supplements and substitutes for your bees to eat. It may also mean not taking honey for yourself so your bees have enough to sustain themselves throughout the winter.

Whether it is your bees turning robber or you are invaded by bees from another apiary, robber bees are something that you do not want or need around your hives or colonies.

Parasites

Varroa Mites

Varroa mites feed on the bodily fluids of the honeybees in every stage of life: larval, pupal, and adult. Seen on the bee as a small red or brown spot on the thorax (and visible by the eye), the varroa mite carries a virus that causes noticeably deformed wings on the honeybee.

While the varroa mite is admittedly more of a problem during the winter preparation time or in times of poor foraging (both of which are periods of low colony population), it can be a serious threat to your hives. The varroa mite has almost eliminated whole colonies in some areas, as well as causing problems in apiaries, although, in some of these places, the bees are recovering and making a comeback. It is also thought that the varroa mite may be a contributing cause of colony collapse disorder, which is further discussed in Chapter 13.

A varroa mite. Photo courtesy of Wikimedia Commons.

Fortunately, there are treatments available for honeybees against the varroa mite. Some treatments are chemical based, while others are mechanical or manual treatments.

The substances used in chemical treatments include formic acid, oxalic acid, fluvalinate, thymol, and coumaphos. Although it is said that these chemicals should not cause any problems with the honeybees, they are not to be used during the time that honey is being produced when intended for marketing or consumption.

Mechanical or manual treatments of the varroa mite include drone-brood sacrifice, which is the elimination of the brood. Powdered-sugar dusting of the bees is also said to work, as it encourages the bees to clean themselves, leading them to dislodge some of the mites. Screen bottom boards on the hive are also recommended when using this technique, as it allows dislodged mites to fall through the cracks instead of into the hive.

These are not the only treatments available for a hive dealing with varroa mites, but they are the most commonly used. However, there are a variety of resources available to the novice beekeeper for treating this and other infestations. You should always seek the treatment method that is best for you, your bees, and your hive.

Acarine Mites

Believed to have come to the United States through Mexico, **acarine mites** (also known as tracheal mites) infest the airways of the honeybee. The mature female mite will then make her way out of the bee's airway and out onto the bee's hair. At that point, it waits to transfer to young bees, where it will again infest the airway and begin to lay eggs.

Acarine mites almost wiped out the British Isles' bee population in the early twentieth century. As a result, the Buckfast bee was developed at Buckfast Abbey.

Treatment for the acarine mites can be pretty simple through the use of grease patties. Grease patties are one part vegetable shortening combined with three to four parts of powdered sugar. The patties are then placed on top of the bars of the hive's outer cover.

The bees will then nibble at the little cakes, and, when they do, the shortening makes it almost impossible for the mites to infest the young bees. This, in turn, causes some of the mites to die before they are able to locate a young bee and reproduce, as a young bee is necessary for the mites' reproduction process.

Wax Moths

The **wax moth** feeds on the wax of the honeycomb, used brood cells, and cell cleanings, all of which contain essential proteins for the development of the wax moth larvae. This destruction of the honeycomb may cause stored honey to spoil and/or become contaminated. It can also kill the honeybee larvae.

The wax moth will spread rapidly at high temperatures, usually at 90°F and above. However, in regions where this type of temperature occurs only occasionally, the hive will experience few problems with the wax moth (unless it is already a weak bee colony).

There are a few treatments for hives troubled by the wax moth. Two of the most common methods are strong hives taking care of the problem itself, with the honeybees killing and cleaning out the wax moth larvae and the webs that the larvae create to move around on and then leave behind. The second treatment takes advantage of the fact that the wax moth can be killed by freezing. So, in colder climates, hive storage in unheated sheds, barns, or outdoors could also work as a treatment.

However, with all that said, the stronger your colony is, the more that it will be able to protect itself from the wax moth.

Small Hive Beetles

The **small hive beetle** is a small, dark beetle that lives inside the hive; it is a scavenger of weak hives/colonies. The small hive beetle will cause considerable damage within the hive by tunneling through combs, ruining the combs, and killing the brood. The beetles can even contaminate the honey, rendering it unsalable by the keeper at market and unpalatable to the honeybees themselves, leaving it useless to all involved.

Thankfully, controlling the small hive beetle is not a complicated matter. The larvae may be trapped as they try to get down to the soil. Alternatively, the soil in front of the infected hives may be safely treated with predatory soil nematodes.

Nematodes are nonsegmented worms, usually one-five hundredth of an inch in diameter and one-twentieth of an inch long. They are also called roundworms. These nematodes will attack the hive beetle larvae.

Cleanliness will also play a part in controlling small hive beetles. Do not leave your cappings exposed and do not leave filled supers standing. As a side note, if you have fire ants, they may also pray on the pupating beetles.

Fungal Infestations

Yet another problem that the colony/hive may have to deal with at some point is fungal infestations. Two examples of this problem are nosema and chalk brood.

Nosema

Now considered a fungus rather than a parasite, **nosema** is a unicellular fungus that gets into the intestinal tract of the adult honeybee. Nosema reproduces by forming spores, which are then passed and spread in the bees' waste. As a result, the bees can run into their biggest problems when dealing with nosema in those circumstances in which they are unable to eliminate waste from the hive. They can then develop dysentery.

There are two species of nosema: *ceranae* and *apis*. Nosema ceranae can cause the rapid decline of the colony's population, can affect the hive at any time of the year, and, worst of all, has no observable symptoms.

Nosema apis is the biggest problem in spring and winter. However, heavy summer rainfall can also contribute to the problem. It is also the most common and widespread of the two variants, and has the ability to wipe out entire colonies.

In its dormant stage, *Nosema apis* is long lived, as well as being resistant to extreme temperatures and dehydration. A common sign of an infected hive or colony is unusual feces on the outside of the hive; on the inside, the most noticeable symptom is combs covered with brown freckles.

Treatment of nosema (both varieties) include increasing ventilation in the hive as well as treating with Fumagilen B, which renders nosema unable to attach to the cells in the honeybee gut, therefore leaving the fungus unable to reproduce.

Treatment for the apis strain also includes thoroughly cleaning the hive and removing any contaminated combs. Also, although cold does nothing to kill *Nosema apis*, heat treatment of the infected hives for 24 hours will.

Two more treatment options are transferring all bees in the infected hive into a clean hive and re-queening whenever necessary. This can be done even by beginner beekeepers, but, if you are hesitant, contact your local beekeeping association or extension office to ask for some guidance from an experienced beekeeper.

Prevention of nosema includes reducing stress in the hive, removing any contaminated frames, relocating the hive to warmer, dryer locations, rotating hive sites, re-queening as necessary to help keep the hive strong, and, finally, good hygiene of both the beekeeper and the equipment.

It may also be worthwhile to note that the Caucasian bee types may be less resistant to nosema than other types of honeybees.

Ascosphaera apis (Chalk Brood)

Another fungal problem that colonies may face is chalk brood, or **Ascosphaera apis.**

Chalk brood infests the gut of the honeybee larva. There, it competes with the larva for food, where it then causes the larva to starve. After the honeybee larva dies, it will then be devoured and appear white and chalky, hence the name chalk brood. It also causes mummification of the brood.

Chalk brood will rarely kill an entire colony, but can

substantially weaken it. Hives can usually recover if ventilation in the hive is increased.

As with other problems that can affect your hive or colony, stress can contribute to the problem. Broad temperature changes may trigger the problem as well. A damp or rainy spring is a common cause of chalk brood.

Treatment and prevention of chalk brood are pretty straightforward and include destroying infected combs and making sure that equipment is clean before use, between hives, and after use. You may also find that you will need to re-queen.

Bacteria

Bacterial problems can also plague your hives. A few of the more common bacterial problems are as follows.

American foul brood is caused by the larvae of a spore-forming subspecies of *Paenibacillus*. It is the most widespread and destructive of the existing bee brood diseases.

Young honeybee larvae that are less than 24 hours old are the most susceptible to the infection, but larvae up to three days old can remain at risk of infection through the ingestion of spores in their food. However, the spores will die in larvae that are over three days old in age.

Infected honeybee larvae will die after being sealed in their cell by nurse drones. Also, although the vegetative form of the bacteria will die with it, it will first produce millions of spores, with each dead honeybee larva containing up to 100 million spores. Although these bacteria affect only the honeybee larvae, they can be deadly to the entire brood.

Unfortunately the Paenibacillus larvae are visible only under a high-powered microscope; however, the method of treatment response is pretty straightforward with the shook-swarm method. The shook-swarm method is simply shaking the adult bees from an old set of frames into a new hive. Originally used as a way to control swarming, the shook-swarm method can also be used to replace a brood comb in order to reduce an existing problem with disease or reduce the risk of disease.

European foul brood *(Melissococcus plutonis)* is a bacteria that infects the midgut area of the honeybee larvae. European foul brood is much less deadly to a colony or hive than the American foul brood. However, though it does not form spores as the American variant does, the European brood *can* survive the winter.

European foul brood is often considered a stress-related disease, meaning that it would usually be dangerous only to an already stressed hive, one which is either undergoing a preexisting infection or struggling to find adequate food resources. A healthy hive will usually survive its encounter with the bacteria.

Symptoms of European foul brood include dead and/or dying larvae that will appear as they are curled upward with a brown, yellow, melted, or deflated look. The tracheal tubes may also be dried and rubbery.

As with American foul brood, the best treatment for European foul brood is the shook-swarm method, followed by thoroughly cleaning the old hive.

A final example is stone brood. **Stone brood** is a bee brood disease caused by the fungi *Aspergillus flavus, Aspergillus fumi gatus*, and *Aspergillus niger*. Stone brood affects both sealed and unsealed broods. Although it is rare and not as serious as other brood diseases, it should be noted that this fungi can also cause respiratory disease, not only in other animals, but in humans as well.

It can be difficult to identify stone brood when the fungi are in their early stages, but (unfortunately) the fungi are rapid growers. They will then show a whitish-yellow ring near the head of the infected larvae. The larvae may also be covered in yellow-green, gray-green, or black, powderlike spores, with the color of the spores depending on which of the strains that you are dealing with. They cause mummification of the brood, and the spores can overrun and fill the cells that contain the infected larvae.

Spores are common on moldy hay, as well as being present in soil. The spores can also spread through foodstuffs, contaminated equipment, by robber bees, and swarming. Both robber bees and swarming can carry spores from place to place.

Checking for evidence of stone brood basically requires examining brood frames and floor debris, again, using shook-swarm. As the bees are gently shaken from the frame, it is easier to spot the problems. Mummies can be spotted easily, and may even fall out of their cells. Adult bees may tear the cappings off the dead larvae's cells as well.

Although treatment is nonspecific, increased ventilation and re-queening are two options. Proper management is also a great help. Similar to chalk brood, good practices include cleanliness (a stone brood can spread by using contaminated equipment), having the hives in a warm, dry location, and having strong colonies. It is also a good idea to remove any mummies and destroy combs with large numbers of mummies in them.

In the end, there are a number of diseases and parasites that can affect the colony or hive. While this discussion touches on only a few, it is a good idea for new beekeepers to try and familiarize themselves with those most common within their areas and regions.

Predators

As with any other livestock, there are also other predators that can go after a colony or hive. Although the worst predator that the honeybee can face is the aforementioned parasite, the varroa mite, insects, spiders, reptiles, amphibians, birds, and some mammals can also pose a threat to honeybee colonies and hives.

The following are a few examples of threats that prey on the honeybee. Although we will not get as in depth as with diseases and parasites, this will give you a good idea of a few of the common predators that you may face with your bees. Some may be difficult to prepare for, while others may have simple, common sense solutions.

Wasps and hornets can be difficult to control, and the results of their preying on honeybees are significant.

In tropical areas, **ants** can destroy entire colonies, and their work can be quick. In trying to get a handle on these predators, it is suggested that you visit local extension offices or even pest-control companies so you can review your particular situation, and they can give you the safest way to remove the threat from your bees.

Frogs, toads, and lizards can also be problems for your hives, although their potential for damage is minimal compared to others. The threat can be easily eliminated, or at least reduced, by simply eliminating standing boards from the hives.

There are some mammals that will also prey on your hives. The two most common predators that will be briefly touched on are skunks and bears.

Bears can tear hives apart. Contrary to popular (and storybook) belief, the bears are actually going after the fat and protein rich pupae, larvae, and eggs in the brood comb and not the honey, although they will eat the honey. Also, the bears do get stung in the process, but, when they are done, they will shake the bees off as they walk away from their mess.

While your fencing may be able to help some, it is still a good idea not to keep hives at the edges of woods, especially when bears are known to live in your area. Although it will not totally prevent bears from invading your hives, they may be less likely to come after your bees if they are away from the woods.

Another mammal that preys on honeybees and is even more common than the bear is the skunk. **Skunks** can destroy an entire hive in only a few nights.

A skunk will approach the hive and scratch on the front of

it. In turn, the workers that are on guard duty will come out and check to see what is going on. As soon as a few guards step out, the skunk will devour them. As each wave of guards comes out to check, they will be caught and devoured as well. If the skunk finds the hive easy pickings (if the placement of your hive is easy to reach without being too close to human habitations), it will continue to come back to the hive until it has emptied the hive of the bees. Then, when the bees are gone, the skunk will go after the honey, wax, and pollen if it can find its way into the hive without too much difficulty.

Fencing will go a long way to keep out a skunk. Chicken wire will work well. Choose some that will be strong gauge, but with small openings, like one and a half to two inches. As skunks will dig, any fencing should be sunk at least eight to twelve inches down, or they may dig under the fence and get to your hives anyway.

This has been just a brief overview as to what can go after your bees and how to take care of (or at least control) the problems, keeping your bees and honey safe.

CHAPTER 11

A YEAR IN BEEKEEPING

······························

One more element to consider when determining the ease with which you can keep your honeybees is the seasons. Whether you live in a cold, cool, or tropical climate, there will be seasonal weather issues.

On the whole, weather conditions can both help and hinder your beekeeping efforts, even to the point of encouraging or killing parasites and disease. Now, let us look a little further at the seasons and how they can affect the colonies and beehives.

Winter

Winter is the hardest time of the year for your bees and is the time when they can suffer the most losses. Bees can even get hypothermia. While the season, with its cold temperatures, snow, and ice (in many areas), can take its toll on a hive, many problems are also due to the mistakes of the beekeeper.

One major mistake the beekeeper can make is not leaving the bees enough honey to sustain them throughout the winter. Although we have discussed that supplemental food may be left for the bees, the irrefutable truth is that there is nothing better for your hive than its own honey, especially in the winter. The number to remember is that between 60 and 80 pounds of honey left in the hive should suffice (some even say up to 90 pounds).

Another problem that can cause harm to your bees is bad ventilation in the hive. Warm air from the hive meeting the cold surface of the hive's roof forms ice, which, in turn, melts back into water as it warms up. The water then drips back into the hive, creating a wet hive. While the installation of a top hive entrance will usually solve this problem, the hive still needs proper ventilation regardless.

Still another problem is failing to check for parasites and diseases in the fall. Left unchecked, this can cause a weak hive, resulting in further problems within the hive and colony in the spring.

After you have done your checks, cover hives if necessary. (This will depend on the region you are in. It will not be necessary in tropical or temperate areas, where severe winters are mild or nonexistent.)

As a brief note on honeybee characteristics, it is worth mentioning that bees do not hibernate for the winter. They cluster in the hive. Generating heat by vibrating their wing muscles (without moving their wings), the bees cluster to keep warm. If there is a brood in the hive, the adult bees will cluster around it, keeping the brood warm as well. During this time, any drones left will be forced out to conserve food. While the honeybees will normally retreat to their hives for the winter, do not be surprised if you see some out flying around on unusually warm winter days.

Spring

Spring can be unpredictable because, at this time, especially in early spring, the weather and temperature are still changing frequently and unpredictably. However, it is also the time to perform a few necessary chores with the hive.

Spring can be a good time to split your hives. Splitting the hive will reduce the colony size and will hopefully discourage swarming due to lack of space. Splitting also helps with mite control, as it gives the beekeeper the chance to do a hive inspection. It also allows an increase in the number of hives for honey production. Also, depending on how much honey is left in the stores, and depending on where you are, you may need to offer your colony supplemental food until the pollen and nectar are once again fully accessible to the honeybees.

As far as splitting a hive, it is basically like splitting a plant. When you have too many plants in a pot, you need to remove some and put them in a new pot. In much the same way, when your hives begin to get overcrowded, it is to the benefit of beekeepers and their bees to split the hive. Do not forget that you will also need to queen the new hive.

Summer

With summer and its hot, hot days, the colony will need and use a lot of water: an average of a quart to a gallon of water per day, depending on temperature and hive size.

While the bees may find water for themselves in nearby lakes, ponds, rivers, springs, and even in temporary puddles, you may also want to create water sources for them by leaving water dishes near the hive or in the garden. Do not forget to add something for the bees to stand on so they cannot drown. If you have a soaker hose going in your garden, I have found that the bees will use this as a water source as well. It actually works perfectly for them.

Ventilation is also very important in the hives. Screen bottom boards and ventilation openings in the bottom will help aid air circulation. However, if the hive still gets so hot that you notice the beeswax melting, you will need to allow for some shade as well as ventilation.

As far as working with your bees and anticipating their temperament, this is basically their time to go out and do what they do, which is hunt, forage, and create honey, while going about their daily hive chores.

It should be noted that, if you live in a warm or tropical climate, you will probably be doing some of the summer chores a bit more often and for a longer period of time than a beekeeper who has a hive in a more temperate or cool climate.

Fall

Fall is usually honey harvest time. Yet remember to leave enough so the bees can survive the winter. If you think that the bees will not have enough honey for their winter stores, then do not harvest any honey for yourself or for market from that particular hive. This is also the time to once again check and treat for disease and parasites.

Preparation for the winter should begin at this time. Efforts such as reducing the hive entrance (making the hive entrance smaller), making sure there is proper ventilation, and installing mouse guards so mice cannot get into the hives during the winter will help your colonies through the season.

You will find that the queen will stop laying in late fall/early winter. This is due to her limited food stores, as the workers focus on insulating their hive. Again, any drones still in the hive at this time will be driven out of the hive to preserve the limited food stores that the colony will have for the winter.

Fall is also the time that some beekeepers will re-queen if the hive's queen is in her second season or has not been laying well. This preventative practice is due to the fact that she may have as little as a 50-percent chance of surviving the winter at this age. However, this should be done on a case-by-case basis, as you will know your hives and your bees best.

Although there are other jobs that will pop up with the seasons, as well as unexpected things (good and bad), this brief overview of the seasons gives you an idea as to what to expect. It may be easier to keep a yearly calendar of what you need to do with your bees, especially for your first few years with the honeybees, until you are comfortable with your monthly routine. Just remember that it is always subject to change.

CHAPTER 12

BEES, HONEY, AND ALLERGIES

A s helpful and as necessary as bees are, and as healthy as honey is, some people are allergic, even deathly allergic, to one or both. At the same time, honey can actually help other people with their allergies, and bee stings can be therapeutic to someone with severe arthritis. Yet why?

First, let us look briefly at why bee stings can be both deadly and therapeutic.

Bee Stings

Bee stings are a part of life, yet some people are much more affected by them than others. Most of the population would have some pain and a little swelling after a bee sting, perhaps extending to nausea, which, while not life threatening in itself, can be a clear sign of more serious complications. Others may experience more severe reactions ranging from life-threatening situations such as tongue swelling, breathing difficulties, and the worst-case scenarios of anaphylactic shock and cardiac arrest.

Approximately two million people in the United States are allergic to bees, with approximately 50 deaths per year. You actually have higher odds of death by lightning or flu than by a bee sting. So, for those who are allergic, why is it so?

Those who are allergic to bee stings are actually allergic to the venom the bee produces, not the stinger or even the bee. This is due to the body producing antibodies to the venom's allergen. In turn, the antibodies react, producing chemicals and histamines, which can then cause swelling of glands, membranes, and cells.

Some people do not even know that they are allergic to bee stings until they get stung. On the other hand, some people may have no reaction at all the first time or two (or even three times) they get stung; then, all of a sudden, they can show signs of allergies or have a severe reaction.

One of the most common things used to treat someone with bee-sting allergies when stung is an epinephrine injection. However, some people have also built up a tolerance through small, then, later, larger doses of the venom itself, with boosters afterward. Most people, though, carry the injection kits with them in case of a sting. This gives them time to get to a doctor or hospital.

There are also several home remedies for bee stings. A few examples are:

- Covering the sting with honey and reapplying as necessary for the pain
- Using aloe-vera gel on the sting
- Using apple-cider vinegar on the sting
- Crushed lemon-balm leaves
- Making a paste of baking soda and water, and then applying to the sting

I have also found (firsthand) that if you are outdoors and are near some mud, placing some on the affected area can also help to soothe the sting.

There are a number of other home remedies available, but, before you use any, it is recommended to read further about them. Also, if you show any signs of an allergic reaction or know that you are allergic to bee stings, get to a hospital immediately.

Finally, there is one thing to remember: when you are stung, the faster you can remove the stinger, the less venom will be released into your body.

|||||||||||||||||||||||||||||||||||||||||||||||||||||||||||||||||||||||||||||||||||||||||

Honey Allergies

Can someone be allergic to honey? Sure, just like any other food. Symptoms include runny nose, swelling of the lips and/or tongue, itchy throat, and hives, among other reactions. As with bee stings, the worst-case scenario can also be anaphylactic shock. Allergies to honey can lead to weakened immune systems or infection, too. Treatment usually includes an antihistamine when symptoms start.

The good news is that, if you *are* allergic, honey is easy to avoid. It is still not used in food preparation nearly as much as sugar, and, many times (although not always), products are labeled up front as being made with honey. However, as with any other allergy, it is important to check the ingredient list, or, if at a restaurant, just ask. One interesting fact: it is quite possible to be allergic to bee stings, but not honey.

Also, please note that honey should not be fed to children less than one year of age, due to the risk of botulism. This is because, at this age, their immune systems are not developed enough to fight the botulism spores from the dust and dirt that often make it into the honey.

|||||||||||||||||||||||||||||||||||||||||||||||||||||||||||||||||||||||||||||||||||||||||

Apitherapy and Honey for Allergies

On the other side of the coin, bee stings and honey can be therapeutic. First, let us look at the basics of apitherapy.

Apitherapy, also known as bee-sting therapy, is a folk remedy that has been used in many countries for centuries and is today considered a homeopathic remedy. Used by historic figures such as Alexander the Great and Charlemagne (who supposedly used it to cure his gout), today, bee-sting therapy has been used for arthritis, multiple sclerosis, Lyme disease, and carpal tunnel, among other ailments.

The bee's venom, which is the source of the sting's healing properties, is a rich source of enzymes and biogenic amines, along with a number of other components with pharmaceutical properties. Although it is still unknown as to why the venom works the way that it does, it is believed to modify how the immune system functions, as well as contributing to an increased production of cortisol.

Traditionally, live bees have been (and are still) used to sting and inject venom into the affected area or areas. However, the venom can also be injected through applying creams or ointments directly to the ligaments, but it is said that using the sting method, which supplies pure venom, is the best method.

It should be noted that bee-sting therapy needs to be done under the care of a doctor or other licensed practitioner, due to the risk, albeit slight, of an allergic reaction.

Honey can also help in dealing with seasonal allergies and to help alleviate symptoms. Many people say that they can fight their allergies with the help of local honey. Due to the fact that the honey is likely to be produced by bees in the area where the allergy sufferer lives, the honey is said to help build immunity to the local pollen.

However, research on this subject is divided. Some researchers and medical professionals say that local honey does not work in helping to combat seasonal allergies. Others say the complete opposite. Among those individuals who are actually trying it or have used it, though, many say that it does help.

The typical recommendation for those using local honey for allergy relief is one teaspoon per day, starting a few months before pollen/allergy season begins in order to allow the system to build up immunity.

If you are considering trying local honey for allergy relief, remember that, in some cases, honey *can* cause a severe allergic reaction. So, if you know or think that you may be allergic to honey, do not use it.

CHAPTER 13

COLONY COLLAPSE

··

Something that has been causing mayhem in the honeybee world is the phenomenon of colony collapse. Although it is uncertain exactly what is causing this disorder, it has been having a devastating effect on the honeybees, including those in apiaries, worldwide.

Colony Collapse Disorder, also known as CCD, occurs when worker bees disappear without warning or apparent cause. Known to have been around since as early as the 1900s, when it was first observed, it was called the "mystery disease" or the "disappearing disease." In 1906, during an outbreak of CCD in the United Kingdom, the cause was later attributed to a combination of weather, inadequate foraging, and an underlying chronic bee-paralysis virus.

From there, it has continued to occur throughout the years, but has recently become a much bigger concern. It was not until 2006/2007, when losses grew to significant numbers in North America, that it became known as Colony Collapse Disorder. Besides North America, CCD has also invaded the Netherlands, Italy, Belgium, Greece, Spain, France, and Portugal, along with possible problems in Switzerland and Germany. Almost one third of the hives in the United States have been lost due to CCD.

Possible causes of CCD include, but may not be limited to:
- Varroa mites
- Disease
- Stress due to environmental change
- Pesticides
- Malnutrition
- Genetically modified crops
- Cell-phone towers

Although the last two are just theories, some claim to have proof that they are affecting the bees, though no such proof has of yet been widely accepted. One prominent theory for the decrease in honeybee population suggests that the limited genetic base of commercial bees has left them more susceptible as a group to certain threats and diseases.

However, it is most likely that CCD is caused by a combination of problems, which seems to be the theory that many are leaning toward.

Although no one knows for sure what the cause is, CCD does have symptoms, which include abandoned hives with capped broods, few to no workers with the queen still in the hive, still a presence of food in the hives, not enough workers, or all the workers that are there are young.

However, should you find dead bees, it does not mean your hives have become victim of CCD, especially if those bees are found outside of the hive. However, as this may be a sign of poisoning by pesticides, so it is certainly a cause for concern.

Disappearance due to CCD has also been affecting feral or wild honeybees. However, those keepers who are using organic practices with their beekeeping claim to be little affected from CCD, due to the fact that their bees are kept without the use of pesticides to control problems, and that the keepers are, instead, trying to mimic more natural keeping. Also, it does appear to be true that organic honeybees do not seem to have the stress factor.

Although little is known about this devastating problem, beekeepers and researchers are diligently trying to find a definitive reason or reasons behind CCD, with the hopes of controlling or eliminating it in the near future.

FINAL NOTES

The honeybee is an amazing feat of nature that packs a lifetime into a few weeks. They are extremely well organized, with every one knowing its place and job from birth, and they produce one of the healthiest foods in the world. They are also important to our own food supply, and for that alone they deserve our respect and admiration.

The purpose of this book is just to scratch the surface of these fascinating insects, and is meant only to give prospective beekeepers a window into the world of the honeybee. Should you decide to pursue keeping honeybees, you will be entering into a fascinating, self-contained society that will quickly catch you up in the magic of the honeybee.

Enjoy!

FUN FACTS

· ·

- Aztec and Mayan carvings are full of bees, honeycombs, and pollen.
- Ancient cave paintings show that the practice of honey collection and beekeeping dates as far back as the Stone Age.
- When substituting honey for cooking, substitute ¾ cup of honey for each cup of sugar. Reduce other liquids by ½ cup for every cup of honey used (this is due to the added moisture the honey will provide).
- Honey can help keep baked goods moist and fresh when used as one of the ingredients.
- Honey can range in color from white to golden or dark brown. The darker the color of the honey, the stronger the flavor.
- In the United States, approximately one-third of all the food that we eat is derived from honeybee pollination, whether directly or indirectly.
- The population of a colony of honeybees typically peaks in mid-summer, and can reach 60,000 to 80,000 bees per colony.
- Honeybees contribute over $14 billion to the value of American crop production.
- A colony of honeybees (around 30,000 bees) can pollinate one acre of fruit trees.
- A bee's brain is only about the size of a sesame seed, yet it has an amazing capacity to learn and remember things, and can make complex calculations in regard to distance and foraging efficiency.

RECIPES

. . . .

I would like to thank the National Honey Board
(www.honey.com) for use of their recipes for this book.

(All recipes courtesy of the National Honey Board.)

Honey Yogurt Dumplings with Apples

Dumpling Batter:

1 cup all-purpose flour

4 teaspoons baking powder

1 teaspoon ground cinnamon

⅛ teaspoon salt

1 egg

6 tablespoons low-fat plain yogurt

1 tablespoon honey

1 tablespoon 2% low-fat milk

1 teaspoon grated orange peel

Apple Mixture:

4 cups apple slices

2 cups cranberry juice

½ cup honey

1 cinnamon stick or ¼ teaspoon ground cinnamon

¼ teaspoon ground nutmeg

Combine flour, baking powder, cinnamon, and salt in a large bowl. Mix together egg, yogurt, 1 tablespoon of honey, milk, and orange peel in a separate large bowl; stir into the flour mixture to form a moist batter. Combine apples, juice, the remaining ½ cup of honey, cinnamon stick, and nutmeg in a heavy, large skillet; mix well. Bring to a boil over medium-high heat. Reduce the heat to low. Drop tablespoonfuls of batter over the hot apple mixture. Cover and simmer for 15 to 20 minutes or until the dumplings are cooked through and a wooden pick inserted near the dumplings' centers comes out clean.

Bee Berry Sorbet

1 package (16 oz.) frozen raspberries
¼ cup honey
¼ cup fresh lime juice, including pulp
½ teaspoon grated lime peel
1 cup water

Puree raspberries in blender or food processor. Strain through fine strainer using spoon to press puree through strainer into medium bowl. Add remaining ingredients; mix well. Pour into canister of ice cream maker. Freeze according to manufacturer's directions.

Freezer Method: Pour raspberry mixture into 9-inch freezer-safe pan. Place in freezer for 3 to 6 hours or until firm. Transfer mixture to mixer bowl. Beat with an electric mixer until slushy but not thawed. Return to pan and freeze for 2 to 4 hours or until firm.

Makes 6 servings.

Honey Almond Biscotti

½ cup butter or margarine, softened
¾ cup honey
2 eggs
1 teaspoon vanilla extract
3½ cups all-purpose flour
2 teaspoons anise seeds
2 teaspoons ground cinnamon
½ teaspoon baking powder
½ teaspoon salt
¼ teaspoon baking soda
1 cup dried cranberries
¾ cup slivered almonds

Using an electric mixer, beat butter until light; gradually add honey, eggs, and vanilla, beating until smooth. In a small bowl, combine flour, anise seeds, cinnamon, baking powder, salt, and baking soda; gradually add to the honey mixture, mixing well. Stir in cranberries and almonds. Shape dough into 2 10-by-3-by-1-inch logs on a greased baking sheet. Bake at 350°F for 20 minutes or until light golden brown. Remove from the oven to a wire rack; cool for 5 minutes. Reduce the oven to 300°F. Transfer the logs to a cutting board. Cut each log into ½-inch slices; arrange on a baking sheet. Bake for 20 minutes or until crisp. Cool on wire racks.

Linguini with Honey-Sauced Prawns

1 pound prawns, peeled and deveined

½ cup julienned carrots

½ cup julienned celery

½ cup diagonally sliced green onions

3 cloves garlic, minced

2 tablespoons olive oil

½ cup water

¼ cup honey

4 teaspoons cornstarch

1 teaspoon salt

¼ teaspoon crushed red pepper flakes

¼ teaspoon crushed dried rosemary leaves

1 pound cooked linguine pasta, kept warm

Stir-fry prawns, carrots, celery, green onions, and garlic in oil in a large skillet over medium-high heat for about 3 minutes or until the prawns start to turn pink. Combine the remaining ingredients (except pasta) in a small bowl; mix well. Add to the prawn mixture; stir-fry for about 1 minute or until the sauce thickens. Serve over pasta.

Honey Barbecue–Glazed Salmon

2 large onions, sliced
2 cups dry white wine
2 cups tomato juice
1 cup ketchup
½ cup honey
⅛ cup Worcestershire sauce
1 teaspoon garlic, chopped
1 teaspoon chili powder
Salt and pepper, to taste
8 Alaska salmon steaks (6 ounces each)

Combine onions and white wine in a medium saucepan. Bring to a boil over medium-high heat. Add the remaining ingredients (except fish) and stir well. Reduce the heat to low and simmer for 1 hour; remove from the heat and puree in a blender or food processor; set aside. Place salmon steaks in a lightly oiled baking pan and baste with the sauce. Bake in a preheated, 425°F oven for about 6 minutes; turn and baste. Bake until the fish just flakes when tested with a fork.

Balsamic Onions with Honey

3 large red onions (about 3 pounds)

1 tablespoon plus ¼ cup water

6 tablespoons honey

¼ cup balsamic vinegar or red-wine vinegar

3 tablespoons butter or margarine, melted

1 teaspoon paprika

1 teaspoon ground coriander

½ teaspoon salt

⅛ teaspoon ground red pepper

Peel onions and cut crosswise into halves. Place cut-side down in a shallow baking dish just large enough to hold the onions in a single layer. Sprinkle with 1 tablespoon of water; cover with foil. Bake at 350°F for 30 minutes. Combine honey, vinegar, the remaining ¼ cup of water, butter, paprika, coriander, salt, and red pepper in a small bowl. Remove the onions from the oven and turn cut-side up. Spoon ½ of the honey mixture over the onions. Bake uncovered for 15 minutes more. Baste with the remaining honey mixture; bake for 15 minutes more or until tender.

Serving Suggestion: Serve with poultry or pork.

Creamy Honey-Sesame Dip for Vegetables

¾ cup nonfat mayonnaise

¼ cup rice vinegar

¼ cup honey

3 tablespoons toasted sesame seeds

1 tablespoon grated fresh gingerroot

1 small clove garlic, minced

¾ teaspoon oriental sesame oil

⅛ teaspoon crushed red pepper flakes

Salt, to taste

Whisk together mayonnaise, vinegar, and honey in a small bowl. Add the remaining ingredients; mix thoroughly. Dip may be stored tightly covered in a refrigerator for up to 1 week.

Serving Suggestion: Serve with assorted fresh vegetables.

Honey Lemonade with Frozen Fruit Cubes

1½ cups lemon juice

¾ cup honey

9 cups water

28 small pieces assorted fruit

Combine lemon juice and honey in a large pitcher; stir until the honey is dissolved. Stir in water. Place 1 to 2 pieces of fruit in each compartment of 2 ice-cube trays. Fill each compartment with honey lemonade and freeze until firm. Chill the remaining lemonade. To serve, divide the frozen fruit cubes among tall glasses and fill with the remaining lemonade.

Makes 28 Frozen Fruit Cubes.

Spiced Honey Butter
(Recipe developed by Carol Stevens, Red Star Yeast and the National Honey Board.)

½ cup butter or margarine, softened
¼ cup honey
1 teaspoon grated orange peel
½ teaspoon ground cinnamon

Combine all ingredients and mix well.

Serving Suggestion: Serve with biscuits, bread muffins, or scones.

Bee Birthday Cake

Cake:

Cooking spray

All-purpose flour, for dusting pans

2 cups white whole-wheat flour, sifted

2 teaspoons baking powder

1½ teaspoons cinnamon

¼ teaspoon baking soda

¼ cup butter, softened

2 eggs

1 cup honey

1 teaspoon vanilla

⅔ cup 1% milk

Frosting:

8 ounces cream cheese, softened

¼ cup honey

½ teaspoon vanilla extract

Cake:

Heat an oven to 350°F. Spray two 8-inch cake pans with cooking spray and dust with all-purpose flour. Whisk together whole-wheat flour, baking powder, cinnamon, and baking soda. In a stand mixer with a paddle attachment with electric beaters, cream butter on medium speed until light and fluffy. Add eggs 1 at a time, mixing well after each addition. Add honey and vanilla, and beat until smooth. On low speed, add the flour mixture to the mixer alternately with milk, starting and ending with the flour mixture, and mixing just until blended. Portion the batter into prepared cake pans, dividing it evenly. Bake for 20 to 25 minutes or until the top of the cake springs back when lightly pressed. Cool the cake in pans for 15 minutes; unmold onto a rack and cool completely.

Frosting:

Beat cream cheese, honey, and vanilla until light and fluffy. Spread ½ of the frosting onto one layer, place a second layer on top, and spread the remaining frosting on top. If the frosting is soft, refrigerate for about 30 minutes or until the frosting starts to firm up; cut into 10 pieces.

Grilled Portobello-Mushroom Salad with Greens, Honey Vinaigrette, and Roquefort

⅓ cup honey

¼ cup balsamic vinegar

3 tablespoons soy sauce

2 cloves garlic, coarsely chopped

⅓ cup olive oil

4 (3 to 4-inch) portobello mushrooms, cleaned with stems removed

¼ cup bacon, chopped (or 1 ounce cooked bacon bits)

8 cups mixed baby greens

Honey Vinaigrette (recipe follows)

½ cup crumbled Roquefort or blue cheese

Snipped chives, for garnish

To make Honey Vinaigrette: In the container of an electric blender, blend honey, vinegar, soy sauce, garlic, and ¼ cup of oil until smooth; set aside.

Brush mushrooms on both sides with 1½ tablespoons of oil; place on an indoor grill or in a preheated nonstick skillet over medium-high heat. Cook for about 5 minutes, turning occasionally just until tender. Transfer to a nonreactive container gill-sides up. Pour the marinade over the mushrooms; cover and refrigerate for 2 to 4 hours, basting with marinade occasionally. If using raw bacon, sauté the bacon until lightly browned. Remove to paper towels to drain; set aside. Drain, and then reheat the mushrooms for 1 to 2 minutes on an indoor or outdoor grill, turning once. In a large bowl, toss greens with ⅓ cup (or to taste) of Honey Vinaigrette. Divide the greens equally among 4 individual serving plates. Halve the mushrooms. Prop ½ of the mushrooms on the others on each salad. Divide the cheese and cooked bacon bits among the salads. Sprinkle with chives.

Chewy Monkey Bars

3 cups miniature marshmallows
½ cup honey
⅓ cup butter or margarine
¼ cup peanut butter
2 teaspoons vanilla
¼ teaspoon salt
2 cups rolled oats
4 cups crispy rice cereal
½ cup flaked coconut
¼ cup peanuts

Combine marshmallows, honey, butter, peanut butter, vanilla, and salt together in a medium saucepan. Heat the mixture over low heat, stirring constantly. In a 13-by-9-by-2-inch baking pan, combine oats, rice cereal, coconut, and peanuts. Pour the honey mixture over the dry ingredients. Mix until thoroughly coated. Pack the mixture firmly into the pan. Cool and cut into 24 bars.

RESOURCES

Books

Aebi, Ormond, and Harry Aebi. *The Art & Adventure of Beekeeping. Santa Cruz, California: Unity Press, 1975.*

Cale, Gladstone Hume. *Beekeeping for Beginners. Carthage, Illinois: Hancock County Journal, 1949.*

Kelly, Walter T. *How to Keep Bees and Sell Honey. Clarkson, Kentucky: Walter T. Kelly Co., 1958.*

Beekeeping. New Brunswick, New Jersey: Boy Scouts of America, 1957.

Periodicals

Countryside Magazine (www.countrysidemag.com)
One of the first in self-sufficiency. Lots of articles on beekeeping.

Mother Earth News (www.motherearthnews.com)
One of the first magazines for those interested in homesteading and self-sufficiency. A variety of articles about bees and beekeeping, including their upkeep and use.

Acres U.S.A.: "A Voice for Eco-Agriculture" (www.acresusa.com)
Excellent magazine for sustainable and organic farming. Lots of articles for the small and backyard farmer.

Organic Gardening Magazine (www.organicgardening.com)
Magazine for the organic gardener and small farmer. Covers rural, suburban, and urban, all across the country. Includes occasional articles about bees, honey, and its uses.

Bee Culture: The Magazine of American Beekeeping (www.beeculture.com)
Focuses entirely on beekeeping for both the hobbyist and small commercial beekeeper. Covers rural, suburban, and urban beekeeping.

Websites

New Century Homestead (www.newcenturyhomestead.com)
Workshops and programs. Feel free to contact with questions on any aspect of backyard farming.

HolisticMD (www.holisticmd.org)
Website for holistic medicine. Includes information on bee-venom therapy.

Center for Ecological Apiculture (www.thiele-und-thiele-consult.de)
Excellent information on beekeeping. German site in English.

BeePollenBuzz.Com (www.bee-pollen-buzz.com)
Excellent site for information on royal jelly and its uses.

WebMD (www.webmd.com)
Online medical information site.

www.drgrotte.com
Has excellent information on honey as medicine.

www.honeyo.com
Various information on bees, beekeeping, and honey.

Honey Bee Suite (www.honeybeesuite.com)
Excellent general bee information.

The Hive and the Honeybee (http://bees.library.cornell.edu)
Excellent general bee information.

E. F. Phillips Beekeeping Collection (http://westmtnapiary.
com/bee_diet.html)
Great information on a bee's diet.

www.biobees.com
This website has lots of bee information, including plans on
building one style of beehive.

MadeGood.org
Plans for frames.

beespace.net
Information site and hive plans.

Buzz About Bees.net
Free hive plans.

www.beethinking.com/top-bar-hives
Top-bar hive plans.

www.beethinking.com/warre-hives
Information on Warré hives.

www.buildingbeehives.com
Information website by Howland Blackiston, the author of
Building Beehives for Dummies and Beekeeping for Dummies.

www.extension.org
Cornell University's eXtension site.

Apps
(The following apps are free of charge.)

Bee Smart- Pollinator Gardener
Enter your zip code, and a list will pop up of plants native to that area that will attract pollinators.

Beehive Manager
Keep track of your hives and their locations if you are keeping them somewhere other than your own home.

MY BEEKEEPING JOURNAL

MY BEEKEEPING JOURNAL

_____

_____

_____

_____

_____

_____

_____

_____

_____

_____

_____

_____

_____

_____

_____

_____

_____

_____

_____

_____

MY BEEKEEPING JOURNAL

MY BEEKEEPING JOURNAL

MY BEEKEEPING JOURNAL

_____

_____

_____

_____

_____

_____

_____

_____

_____

_____

_____

_____

_____

_____

_____

_____

_____

_____

MY BEEKEEPING JOURNAL

MY BEEKEEPING JOURNAL

MY BEEKEEPING JOURNAL

_____

_____

_____

_____

_____

_____

_____

_____

_____

_____

_____

_____

_____

_____

_____

_____

_____

MY BEEKEEPING JOURNAL

_____

_____

_____

_____

_____

_____

_____

_____

_____

_____

_____

_____

_____

_____

_____

_____

_____

_____

MY BEEKEEPING JOURNAL

MY BEEKEEPING JOURNAL

MY BEEKEEPING JOURNAL